D1488607

ARVN

ARVN

Life and Death in the South Vietnamese Army

Robert K. Brigham

University Press of Kansas

© 2006 by the University Press of Kansas

Published by the University Press of Kansas (Lawrence, Kansas 66045), which was organized by the Kansas Board of Regents and is operated and funded by Emporia State University, Fort Hays State University, Kansas State University, Pittsburg State University, the University of Kansas, and Wichita State University

Library of Congress Cataloging-in-Publication Data

Brigham, Robert K. (Robert Kendall), 1960–
ARVN : life and death in the South Vietnamese Army / Robert K. Brigham.
p. cm. — (Modern war studies)
Includes bibliographical references and index.
ISBN 0-7006-1433-8 (cloth : alk. paper)
1. Vietnam (Republic). Quân luc. 2. Sociology, Military—Vietnam (Republic)
I. Title. II. Series.
UA853.V48B86 2006
959.704′342—dc22
2005033830

British Library Cataloguing-in-Publication Data is available.

Printed in the United States of America
10 9 8 7 6 5 4 3 2 1

The paper used in this publication meets the minimum requirements of the American National Standard for Permanence of Paper for Printed Library Materials Z39.48-1996.

FOR MY WIFE, MONICA CHURCH, AND
OUR DAUGHTER, TAYLOR CHURCH BRIGHAM

CONTENTS

*A photograph section appears
following page 102.*

PREFACE

This book examines the experiences of the Army of the Republic of Vietnam (ARVN) during the American war in Vietnam, 1955–1975. Because it explores the lives of ordinary men engaged in a commonplace pursuit through diaries, memoirs, letters, oral interviews, and novels, it is a social history. Unlike most recent social history, however, it focuses on the impact of a war on the lives of the people whom it affected most. Because this story focuses on war, it is also military history. Unlike most military histories, however, it is primarily concerned with the soldier's experience outside battle. This is not the story of men and maneuvers during the Vietnam war, or even the story of the ARVN in battle. Rather, it is a glimpse into the lives of ARVN enlisted men. I purposefully take the soldier's-eye view beyond the battlefield into recruiting centers, barracks, food lines, training centers, and hospitals. I listen to former combatants tell about their pay, their families, their leaves and rotations, and their patriotism. In all of this, I focus on the army as a social organism. This emphasis forces me to ask questions not usually associated with the study of warfare.

For example, how did army life restructure family behavior? What did soldiers think about barracks life in provinces far away from home? What held this collection of individuals together—was it allegiance to the idea of the army itself? Did being part of small units that lived and fought together foster community ties and patriotism? Did having families attached to military units aid in the creation of community ideals? Did the ARVN draw from existing village attachments or regional solidarity? In answering these questions, I hope to get to know ARVN soldiers better, to get a fuller understanding of the Vietnam war, and to examine the problems associated with U.S. nation-building through military intervention.

The ARVN was born in 1955, when the United States had great faith in modernization and nation-building as weapons of the cold war. U.S. officials argued that they could create a new army out of the remnants of the old Vietnamese National Army that the French had grudgingly organized to help put down the Communist revolution. It was reorganized in the late 1950s by Americans connected to the Military Assistance and Advisory Group (MAAG) who were helping the newly created Republic of Vietnam (RVN, or South Vietnam) establish a counterrevolutionary alternative to Ho Chi Minh's Communists south of the seventeenth parallel.

These Americans helped shape the ARVN in America's image and initially prepared the ARVN to battle a communist-led insurgency. MAAG's successor, the Military Assistance Command–Vietnam (MACV), led by General William Westmoreland, pushed the ARVN aside in 1965, believing that only American soldiers could properly defend South Vietnam. The ARVN was relegated to a static security force and became completely dependent upon the United States for supplies, aid, and orders of battle. During the last stage of the Vietnam war, 1969–1975, the ARVN was given more offensive military responsibilities, but by that time its weaknesses were apparent.

The term "ARVN" is often used to describe all military forces in Vietnam fighting for the political survival of South Vietnam. More accurately, it refers only to the army within the Republic of Vietnam Armed Forces (RVNAF). RVNAF also included an air force, a navy, marines, rangers, regional and popular forces, and civil defense forces. In 1956 the ARVN was organized into four conventional field divisions and six light divisions. It was reorganized in 1959 into seven infantry divisions and three corps headquarters in order to better deal with the communist-led insurgency and to make the most of U.S. advisory efforts. From 1964 until late in 1968 the ARVN force structure primarily comprised ten infantry divisions in four corps headquarters. During these years of the heaviest fighting ARVN troop numbers soared over 700,000. In the last six years of the war, 1969–1975, there were over one million ARVN soldiers serving in eleven infantry divisions, making the ARVN one of the world's largest armies.

For the purposes of this study, I focus only on the ARVN enlisted men serving in these infantry divisions. It is their lives that were affected most by the disruption of village life, their service that was most closely connected to the Americans, their bodies that made up the bulk of RVNAF forces. They are also the soldiers who suffered most from the burdens of negative stereotyping, taking more than their share of the responsibility for the American defeat in Vietnam.

Indeed, the ARVN is one of the most maligned armies in modern history. Friend and foe alike have criticized it, calling it "corrupt," "lazy," "cowardly," and "incompetent." Naturally, the Communists in Hanoi called the ARVN "a puppet army," "the lackey army," "imposters," and "rebels without a cause."[1] More troubling was criticism from the ARVN's allies. U.S. secretary of defense Robert S. McNamara (1961–1968) concluded early in the war that the ARVN was "weak in dedication, direction and discipline."[2] U.S. ambassador to Vietnam Frederick Nolting told colleagues in Washington that ARVN malfeasance was "a chronic problem."[3] George Carver of the

Central Intelligence Agency's Vietnamese affairs staff concluded in July 1966 that the ARVN was "not pulling its weight."[4] John Sylvester, Jr., Binh Long Province senior adviser with the U.S. Army, wrote in September 1969 that "the ARVN was . . . lazy and gutless . . . content to let the Americans do the fighting and dying."[5] Joseph Treatser, who covered the war for the *New York Times,* concluded that the ARVN was little more than an "armed mob."[6] Journalist Neil Sheehan wrote that the ARVN had "an institutionalized unwillingness to fight."[7] Another journalist, Frances FitzGerald, concluded that the ARVN was never more than a collection of individuals.[8]

To be sure, the ARVN lived up to these negative views at times. However, it was also made up of deeply patriotic soldiers. For example, Nguyen van Hieu served for years in the ARVN despite being officially blind in one eye because he believed in the anticommunist cause. Others, such as Ngo van Son, fought on despite receiving several wounds in battle. For Nguyen van Thinh, service in the army was the highest calling of a patriot, even though the RVN had imprisoned two of his brothers for their political activities. Hoang Trinh believed that he had a responsibility to protect the nation, even if he could not define what the nation was. The ARVN lost over 200,000 men in combat, some of whom must have been committed to a counterrevolutionary alternative. Others were not as committed to the idea of national freedom through support of the Saigon government but saw their service in the ARVN as support for an alternative civil-military structure that might one day come to power.

Most ARVN soldiers, however, were ambivalent about service in the army because of the lack of proper ideological training and the recognition that the RVN was not a legitimate political entity with a cultural or historical precedent in Vietnam, two requirements for a viable future. Furthermore, because of their experiences in the service of the RVN, many ARVN troops distrusted their own government. Once this occurred, the ARVN created a subnational culture that redefined the meaning of the war. Believing fully that Saigon was no match for Hanoi and that the Americans had pushed the ARVN aside, ARVN troops focused on their families' survival.

My sources for this story are South Vietnamese government records located at Trung Tam Luu Tru Quoc Gia–II (National Archives Center–II) in Ho Chi Minh City, Vietnam, combined with official U.S. government reports found at the U.S. Army Center for Military History in Washington, D.C.; the U.S. Army Military History Institute in Carlisle Barracks, Pennsylvania; and the National Archives in Suitland, Maryland. I also found key items in the John F. Kennedy and Lyndon Baines Johnson Presidential Libraries.

I have also conducted hundreds of interviews with former ARVN soldiers, mostly during the 1990s in Vietnam and the United States. Since many of the issues discussed in these pages remain controversial, some Vietnamese were willing to speak openly only on the condition that they remain anonymous. I delivered typed questions to my subjects before the actual interviews took place. I have made every effort to minimize the problems typically associated with oral histories. The losing army does not usually get a chance at writing history. Former ARVN soldiers have a particular viewpoint that is shaped by the military and political realities of their lives during the war and since the fall of Saigon in April 1975. Whether the ARVN enlisted man escaped to the United States or remained behind in Vietnam also plays an important role in how the war is remembered.

This dependency on memory presents several problems. For one, memory is a social and cultural force. It often adapts itself to the needs of a society. Over time, those needs may turn memory into myth. In his recent prizewinning book on Civil War memories, *Race and Reunion: The Civil War in American Memory*, David Blight argued that myths are "the deeply encoded stories from history that acquire with time a symbolic power in culture."[9] In his classic 1957 study, *Mythologies*, Roland Barthes suggested that myths are clusters of ideas and values that have "lost the memory that they were ever made."[10] Myths separate themselves from historical fact, Barthes concluded, by repetition and because of their usefulness to society. When a culture wants to forget an event, or remember it in a different way, consensus usually leads in that direction. I have no doubt that such a process has taken place within ARVN communities.

Therefore, I have used most of the interviews to add a human touch to events described in the written record or to clarify points made elsewhere. Most former ARVN soldiers appear in this manuscript in the form of quotations that highlight and expand upon an idea represented in the source material. I rejected hundreds of interviews for inclusion in this book because they simply did not have any support in the written record or in the memories of others. It is also true that I am trying to capture the perceptions of former soldiers involved in one of the most tragic events of the cold war. Their responses to my questions are interesting in and of themselves, and are sometimes used to emphasize a particular point of view and not to substantiate a fact.

During ten years of researching and writing this book, I have amassed countless debts that I now gratefully acknowledge. My interest in sociomilitary history began in the mid-1990s when I was a participant in a faculty seminar at Vassar College taught by the noted military historian John Keegan. I thank John and my colleagues in that seminar for their thoughtful insights into this complicated history.

I have received enormous grant and fellowship support to complete this project. First, two deans at Vassar College, Barbara Page and Ron Sharp, helped provide grants to fund travel and research expenses. I thank former president of Vassar College Frances D. Fergusson for many conversations about Vietnam, including thoughts shared on a trip there in January 2004. I thank Bennett Boskey for his generous support of Vassar and me. It has also been my good fortune to receive grants of varying kinds from the Smith Richardson Foundation, the National Endowment for the Humanities, the Society for Historians of American Foreign Relations, the Lyndon Baines Johnson Foundation, the Delmas Foundation, and the Mellon Trust.

I thank Mark Bradley, Fred Logevall, David Anderson, Robert McMahon, Richard Immerman, Lloyd Gardner, Ngo Vinh Long, David Elliot, Duong Van Mai Elliot, Marilyn Young, Mary Ann Heiss, James Hershberg, John Prados, Ellen Pinzur, Jessica Chapman, John Lee, Kyle Longley, James Blight, Janet Lang, and Chen Jian for their comments on various parts of this book. Frances FitzGerald shared her ideas with me at several important points in the research. My colleague James H. Merrell, a friend for all seasons, read the entire manuscript and made valuable suggestions.

I wish to thank the many universities, colleges, and libraries that have invited me to lecture and supported my research over the past decade. They cannot all be listed individually, but special thanks go to four in particular: the University of California at Santa Barbara, which provided a thoughtful forum for this project when it was in its infancy; the Columbia University Seminar, where I received valuable comments and suggestions; Clare College at Cambridge University, where I was Mellon Senior Visiting Scholar and hosted by Anthony Badger, who introduced me to the Americanists at Cambridge; and the University of Miami, where Charles Neu gave the book one final airing before publication at a National Endowment for the Humanities seminar on the Vietnam war.

Several librarians, administrators, and archivists paved the way for me to conduct efficient and useful research. Ted Gittinger at the Lyndon Baines Johnson Presidential Library and Jeffrey Clarke at the U.S. Army Center for Military History were particularly helpful, as was Charles Shaughnessy at the National Archives. Thomas Blanton and Malcolm Byrne at the National Security Archive and Christian Ostermann at the Cold War International History Project provided needed documents and support.

To the many Vietnamese families who opened their homes to my research assistants and me, I owe special thanks. Their kindness and willingness to talk about the painful past was an inspiration, and their dedication to their families is commendable.

I owe special thanks to my colleagues in the History Department at Vassar College, who have provided cheer and assistance. I am particularly grateful to Nancy Bisaha, Mita Choudhury, Miriam Cohen, Rebecca Edwards, Michael Hanagan, Maria Hohn, Ben Kohl, James Merrell, Lydia Murdoch, Leslie Offutt, Miki Pohl, Ismail Rashid, David Schalk, Josh Schreier, Norma Torney, and Tony Wohl (and all the kids!).

Thanks go to Scott Morrison, Cathy Baer, John Mihaly, Ed Pittman, Steve Rock, and Chris Roelke for their support and friendship. Thu Nguyen has been a helpful friend throughout this project. To Brian Trapp and Bill Kay, fair winds.

My students at Vassar have been a source of great inspiration and support. Their influence pervades these pages far more than these words of thanks indicate. From my earliest forays into this topic, student research assistants have aided my work immensely. They include Amanda Bennett, Megan Betts, Keely Jones, Chris Johnson, Jaime Alexis Fowler, Injy Carpenter, Lucy Amory, Jerome Sherman, Tim Shea, Kelly Shannon, James Wilson, Kaveh Sidigh, Greta Lundeberg, Nicole Darling, Erin James, Tawny Paul, Carrie Maylor, Gabe Tigerman, Wendy Matsumura, Veronica Plaut, Sam Hardy, and Debbie Sharnak, all of whom helped with the research. Le Phuong Anh and Barbara Brannon came into the project at key times to help with research. Michael Briggs at Kansas has been a kind and thoughtful editor. His equanimity, patience, and good humor have sustained me in many ways.

I am grateful for the support and friendship of three mentors: Owen "Steve" Ireland, Frank C. Costigliola, and George C. Herring. Steve sparked my interest in history when the war in Vietnam was a recent memory. Frank introduced me to the joys of teaching and research. George Herring has been a friend to an entire generation of Vietnam war scholars. It is difficult to categorize the many things he has done for the book and for me. I owe him more than I can ever repay.

From beginning to end of this project, my family has shared with me its frustrations and satisfactions. They have tolerated my long absences, and their support has sustained me over the years. My mother, Marjorie Brigham, and Jane, Jessica, and Jon Earthrowl have provided pleasant distractions, as have Anita, Joe, and Nancy Church, and Claire Dufour. Thanks too to Claire and Richard Komulainen. I want to extend a special thanks to the Bradfords in Dartmouth, Massachusetts.

ONE

CONSCRIPTION

In the Republic of Vietnam of the mid-1960s, as in the United States, citizens' attitudes toward military service varied widely—and underwent momentous change. In the early years of the war, from 1955 to 1960, most ARVN troops had volunteered. After 1960, however, with significant changes in the draft laws, the government had to force more and more young men into the army. What started out in 1955 as a rather innocuous course of compulsory military service for all able-bodied twenty- to twenty-two-year-olds ended in 1975 with one in six South Vietnamese males serving in the active military and the full mobilization of all males from sixteen to fifty years old.[1] Even at the height of World War II, most nations did not resort to these drastic measures to raise an army. To fully appreciate the experience of ARVN troops, then, and to better understand their ideas and actions, we must first examine how they came to serve.

Conscription, according to the military historian John Keegan, is a form of "tax." Like all taxes, such a levy eventually has to be beneficial to those who paid it.[2] It now seems clear that the ARVN's draft policies ran counter to the rhythm of life in the countryside and alienated peasants from the government. Instead of devising enlightened draft laws recognizing that sons were important social and economic contributors for most rural families, the ARVN drafted young men for long periods with little regard for the consequences. The government in Saigon insisted that service in its name "was a national requirement of all."[3] "We had the right and the need to draft young men," argued one former official. "It was the obligation of every young man to serve the national interest as long as the government demanded."[4]

Such harsh measures were new to military life in Vietnam. Throughout its history the nation had conducted successful drafts based on flexibility and an understanding of the organic nature of the relationship between the army and the general population. As early as the eleventh century, the late Ly Dynasty had introduced conscription to Vietnam. All male inhabitants in the realm were registered and classified according to their military eligibility in six categories: princes, mandarins, professional soldiers, special professions (doctors, actors, monks), all others between eighteen and sixty years old, and the aged and sick. The bulk of a drafted army came from the first three categories. When the nation needed to raise an army, there was a conscious effort not to deprive a village of all of its young men.[5]

Conscription was based on the principle that each village owed the emperor a portion of its men to serve as soldiers. How many men depended upon the population and location of the village. Provinces suffering from floods or droughts did not have to provide soldiers. There were also family exemptions to make sure that some able-bodied men were left at home to care for family farms. No family was required to send an only son to the army. Most important, military assignments were temporary—four months out of the year—allowing soldiers to return home to help with rice production.[6]

In the fifteenth century, the late Le Dynasty (1428–1788) introduced a series of service reforms that laid the foundation for Vietnam's modern civil-military code. First, the Le emperors divided the inscribed population into six new categories: able-bodied *(trang hang),* the military who remained at work in the fields but who could be called upon for active duty at any time *(quan hang),* simple inhabitants *(dan hang),* the aged *(lao hang),* the mercenaries hired out as laborers *(co hang),* and the indigent *(cung hang).*[7] The new classifications gave greater flexibility to the Le leaders, even as they expanded Vietnam's borders with military victories over the Cham and Lao. This categorization also made conscription more democratic by increasing merit deferments.

Beginning in 1435 the bulk of regular soldiers conscripted into the army came from large families that were sufficiently wealthy in land and sons that the temporary loss of one son would not cause great hardship. The soldier's family was charged by the village for his upkeep, in return for which the village subsidized the family by giving it either an allowance, a tax exemption, or a concession that allowed it to use a portion of the communal farmland owned by the village. Desertions were registered with the village, which would be required to supply the army with another soldier.[8]

For nearly a thousand years, this system worked well. Flexibility was the cornerstone of Vietnamese conscription, and national political leaders had little difficulty raising armies to fight the Han, Sung, Mongols, Cham, Lao, and Ming. Families and villages understood that there were limits to the sacrifices they would have to make in service of the nation. Conscription, therefore, was associated not with pain and suffering but rather with limited civic responsibility. Central authorities recognized that the army was also a social tool, and when not pressed into service, the emperor often used troops to help peasants in the field. Indeed, *quoc gia* literally means "nation-family." Although the links between family, village, and the nation are overly determined and rely on universal understandings of Confucianism in

Vietnam that have been overstated, the party did create the perception that such a cosmology existed.[9]

In the twentieth century Vietnam's Communist Party understood the importance of developing a conscription policy that reflected past customs as well as the country's present needs. In 1945 the Democratic Republic of Vietnam (DRV) passed a conscription law that called all young men to service.[10] However, party officials were careful to make sure that new recruits understood that the army was a logical extension of the family and village. Leaders in Hanoi stressed the links between peasant customs and the party's nationalistic and patriotic cause. By promoting the concepts of *dan toc* (the people) and *quoc gia* (the nation), the party extended family obligations to the larger community and state.[11]

To cement this bond, army officers replaced village elders in key aspects of social life. They conducted marriages, supervised burials, and provided financial support to families of wounded soldiers.[12] As in the past, the army was also used to maintain agriculture. Cadres not in active service helped with rice cultivation in the Red River, including large irrigation projects that actually increased the rice yield in a time of war.[13] As will be discussed later, the army of the National Front for the Liberation of South Vietnam (NLF), the People's Liberation Armed Forces (PLAF), went to great lengths to create a military force that was flexible and sympathetic to the lives of village families.

Not all Communist soldiers felt this filial tie to the army. Scores of memoirs and semiautobiographical works of fiction provide a more complete understanding of life in the PLAF, or People's Army.[14] What we see through this lens is that military service took its toll on all peasant families, Communist and non-Communist, especially the scores of families that had sons and brothers fighting on both sides.[15] Still, if the result fell short of an organic people's army with ties to Vietnam's past and reverence for the role of the family in national life, such an army was still the stated goal. In theory, the People's Army of Viet Nam (PAVN) and the PLAF were committed to the relationship of the individual to the army along traditional lines. As one former PAVN general recalled, "Our goal was to remain true to Vietnam's past. We still held dear that notion that service in the army should not destroy family and village life. After all, that is what the war was all about."[16] During the French war (1945–1954), Vietnam's modern, anticolonial army functioned as a people's army, drawing support and inspiration from local communities.[17]

The ARVN, however, had a very different experience. Beginning with the army's birth in 1955, Saigon turned its back on Vietnam's past. Slowly at first, but then with alarming speed, the South Vietnamese government developed a conscription policy that defied both history and the reality of peasant life. In sharp contrast to the Communists, it did not tie the army to Vietnam's past. Nor did it show any empathy with the needs of peasant families. Instead, Ngo Dinh Diem, South Vietnam's first president, charted what he called "an independent course."[18] That course would bring the ARVN into conflict with the people of South Vietnam and begin the process of alienation that would plague the army throughout its twenty-year existence.

A MODERN ARMY

Why did the ARVN turn its back on centuries of tradition and success in raising an army? The answer lies in its relationship with its major ally, the United States.

Beginning in 1955 with the birth of the Republic of Vietnam (RVN), known in the West as South Vietnam, U.S. military advisers assigned to the Military Assistance and Advisory Group (MAAG) put pressure on the government in Saigon to field a modern, regular army to defend against a cross-border invasion by the Communists. MAAG was the first U.S. command group to work within Vietnam and was responsible for training the newly created army. MAAG advisers worked closely with South Vietnamese military leaders and politicians to create an army capable of withstanding a communist attack. Most MAAG officials accepted the 1954 division of Vietnam as national boundaries and believed that any attack against South Vietnam would come from the north. The thinking among American leaders in Washington and Saigon (the capital of the new nation) reflected previous U.S. combat experience in Korea. The general outlook of U.S. Army doctrine in 1955 was that revolution could not be instigated or successful without the support of an external sponsoring power.[19] Experience in Korea had taught that the guerrillas now operating freely in South Vietnam were the early warning of cross-border conventional attacks, considered to be far more serious than any local insurgency.[20]

The focus of MAAG's efforts in Vietnam, therefore, was to prepare the RVN's new army to combat this invasion. Specifically, MAAG military planners called for the RVN to create an army (with U.S. aid and advice) that would occupy blocking positions while U.S. forces in the Pacific Command would secure air and sea facilities in South Vietnam, then deploy to occupy blocking positions north and west of Saigon. After the invasion had been contained, a counteroffensive would be undertaken, featuring an ambitious joint airborne, amphibious, and ground attack on North Vietnam.[21]

Initially, ARVN military leaders opposed the American plan. Generals Nguyen van Vy and Tran van Don argued for the creation of mobile units from the former Vietnamese National Army battalions organized under the French. These smaller units were more organic and would be equipped only with 105-mm howitzers, which were light and mobile. The ARVN would recruit infantry battalions locally, as the Vietnamese had for centuries. These battalions would then conduct local antiguerrilla and civic action operations.[22] This cellular people's army would be motivated by strong personal ties to an area to protect local villages. The ARVN would also create a series of special forces and counterguerrilla groups in the Central Highlands to choke off the invasion that so many Americans in MAAG feared was coming from North Vietnam.

In developing their plan, ARVN military officials suggested to their U.S. counterparts that this type of army was more consistent with Vietnam's past and "was the best way to combat the Communists" who were already in the villages of South Vietnam.[23] In his memoir of the period, a frustrated General Don wrote that Vietnamese "arguments unfortunately fell on deaf ears."[24]

President Diem was in a difficult position. If he did not accept the American plan, MAAG leaders warned that it would be impossible for them to send aid to South Vietnam. Furthermore, MAAG officials claimed, if the ARVN were not reorganized into heavy divisions on the U.S. model, American advisers would be ineffective.[25] The force structure and the doctrine had to match if South Vietnam were to play an active role in its own defense.

Diem understood precisely what MAAG leaders meant. If his country declined to develop a South Vietnamese army in accordance with U.S. directives, there would be no military aid. If Diem went his own way and the ARVN failed, the United States would have no choice but to take over the war entirely. Diem, on the record as officially opposing the introduction of U.S. combat troops to South Vietnam, was especially fearful that American advisers would give way to American troops.[26] The few internal records available from the Diem period suggest that he agonized over his ally's wishes to create a conventional army based on U.S. war doctrine.[27] He understood his own generals' opposition to the American plan, and, some of his aides suggest, he also feared that he was going against accepted military practices and Vietnamese traditions. One of Diem's closest advisers reported after the war that few decisions weighed as heavily on South Vietnam's first president as the one to mold the ARVN in the U.S. image.[28] Diem also recognized that his own generals had a different vision for the army; it would be hard to face them on tough issues again if he did not support them in this first round of negotiations with their benefactors in Washington, D.C.

Eventually Diem's domestic needs overrode his generals' arguments. From 1956 onward, he continually supported MAAG force-level projections as the way to keep "American troops out of South Vietnam" but also to keep U.S. dollars flowing into the country.[29] He believed that U.S. aid would help South Vietnam modernize, and only through this process did he feel that the RVN would be able to stand up to the Communists. To make his point, Diem once told MAAG leader General John O'Daniel, "We cannot survive as a nation without industrialization"—which U.S. aid would make possible.[30] Yet Diem and some of his closest advisers also criticized U.S. aid programs. "American aid could become a sort of opium paralyzing the country," warned Diem's brother, Ngo Dinh Nhu.[31] The trick was how to get the right kind of U.S. aid without surrendering sovereignty.

Diem found the answer to this puzzle inside his own army. He held the Americans at bay by supporting MAAG requests for a larger, more conventional army. Given the American war plan, it would be hard for Diem's critics to attack him for creating a modern army on the U.S. model. If U.S. aid to South Vietnam increased dramatically in the right sectors, Diem thought his opponents would be isolated from public support. "It was a bargain with the devil," remembered one former Saigon official.[32] Diem was confident, however, that he could walk this tightrope. Of course, his gamble would eventually cost him his life—Diem was assassinated by his own generals with U.S. backing in 1963. It would also forever cast the ARVN in an inferior military role in defense of South Vietnam, a problem from which the army never fully recovered.

Diem's dependence on U.S. support had a profound impact on life in South Vietnam, but it also shaped the contours of the ARVN. Instead of creating a small regular army supported by special forces, Diem knowingly endorsed a massive military buildup. One of Diem's most trusted aides, Nguyen van Vy, once commented that the president "held his nose and signed the papers" approving overall troop-level requests.[33] The agreement must have been a difficult decision for Diem, who was customarily cautious in dealing with the Americans. In a conversation with reporter Marguerite Higgins, Diem once wondered, if the United States ordered South Vietnam around "like a puppet on a string . . . how will it be different from the French?"[34] Still, Diem met every MAAG request to increase the size and scope of the ARVN.

By 1957 the government in Saigon was offering its own initiatives to expand the ARVN, often anticipating MAAG suggestions. An official ARVN history, *Quan Doi Viet Nam Cong Hoa* (Republic of Vietnam Armed Forces), published in Saigon in 1962, stated that the army started with loosely organized small infantry units but eventually moved toward large units that, it claimed, better met the needs of the war.[35] MAAG officials were still waiting for an attack by North Vietnam across the seventeenth parallel. Once this process was in motion, it was difficult to stop. U.S. advisers seemed content with quantity even when the quality of the ARVN diminished. By the end of the Vietnam war, the ARVN was one of the world's largest standing armies.

THE DRAFTS

Unlike most modern armies in a time of war, the ARVN was built on the draft. Although Saigon officials were fond of saying that most in the army "had volunteered out of a spirit of patriotism," the ARVN had unusually high numbers of conscripted men.[36] In the early years of the war (1955–1960), according to Jeffrey Clarke, chief historian at the U.S. Army Center for Military History, "voluntary enlistments satisfied over half of the personnel requirements" of the ARVN.[37] However, by 1961 the number of volunteers had dropped dramatically. As security in the countryside became more tenuous and the length of mandatory service in the ARVN increased, the government had to force more and more young men into the army. Nguyen van Hieu, a former ARVN corporal, suggested that the experience of most ARVN troops was like his own: "We joined the army against our will because the alternatives were so dire."[38] These alternatives included jail time in the hands of Diem's secret police, something most peasants feared more than the war itself.

Hieu's story is repeated in hundreds of ARVN memoirs and in nearly three hundred interviews conducted for this book.[39] The nationalistic surge that customarily occurs during war often yields a high number of volunteers for military duty. This never happened in South Vietnam. Over the course of the ARVN's twenty-year life (1955–1975), drafted soldiers represented about 65 percent of the army's total troop levels, making it one of the most heavily conscripted armies in history.[40]

The government not only drafted its army but it did so with a capricious and oppressive selective service system. From 1955 until 1959 only twenty- to twenty-two-year-olds had to serve in the armed forces.[41] Peasant families knew that their young men would be gone for no longer than one year. New recruits understood that they would spend four months in training and only eight months in active service. This system had flexibility and a definite endpoint. The personal hardships created by the draft were minimized because new recruits and their families could plan on the return of sons from war. "It was easy to find someone to help with the rice farming," reported Nguyen van Khai, a peasant from a small village near My Tho. "My son was only gone for a year," he recalled, "so I bartered with my neighbor to get the services of his son who was not yet of draft age."[42]

By 1959, however, manpower shortages forced the government to increase the length of service from twelve to eighteen months. In 1961 the commitment was extended to twenty-four months. Huynh van Hung, the father of two draft-age sons, claimed that the additional service time disrupted South Vietnamese society sufficiently to provoke animosity in the countryside: "Everyone in my village who had sons began to doubt the government. In three short years Saigon had doubled the length of time our sons were expected to serve, and yet security in our village was worse than it ever had been. What were they doing with our boys? We got so little for our sacrifice. To this day, I do not think the leaders in Saigon understood what a hardship it was to send your boys off to war. Fields went unplowed. Rice went unplanted. Families fell apart."[43] The government offered no official justification for the revision of its draft laws, only that "the needs of the First Republic have changed."[44]

One response to critics of the government could have been that the war was going badly for it and its ally. From the birth of the ARVN in 1955 until late 1960, the army and South Vietnam's secret police had enjoyed considerable success. Diem filled his jails with suspected Communists and decimated party cells. According to the party's own records, Diem's purges inflicted serious damage.[45] In response to these attacks, some Communist Party members pushed for retaliatory strikes. Le Duan, a southerner who became the party's secretary general in 1960, urged the North Vietnamese government to take a more active role in the struggle against Diem.

Since the signing of the Geneva Accords in 1954, which had divided the country at the seventeenth parallel, the party had accepted Moscow's strategy of political struggle to unify the country. The party had warned cadres in the South not to take up arms against the government, and this warning had given Diem free rein. In 1956 Le Duan presented a special report to the Political Bureau in Hanoi, arguing that the time had come to take up arms against South Vietnam. He suggested that there was "no other path for the people of the south but the path of revolution."[46] After significant debate, in 1959 party leaders eventually endorsed Le Duan's proposals. The Political Bureau concluded that "self-defense and armed propaganda forces are needed to support the political struggle, and eventually those armed forces must carry out a revolution to overthrow U.S.-Diem. . . . The revolution in the south is to use a violent general uprising to win political power."[47]

As Le Duan's star continued to rise, he argued even more forcefully for armed struggle in the South. In January 1959 he urged the Political Bureau to adopt a strategy of violence and organize a broad-based united front directly under the party's control. The party, known in Vietnam as the Lao Dong (Workers' Party), accepted these requirements because it was losing control of events in the South. Diem had so depleted party cells through his own terror campaigns that many southern Communists called these the "darkest days of the revolution."[48] In May 1959 the Political Bureau approved what became known as Resolution 15 and declared that the time had come "to push the armed struggle against the enemy."[49] By the summer of 1959 southern cadres had received "the green light for switching from political struggle alone to political struggle combined with armed struggle."[50]

In September 1960, at its third national congress, the Lao Dong selected Le Duan as its new secretary general and approved the formation of a united front to overthrow the Saigon government. Following this dictate, on December 20, 1960, at a secret meeting in the jungle of Tay Ninh Province, near Vietnam's border with Cambodia, sixty Vietnamese revolutionaries met to proclaim the formation of the National Front for the Liberation of South Vietnam (NLF).

The NLF, known derogatorily in the West as the Vietcong, immediately pushed the armed struggle against Diem. In a matter of months the revolution had successfully replenished cadre levels and made important inroads in the southern countryside. By mid-1961, the NLF had already consolidated its power in the Mekong Delta and had made substantial progress in provinces west and north of Saigon. Only the south-central coastal areas seemed to be under government control. By October 1961 both the U.S. Joint Chiefs of Staff and President John F. Kennedy's National Security Council were considering the introduction of American combat forces to stem the tide of the Communist advance.[51]

Kennedy ultimately ruled out sending troops, but he did accept the recommendations of General Maxwell Taylor, his personal military consultant, who argued that the administration needed to increase the number of U.S. advisers in Vietnam as well as ARVN force levels. Specifically, U.S. military leaders called on South Vietnam to double its number of troops to combat the insurgency and provide security for the people. From 1960 until late 1963 ARVN troop levels rose from 150,000 to 250,000.[52]

Even with this increase, the ARVN did little to stop the Communists. In a number of key battles in the Mekong Delta, the vastly outnumbered

Communist forces inflicted serious damage on the ARVN. On January 2, 1963, for example, ARVN forces from the 7th Division attacked the PLAF's 261st Main Force Battalion at the tiny hamlets of Bac and Tan Thoi, located 37 miles (60 km) southwest of Saigon. Though outnumbered and outgunned, the PLAF stood its ground. It shot down five U.S. helicopters, then retreated under cover of darkness without suffering heavy casualties. The ARVN, in sharp contrast, refused to advance under fire and lost eighty men. This pivotal battle gave the guerrillas confidence that they could overcome the technological superiority of their adversary and proved a harbinger of things to come. The only U.S. response was to increase aid, send more advisers, and promise more support for an even larger ARVN.

The party always responded in kind, however, and in late 1963 the Lao Dong matched the American escalation. In December 1963 the Lao Dong held its Ninth Plenum in Hanoi to assess the situation in South Vietnam following Diem's assassination the previous month. After significant debate, the party endorsed a change in policy. For the first time since the formation of the NLF, it gave priority to the liberation war in the South. According to Le Duan, the most important decision made at the Ninth Plenum was the one to send PAVN main force infantry units to South Vietnam.[53] In a letter to General Nguyen Chi Thanh, the director of the party's southern office (known in the West as the Central Office for South Vietnam [COSVN]), Le Duan argued that the war could be over in a "relatively short period of time" if the Lao Dong took advantage of the chaos in Saigon.[54] Accordingly, on January 12, 1964, the first PAVN units left for South Vietnam by the Ho Chi Minh Trail. During 1964 the number of PAVN troops sent south increased from 7,906 to 12,424.[55]

Again the Americans called on the government in Saigon to increase the size of the ARVN to stop Communist advances. The RVN announced a new mobilization order in November 1964, requiring all male citizens aged twenty to twenty-five to serve. At the same time, the required length of service was increased from twenty-four to thirty-six months.[56] ARVN ranks swelled because of the new draft laws, reaching a total of nearly 350,000 troops.[57] Nonetheless, in early 1965, when an expanded ARVN did little to stop the Communists, the United States introduced ground troops and began an air war over North Vietnam. For three years, as President Lyndon Johnson often complained, the only answer to the vexing problems in Vietnam seemed to be more of everything.[58] With each passing year the United States increased its overall number of troops, and so did the ARVN. When these increases did not change the course of the war, the Johnson administration tried to use air power to save South Vietnam. American bombers repeatedly hit targets inside North Vietnam. Still, by late 1966 the war had reached a stalemate. The government in Hanoi matched each U.S. increase with new troops of its own, nearly tripling the number of PAVN regulars in South Vietnam between 1965 and early 1967.[59]

U.S. advisers with the Military Assistance Command–Vietnam (MACV), which had replaced MAAG in 1962, wanted to see the ARVN further expand its rosters. General William Westmoreland, MACV commander, desired to see the ARVN take over more of the burden of infantry combat against the Communists. The Tet Offensive in 1968 also convinced many civilians in the Pentagon to accelerate that process. In March 1968 MACV announced a two-year plan to enlarge and modernize the ARVN.[60] The ARVN would grow from 685,000 soldiers to 779,154 in 1969 and 801,215 in 1970. According to the plan, the troop increases were to "round out" and "balance" the existing force structure so that the South Vietnamese government could make significant progress toward a "self-sustaining" army.[61] Jeffrey Clarke argued that in Westmoreland's view the only obstacle to enlarging the ARVN was the ability "to mobilize the necessary manpower."[62] By now, however, South Vietnam had grown dependent on U.S. aid, and the government usually responded to MACV troop requests with polite acceptance. It would do whatever it could, through an expanded draft, to meet MACV demands and Communist advances.

In 1968, in response to further advances by the NLF and pressure from the Americans, the RVN announced its new conscription policy. The new draft law tightened deferments, broadened conscription rules, and expanded reserve status, all to add 65,000 men to the military rolls by the end of the year.[63] Specifically, the proclamation extended the conscription age from eighteen to thirty-three, requisitioned technical support services at all levels from those between the ages of thirty-four and forty-five, and recalled all veterans within either age bracket.[64] Males aged eighteen to thirty-three were automatically inducted into the armed forces. Scores of draft letters went out. All discharges were suspended except for documented disabilities. The length of required service was no longer specified; the government assumed that men would now serve until the war was over.

For some that meant seven years of active duty. According to one official U.S. State Department report, if the United States had mobilized the same proportion of its adult male population, it would have sent over eight million men per year to Vietnam.[65] By the end of 1968 one in six adult males in South Vietnam had fought in the ARVN.[66] The total of men under arms soared past 700,000 early in that same year.[67]

However, the increase in the size of the ARVN did little to stop Communist advances, causing many in the countryside to question the wisdom of the draft. "What was the point?" asked Ngo van Linh, a father of two sons drafted in 1968. "We sent our boys to the army and let our families suffer in their absence. The government did little to show us the good this sacrifice brought. All we saw was death and destruction. And the loss of our sons."[68]

South Vietnamese complaints about the ARVN draft did not end with the new mobilization order. Soon after Richard Nixon's 1968 presidential election victory, the military requirements in South Vietnam changed yet again, forcing the ARVN to increase its manpower roster once more. Nixon had come to office promising not to make the same old mistakes in Vietnam.[69] He insisted that the United States sought peace with honor and that he had a plan to accomplish that goal. But one of Nixon's first actions was to resume the air war over North Vietnam and to interdict Communist sanctuaries in Laos and Cambodia. He believed that this combination would eventually break the back of the Communists.[70] Nixon also hoped to convince officials in Hanoi that he would never abandon the Saigon government and that the United States would make a better negotiating partner now than the RVN would later. The cornerstone of his policy, however, was regrettably called "Vietnamization," implying that the South Vietnamese had not been fighting and dying all along.

Initially tested during the Johnson years, "Vietnamization" was the purposeful transfer of most infantry responsibilities from the United States to the ARVN. Nixon would "arm the ARVN to the teeth" in preparation for the day when it could stand on its own to defend South Vietnam against the Communists.[71] In January 1969, in response to Nixon's new initiatives, the ARVN announced its first collective call-up of all men born in 1951.[72] Any male born in that year had to report to his local induction and training center between March and December 1969.[73] Only those in the last stages of their secondary education were excused; however, many of these young men faced the draft when they graduated.[74] According to historian George Herring, overnight the ARVN "had become one of the largest and best equipped" armies in the world.[75] Indeed, following the 1969 mobilization orders, the ARVN soon had more than one million men in arms.[76]

Nghiem Khoa, a Vietnamese man born in 1951, remembered thinking that his life was over when he heard about the new draft law. "I was not worried about being killed in the army. I was worried that my youth would vanish while I served Saigon's needs. I was eighteen years old and just starting my life."[77] Another man born in 1951 recalled, "I kissed my mother good-bye, knowing if I was lucky I would not see her for several years. It was the worst day of my life."[78]

Ngo Chao Minh had just dropped out of Saigon University to help his family cope with the death of his mother when he heard of the new law. "I knew the moment I heard the news that I would be drafted. I remember telling my father that we were no better off than Russian serfs who served most of their adult life in the army."[79] Minh would serve in the ARVN until the fall of Saigon in April 1975. Like many of his comrades, his only reprieve from service in the ARVN was the Communist victory. "I would still be in the army if the war was still going on," a sarcastic Minh concluded in a 1999 interview. "My military service robbed me of time with my family, the chance to marry and have children, and the peaceful life I dreamed of as a boy."[80]

And so it went. Year after year the RVN expanded its troop numbers to meet the ever-changing needs of the battlefield and to satisfy American demands. When 500,000 ARVN troops could not do the job, officials in Washington and Saigon called for 600,000. Expanding the ARVN ranks did little to change the course of the war, but it did alienate the peasants. Few families forgave the government for its oppressive draft.

ECONOMICS OF THE DRAFT

The draft took away South Vietnam's sons for long periods of time, but the large standing army also drained the RVN's resources faster than U.S. aid could replenish them. According to official RVN records, the government spent nearly 15 percent of its gross domestic product to support the ARVN.[81] Diem had accepted the U.S. order to create a large conventional army, but it seemed that much of the resulting aid went to supporting a dysfunctional army. The ARVN never developed into the kind of force its generals hoped for; instead, it imposed a tremendous social, political, and economic burden on the South Vietnamese people. The RVN's former economic adviser, Nguyen Xuan Oanh, noted the irony in a 1989 interview: "Diem had gone against his own generals' advice to secure U.S. aid. But, by 1964, most of the aid was used to support the armed forces. This cycle was never broken."[82]

The vicious circle was not just a national problem. The individual ARVN soldier felt the pull on resources constantly. As Chapter 4 examines in detail, the RVN deliberately allowed the typical ARVN soldier to "slide down the economic ladder in order to keep him from draining the RVN budget."[83] As a consequence, ARVN morale was devastated. "This was not a good combination of outcomes," commented former Saigon official Nguyen van Luong. "We drafted people against their will, causing great pain and suffering to their families. We then lost control of the countryside to the Communists, so we needed a larger army. Expanding the number of troops under arms meant more expense. We eventually could not afford to keep the soldiers comfortable and the country running, so the soldiers suffered. In the end, most of South Vietnam's poor hated us."[84]

In cold economic terms, taking South Vietnam's young men away from their families for three or more years of military service was requiring more than rural society could deliver. One former high-ranking RVN official recalled that few leaders in Saigon understood the full weight of their decisions. "I do not remember one conversation when we asked what the impact of our draft policy would be on peasant families. We were so concerned with stopping the Communists and pleasing the Americans that we forgot to look at our own people."[85] Any investigation by the government would have found dwindling support for its policies and severe hardship in the countryside. Emotionally, peasant families were distraught over their sons' years of service in the ARVN. Economically, they were devastated by the ever-changing conscription plan.

In the countryside Vietnam's subsistence economy was labor intensive, and sons were a chief source of labor. When the spring rains came, softening the soil, farmers and their sons plowed shallow seedbeds. Young men working in teams harrowed the seedbeds, allowing them to dry before they plowed and harrowed again. In the Mekong Delta farmers could repeat this process five or six times. After the rains farmers prepared seedlings for transplant and plowed the fields once more. According to Gerald Hickey, an expert on village life in Vietnam, "the heavy work associated with transplanting require[d] male laborers."[86] The chore of transplanting the seedlings to the paddy fields was usually done in one day and required approximately twelve laborers for every hectare. Obviously, most farmers hired additional laborers to supplement their own families if they had large tracts of land. Tenant farmers required every family member to put in long hours during the rice-growing season. For many in the Mekong Delta, the season never ended. "There was always something to do," remembered Huynh van Cam. "We could get three harvests per year."[87] The first harvest usually occurred in mid-September, the second in December, and the peak harvest in late January through early March.

Harvesting required careful management of labor. The harvest had to be completed as soon as possible because ripened grains of rice could fall to the ground, and spring rains could cause heavy plants to topple over. Men worked long hours to complete the harvest, and each laborer was essential to the process. When the rice was ripe, one young man used a sickle to cut the rice stalks near the ground, while another carried bundled stalks to a third, who employed a threshing sledge to separate the grain from the stalk. Threshing was the most physically demanding of these three tasks, so laborers rotated positions often. A team of three young men could harvest one hectare of rice in about six or seven full working days if weather permitted.

According to official 1967 statistics from Saigon's Ministry of Agriculture, the average landholding farmed in South Vietnam was 1.5 hectares.[88] Thus it would take, on average, three able-bodied male workers nearly ten days for each of the three harvests. Add to this short, intense cycle the need to irrigate fields and prepare for the next planting, and the grueling demands of rice farming become clearer.

When the government decided to expand its draft, it did so on the backs of poor families. Since most young men aged twenty to twenty-five lived in rural areas in South Vietnam—about 80 percent between 1960 and 1975— and most belonged to farming families, ARVN conscription laws struck deep into the heart of peasant life. Cao van Thu, a former RVN intelligence analyst, suggested that the lack of ideological positioning by the government made the human cost seem more unbearable. Thu explained:

> We in the government clearly understood that the North Vietnamese Army had a heavy-handed conscription policy that called most citizens to universal military service. The record shows at a Communist Party Plenum in March 1957 [the Lao Dong's Twelfth Plenum] Hanoi setup [*sic*] a control group in Hai Duong, Nghe An, and Ha Nam Provinces. The draft was met with little resistance, so the party expanded it to all provinces in North Vietnam in April 1960. The reason the draft met with so little resistance in North Vietnam and so much resistance in South Vietnam had nothing to do with the quality of the people being drafted or their families. It had everything to do with how the people were prepared to accept the draft and why such a policy was needed. The Communists did an excellent job in ideological training, even if the party's message was pure propaganda. In South Vietnam we did nothing to prepare the countryside for the needed sacrifice.[89]

Peasant families did not need a government analyst to tell them that the ARVN draft was a hardship. Losing their sons for three or more years was an unbearable burden for most rural families. In real terms, many farmers lost not only their sons but also their ability to care for their families. Add to that weight the high cost of the war in the countryside and the failed strategic hamlets, and the seeds of discontent become evident.

Not long after the government in Saigon announced its 1964 mobilization order, several villages in the Mekong Delta organized antigovernment rallies calling for an end to the ARVN's new three-year service terms.[90] Nguyen Truc remembered many old men gathering to block roads. "We could not go to Saigon to protest the government's draft policies and our problems with farm help," he said, "so we struck out at the only government presence in our village, a national road. It was kind of pathetic. All of these older men were upset that their sons had been drafted and that there was no one left to farm. Of course, it did us no good."[91] Truc and others wrote letters to the provincial draft boards and appealed to the village notables *(xa truong)* for help, but nothing came of it.

Official RVN records indicate that the government responded to only one appeal. In March 1966 village elders from Thot Not, in Phong Dinh Province, received official notice from Saigon concerning their appeal for a more lenient draft policy. The new government explained that most of the Mekong Delta's labor force had not been drafted into the army, as the elders had suggested, but rather "had left the rural provinces to pursue opportunities in the cities, which were the centerpiece of South Vietnam's modern economy."[92]

The government's reassurance provided little comfort to the nearly ten million people of the Mekong Delta, most of whom made their living from the land. Nguyen Thao, a rice farmer, recalled that labor shortages had always been a problem in the delta, but they had never been as severe as during the American war. "We lived through French imperialism, war against the fascists, a liberation war with the French, and never had we known such problems. In the days before the ARVN draft, if families needed labor they could always hire from local families with more sons. The draft took all of our sons and made farming almost impossible."[93]

Empirical evidence supports Nguyen Thao's claims. In the mid-1960s, Robert Sansom, an economist with the U.S. Embassy in South Vietnam, conducted surveys in Dinh Thuong Province, 37 miles (60 km) south of Saigon in the upper Mekong Delta. The delta was home to nearly 70 percent of the population of South Vietnam. Sansom picked Dinh Thuong because it was far enough from Saigon to be "considered a rural economy . . . rather than an appendage to the urban economy."[94] Sansom's conclusions supported those who claimed that the government had siphoned off South Vietnam's labor supply. In 1966, in a sample drawn from two small villages in Dinh Thuong Province, he found that nearly half of the families surveyed had members away from home.⁹⁵ A population pyramid of those same two villages—Than Cuu Nghia and Long Binh Dien—revealed that in 1966 men ages eighteen to thirty-three were the least-represented group. Of the remaining male population, totaling 404, only 36 were of draft age.⁹⁶ Some of the young men had no doubt been drawn to Saigon and other large cities for economic opportunities, as the government claimed. Others may have joined the guerrilla movement. But, Sansom argued, most left the labor force because the government drafted "large numbers of workers from the rural labor force for both local and non-local military use."⁹⁷ It is no wonder, then, that peasant protests against the conscription policies continued throughout the war.

Compounding the peasants' unhappiness with the government's draft was the belief among many Vietnamese that the Communists had more proactive policies. The NLF went out of its way to make the RVN appear reactive and oppressive by supporting local farm labor exchanges that made up for the labor shortages caused by the ARVN draft. Beginning in 1964, with the advent of the RVN's new conscription policies, the NLF openly formed work-exchange teams to help peasants plant and harvest crops. Poor families could pool their resources to come to the mutual aid of all those in a farming association *(doan the quan chung)*, or they could hire NLF-controlled labor at reduced prices.⁹⁸ The NLF supported this program by charging large landholders high association membership fees and demanding that they pay up to 60 percent more in labor costs for work on their own lands.⁹⁹ NLF cadres enforced these rules vigorously, hoping in the end to scare large landowners away from the villages. If that tactic was successful, the NLF then divided large tracts of land into smaller agricultural plots and reallocated them to local peasants. Smaller plots meant less stress on labor and families. The NLF also reduced rents from 25 percent to 10 percent of annual tenant crop yields, further reducing the need for larger fields and more labor.¹⁰⁰

Over time, of course, the NLF became a victim of its own success. As its land reform campaigns and threats decreased the number of large landholders in the delta, the NLF also reduced its ability to extort money. Financial demands thus grew at a time when the war was expanding rapidly. The consequence was the institution of a special tax, which the NLF eventually applied throughout South Vietnam.¹⁰¹ The tax was at times collected at gunpoint, undoing much of the work that earlier cadres had done to win peasants over to the party's cause.

Still, many Vietnamese believed that the NLF's policies were more in line with the thinking and needs of the countryside. According to Nguyen van

Nhon, the NLF made it possible for him to farm a smaller parcel of land, with better results. "When the Front introduced its land reform campaign in my area in early 1962," Nhon explained, "I farmed a smaller piece of land, but had the same standard of living. I did not have to give the landlord my usual 25 percent and I did not have to hire outside labor."[102] Land reform and the NLF's work-exchange teams made it possible for many tenant farmers and small landholders to survive during the rapid escalation of the Vietnam war. This created more antigovernment sentiment in the countryside and brought thousands of peasants into the NLF fold.

The problem was more than just what the NLF had done right. The South Vietnamese government also failed to manage the ARVN's own economics. In a protracted war, the socioeconomic viability of an army is more decisive than its capacity to win or lose battles.[103] The sheer size and expense of the ARVN, and the RVN's inability to successfully manage its financial affairs, convinced many rural South Vietnamese that service in the army was "a dead end."[104] ARVN pay never kept up with inflation, and real wages for troops fell repeatedly. Aggravating the problem was an inflation rate that hit nearly 500 percent for many household items.[105] Low pay, high inflation, and lengthy military service made life in the army an impossible burden for many of South Vietnam's poor. As the economy continued to falter and the prospects for winning the war diminished, fewer and fewer young men willingly joined the ARVN. General Dong van Khuyen, former ARVN chief of staff, suggested that once ARVN pay dropped noticeably lower than civilian standards and private sector jobs were readily available, "the only factor driving youths of draft age to enlist was the fear of being hunted by the law."[106] The ARVN reflected this social change, and by mid-1966, it was no longer a people's army, a far cry from its early years.

WHO SERVED?

In the early years of the war the ARVN included men from all social strata.[107] "We were an army of the people," recalled Colonel Huong Thuy.[108] Even as the ARVN increased the length of service in 1959 and again in 1961, the army continued to draw its troops from all provinces and income levels. American advisers sent to Vietnam in the early 1960s often commented in their reports that the ARVN seemed to be a representative force.[109]

In perhaps one of the most impressive studies from the early war years, Robert White of the U.S. Army Natick Laboratories created a social profile of the ARVN. In 1963 White conducted extensive research on ARVN infantry units to determine the correct size of uniforms and nature of other equipment needed from the United States. One unintended result of White's "Anthropometric Survey of the Armed Forces of the Republic of Vietnam" was a composite sketch of those who served in the ARVN. According to White's data, the ARVN matched South Vietnam's demographics almost perfectly. For example, only 3 percent of ARVN members had been born in or near Saigon. Most—over one-third—came from the ten provinces of the coastal lowlands (Quang Tri, Thua Thien, Quang Nam, Quang Tin, Quang Ngai, Binh Dinh, Phu Yen, Khanh Hoa, Ninh Thuan, and Binh Thuan); the second-largest group—20 percent—came from the western provinces of the Mekong Delta. In other words, the origins of those serving in the ARVN matched almost exactly the population distribution in South Vietnam. Furthermore, over 70 percent reported that they practiced Buddhism, not Catholicism, a religious pattern that reflected the national demographics.

During the war many U.S. critics of the ARVN suggested that the army was made up mostly of ethnic Chinese, explaining their lack of desire to fight for South Vietnam. Like their counterparts in the PAVN and PLAF, however, nearly 90 percent of the ARVN were ethnic Vietnamese; only 1.6 percent were ethnic Chinese. Montagnards made up the next-highest group, at 7.2 percent. Another interesting fact is that the typical ARVN infantry soldier in 1963 was ten years older (age twenty-nine) than his American counterpart and had, on average, seven more years of military experience. Not only was this an army of the people, it was also an army with years of practice.[110]

All of this changed with the 1964 mobilization act. Instead of an experienced people's army, the ARVN increasingly was an army of those too weak to escape its grasp. Some scholars have interpreted this sea change as a purposeful move to draft members of the urban underclass because they were close at hand.[111] Indeed, statistical studies completed by MACV in 1965 and again in 1967 suggest that a growing percentage of the new ARVN recruits listed cities of 100,000 or more as their hometowns.[112] Geographic information is complicated, however, by the fact that many young men and their families had already left the danger of the countryside for the safety of the cities. The government's internal records suggest that the ARVN matched South Vietnam's demographics throughout the entire war, 1955–1975.[113]

What is most revealing about the makeup of the army following the 1964 mobilization act is how rural Vietnamese tried to protect their young men from military service. Before the new call-up, the government had relied on a recruiting system that demanded cooperation between village elders and provisional recruiting agencies. This complex system was designed to bring all able-bodied men to the attention of the government. The idea was to compile lists of draft-aged men that could be checked against village rolls in order to send out preinduction letters from the government's central post.

The success of this program depended entirely upon factors out of government control. For example, villages only marginally influenced by the NLF often gave up false names for the draft. "We often listed the dead or those already committed to the Communist cause because we could not bear or afford to lose our young men," recalled one village elder.[114] Many elders understood that their fate was often tied to a system that some social scientists have called "moral reciprocity," requiring each member of the village to contribute fully to its economic and social health. As Nguyen Thanh explained, "Our village depended on these young men for survival."[115]

Moral economists such as James Scott have long argued that Vietnamese peasants depended upon closed corporate communities to survive.[116] Scott argued that such communities are more humane and protective because property is owned and farmed in common. The village survives only if everyone shares in the work and the bounty, and this reciprocity ties villagers together morally. According to Scott, when outside influences are introduced—capitalistic land rents, private property, and market forces—the peasants rebel. Samuel Popkin and other political economists have rejected Scott's explanation of the moral economy, theorizing instead the predominance of a "rational peasant" who acts as a judicious problem solver with a sense "of both his own interests and of the need to bargain with others to achieve mutually acceptable outcomes."[117]

It now seems clear that the ARVN draft forced village elders to adopt the moral economy mode of thinking even if this was not culturally predetermined, as Scott suggested. Many villages created elaborate systems of deception to keep their young men out of the draft. For example, in Hoc Man, a small village located just northwest of Saigon, village elders made up fake death notices. In My Tho, a river town in the Mekong Delta, village rolls were often tampered with by the elders.[118] Thus, efforts to recruit new ARVN troops in the countryside met with resistance and purposeful obfuscation. As a result, after the 1964 general mobilization law was passed, the government collected nearly 150,000 undeliverable induction letters from its own central post each year. Most of these letters were from the countryside.[119]

Of course, it was also easier to evade the draft in Vietnam's small hamlets and villages. The French had conducted the last nationwide census in Vietnam prior to World War II. Few records existed, therefore, for many of Vietnam's rural poor, and hopeful young men exploited this fact by turning in false national identification reports when the government demanded them.[120] "It was easy to simply melt into the countryside," remembered one Hoc Man resident. "By late 1966 the government simply had no control over our village. As long as we were friendly to the Vietcong they left us alone. When the police came looking for us, we always had plenty of warning from our friends inside the government. When asked to register, I simply gave a false name."[121] Another potential recruit from the Mekong Delta reported that forged papers were readily available to many young men in his village. "For a few piasters," he remembered, "I could buy papers that said I had a government deferment."[122]

Still, the draft hurt South Vietnam's peasants most. It took the chief source of labor away from families and villages for long periods, and to no avail. The Communists continued to control much of the countryside, making life in the villages of South Vietnam untenable for many. Once American ground troops landed in Vietnam in March 1965, the war was fought almost entirely in rural South Vietnam, adding to the stress of life in the countryside. "We gave up our sons and then had our villages destroyed by our allies," reported Nguyen Thanh, "It was a nightmare that never seemed to end."[123]

DEFERMENTS

Adding to that nightmare was a sense for many drafted by the ARVN that some young men had escaped the draft through illegal deferments. "It was a hellish life," recalled Ngo van Linh, a former ARVN conscript. "I knew that so many had connections and that they used them to evade the draft. It was demoralizing."[124] Indeed, the ARVN had a host of legitimate deferments based on U.S. models that invited corruption. Like most modern armies, it offered deferments for such reasons as poor health, education, religion, primary occupation, and familial burden. However, the abuses of this deferment system created a psychological barrier between the drafted men and the country they vowed to protect. Corruption and abuse in the deferment system alienated many poor Vietnamese who had been forced into the army. Ngo van Chuong remembered the "insult" of being rounded up for the army at the same time that his neighbors "escaped the draft because they knew someone in Saigon."[125]

Usually the abuses in the deferment system came in the traditional areas of draft suspension. For example, educational deferments were routinely granted so that South Vietnam's young men could finish part one or part two of their bachelor's degrees.[126] Few in the ARVN would have objected to this category of deferment, knowing full well that the country needed educated people. However, it now seems clear that many young men who were granted an educational deferment never served in the military.[127] Conscription law specifically stated that those with educational deferments would eventually have to serve the country.[128] Usually the army waited until after the student graduated before sending induction orders.

In scores of instances, however, students with deferments were never sent induction orders. American officials looked into this problem in 1967 and discovered that hundreds, if not thousands, of young men had escaped the draft by attending college or university for long periods.[129] Another favorite tactic was to register as a student overseas and simply never report to Saigon.[130] This type of evasion happened on such a regular basis that the Education Ministry and Saigon's Mobilization Directorate formed a special committee to investigate the problem.[131] In several reports this joint committee complained that the paperwork for individual students was simply too limited to provide grounds for action.[132] Students were attending fictitious schools or had forged academic transcripts showing ongoing matriculation.

The government also granted deferments on religious grounds. Young men of draft age who were clergy of an approved religious order, and had the paperwork to prove it, were given deferments for the entire length of their religious service. Word quickly spread among those drafted that Catholic churches in Saigon, Hue, and Da Nang had established special "clergy" status for favored sons of the church.[133] There is no documentary evidence to support this claim, but it is clear that abuses in the religious deferment category were commonplace. In one official U.S. report, an American adviser warned MACV of a "two-tiered" deferment practice for clergy.[134] Apparently there was a broad interpretation of the religious deferment for Catholics and a "very narrow reading of conscription law" for other religions—particularly for Buddhists associated with the radical Buddhist Institute. Led by Thich Tri Quang, the Buddhist Institute opposed the war and the Saigon government. The institute organized massive rallies against Diem and his successors, believing that a neutral solution to the war in Vietnam was likely if the Americans withdrew and Saigon cooperated with Hanoi. Most followers of Thich Tri Quang believed that they were being discriminated against in draft deferments. "We knew that the Catholics were receiving special treatment," explained Ngoc Cao Hunyh, a former member of the institute, "but there was little we could do about it. We hired lawyers to help us get legal deferments for our monks, but the government usually sidestepped the courts."[135] Compounding this problem, according to Bui Diem, South Vietnam's ambassador to the United States, was the fact that the Buddhist Institute had "no entrée whatsoever" in the Saigon government.[136]

The issue of religious deferments mixed with other forms of perceived discrimination against the Buddhist community to form a hostile climate for leaders in Saigon. Beginning in May 1963 and lasting until the end of the war in April 1975, Buddhists protested various aspects of policy but also the legitimacy of successive South Vietnamese governments. At the core of those protests was the belief, confirmed by many inside the government, that Diem favored Catholics and that his successors were "hostile to protest from the Buddhists."[137]

"We were told every day that this war was about establishing a free and independent South Vietnam," explained one former Buddhist monk, "but the cornerstones of freedom should be religious tolerance and the right to protest the government's actions. We were no better off than those living under communism."[138] Another follower of Thich Tri Quang added that the feeling among many Buddhists was "certainly that Catholics would get deferments, but that we would not."[139] The only option for these Buddhists, they believed, was to protest the deferment policy and the war. And, to Saigon's consternation, Thich Tri Quang's followers did so regularly and to great effect.

As some Buddhists protested the government's deferment policy toward monks, other draft-aged men spoke out against the special treatment given to former Communists who surrendered to the government. In 1963 the RVN established a program called Chieu Hoi (open arms). NLF cadres and Communist sympathizers were offered amnesty and rehabilitation if they turned themselves in to the Saigon government. After one or two months of reeducation, the Chieu Hoi ralliers were released to their home villages. For the next four months they could attend one of the government's retraining programs or attend school. At the end of six months, their names were sent to the Mobilization Directorate. According to the government's own records, however, few men in the Chieu Hoi program ever faced the draft.[140] Many did volunteer for military service because, as one former ARVN officer joked, "there is no soldier like the one newly converted to the cause."[141] Still, many former Communist cadres simply melted into the countryside until the war forced them to choose sides again.

Perceptions of a better life for those in the Chieu Hoi program weighed heavily on the minds of ARVN infantry soldiers because it seemed as if the enemy received better treatment than they did. "How could you give a Communist a deferment from military service after he surrendered to the government?" wondered one former ARVN soldier.[142] Another complained that he was given three weeks to show up for induction, yet someone who had "walked with the enemy against my family" was allowed weeks, even months, before there was any service requirement.[143]

The most common complaint, however, was reserved for those ralliers who never served in the ARVN. Legend and myth regarding the lives of the ralliers were rife, but the overwhelming view held by the ARVN infantry soldier was that those in the Chieu Hoi simply did not serve in the military.[144] According to one legend, "all you had to do to escape the ARVN draft was tell the government that you were a former Vietcong cadre and give them some meaningless maps from the rural provinces."[145] There is no documentary evidence to support charges of widespread abuse in the Chieu Hoi program, but what is important is that so many men drafted into the ARVN *thought* the ralliers were given special deferments, and that this perception helped alienate soldiers from the government.

If it took a stretch of the imagination to find corruption in the Chieu Hoi deferments, it was easy to spot abuse in the suspensions given to "essential personnel."[146] For much of the war, the government routinely granted draft deferments to anyone who was considered employed in a "vital industry,"[147] that is, young men whose employers vouched for their importance to the nation and its international economy. A review board headed by the Defense Ministry was required to look at each case carefully and determine the proper classification for a period not lasting longer than one year. It was standard practice to give year-long deferments for men associated with government ministries and those in key sectors of the economy. It did not take long, however, before most draft-aged men believed that you had to join the Can Lao Party (Can Lao Nhan Vi Cach Mang Dang [Revolutionary Personalist Labor Party]) to enjoy an occupational deferment.

The Can Lao Party was a semisecret organization started during Ngo Dinh Diem's presidency. Most public officials were forced to join the party, and it was nearly impossible to rise in the ranks of the government without membership. The Can Lao controlled the bureaucratic strings in Saigon, and nothing got done without its approval. Made up mostly of Catholics, the Can Lao lost some influence after the coup against Diem. General Nguyen Khanh, who would eventually replace the group of military leaders that overthrew Diem, outlawed the party in 1964. After Khanh's own ouster in February 1965 General Nguyen van Thieu and Air Marshall Nguyen Cao Ky revived the Can Lao. From 1965 until the end of the war ten years later, the Can Lao held influence in Saigon.

Most rural Vietnamese viewed the Can Lao as a distant annoyance that interfered with their lives periodically. For the most part, the party operated "under the radar" of casual government observers.[148] "The Can Lao was more like a nineteenth-century big-city political machine in the U.S.," reported one American official. "It really did not influence policy as much as practice. Contractors, speculators, investors, and others seeking favor from the government had the most contact with the Can Lao. Patronage was its primary purpose."[149]

It now seems clear that the Can Lao's patronage included draft deferments. In scores of official records, draft-aged men in the Republic of Vietnam complained to local officials that those with connections to the Can Lao received occupational deferments while most others served in the military.[150] Because the party dominated the government, the mere existence of these complaints highlights the level of corruption in the deferment system. According to one report, young men from Long An Province complained that "everyone in [their] village was drafted" because they had no ties to the Can Lao Party.[151] Others about to be drafted tried desperately to join the party in order to receive a deferment but found it impossible because they offered the secret organization "no political or economic incentive" for admission.[152] Membership was restricted to those who had actively supported Diem for years, or for political rivals who could be watched more carefully from inside the party. After Thieu and Ky came to power, joining the Can Lao was almost impossible. According to one former Can Lao member, the party never sought out members, nor did it actively run in political campaigns. "It was more like a special club that only those chosen to lead the country were then invited to join. You could not become a member simply by proclaiming allegiance to the government. It was like a Puritan community; only the chosen could join."[153] Membership did have its rewards, as hundreds of young men with connections to the Can Lao received special occupational deferments from military service.

Widespread abuse of the deferment system was just one more way that the ARVN's conscription policy alienated young soldiers and their families from the government. But it also meant that thousands of young men who should have served in the military did not, and the resulting shortfall compromised the ARVN's operational strength. Throughout the war, corruption, draft resistance, and deferments robbed the ARVN of needed manpower. Most battalions never reached their authorized strength, and the figures were even more disappointing in the category "present-for-combat."[154] Eventually inadequate force levels compromised the ARVN and created a cyclical process that added to poor morale. As one former ARVN officer complained after the war, "We had to drag South Vietnam's young men into the army, and once they got there, the army was at half strength. There is nothing worse for morale than building an army like this."[155] Another soldier agreed, adding, "Life became intolerable to those of us unlucky enough to get caught in the army's web."[156]

John Keegan once wrote, "Conscription is for rich states that offer rights—or at least the appearance of rights—to all."[157] South Vietnam never lived up to that maxim. Most citizens of the Republic viewed conscription as arbitrary and oppressive. The draft affected the most vulnerable members of society, exacerbating the estrangement of rural Vietnamese from the government. The official lack of empathy with Vietnam's military traditions and perceived governmental disregard for the needs of peasant families forced many young men to avoid the draft. With the help of village elders fearful of the economic impact of the loss of all their young men to the war, many draft-aged men found a way to beat conscription.

Still, hundreds of thousands were drafted into the ARVN at great cost to their families. Unlike the Communists, the Saigon government made little effort to tie national service to family and village life. Nor did RVN officials offer special services or economic guarantees to the families of those who served. The hardships that developed from having one or more sons serve in the ARVN for extended periods alienated what should have been the government's political base among the many peasant families, fostering the good fortunes of the Communists.

Corruption, deferments, and successful draft resistance also meant that the ARVN never reached full operational strength, and infantry soldiers became further alienated. The fact that at no point in the ARVN's twenty-year history did it attain full battalion strength was repeated often in the ARVN ranks and added to the soldiers' frustration. If a man were drafted into the army and forced to serve, he likely had a sinking feeling that he was one of the "unlucky ones."[158] Once inside the army, many infantry soldiers concluded that "nothing they experienced in the army gave them any faith that the government was viable."[159] Sadly, that judgment was only intensified by the ARVN's training experience.

TWO

TRAINING

Insufficient and inadequate military and political training plagued the ARVN throughout its twenty-year history. From its birth in 1955 until its inglorious defeat two decades later, its troops were never fully prepared for battle or ideologically committed to the national cause. Poor leadership led to dismal training programs that left most soldiers with the sinking feeling that they were "no match for the Communists."[1] ARVN memoirs and postwar interviews have suggested that the greatest fear for infantry soldiers was that they would "die with bullets unfired in rifles."[2] Inferior political training meant that the ARVN never coalesced into an effective fighting force. Because the Saigon government constantly feared a military coup, nationalism and patriotism played an insignificant role in ARVN training. This lack of ideological commitment left a huge void in the political war, a key element to success in Vietnam's civil war, as Ho Chi Minh and his followers well knew.

Another major problem, of course, was that what training programs did exist were almost exact copies of U.S. Army training courses—unmistakable evidence of American doctrinal influence. Tactical training in the early years of the war, 1955–1959, was highly conventional, emphasizing technological resources and maximum use of firepower to win battles. In these early years the Korean war was the model for U.S. strategic and tactical military planners, which affected training programs. With the birth of the National Liberation Front (NLF) in December 1960, however, most U.S. military leaders in Vietnam began to see that the mission in Vietnam had changed. Instead of training for a conventional cross-border invasion, they introduced some innovations into tactical training programs in an effort to cope with the guerrilla tactics of the Communist insurgency.

History tells us that this switch came too late to have much of an impact on the village war in Vietnam. When the war began to go badly in the countryside, American military leaders changed tactical strategy and ARVN training. After Operation Rolling Thunder, the sustained bombing of North Vietnam, that began in early 1965, the ARVN was trained almost exclusively in the U.S. air-mobile strategy. In 1967, when the U.S. national endeavor shifted to pacification, the Military Assistance Command–Vietnam

(MACV) altered ARVN tactical training to reflect the new battlefield realities. In 1969 President Richard Nixon expanded upon Lyndon Johnson's policy of "Vietnamization," and the ARVN's tactical training was once again modified.

In theory, with each tactical shift, MACV redesigned the ARVN training programs to reflect the new strategy. During the planning stages this policy made sense to U.S. military advisers in Saigon, but it did not take long for them to see a total breakdown in the system. Instead of programs designed to turn untested recruits into combat-ready soldiers, most ARVN training courses simply covered written material in U.S. training manuals and did nothing at all to foster political development. ARVN officers were reluctant to take battle-tested soldiers out of the front areas to serve as training instructors; as a result, few live demonstrations ever took place during infantry training. According to one former ARVN soldier, "My training did not prepare me in any way for the trials I would face as a soldier."[3] U.S. advisers constantly complained that poor training was "one of the major causes of the low level of combat effectiveness." Worse, officials in Saigon did not seem to care.[4]

Poor training also led to poor morale, a subject discussed in depth in this chapter. Several social factors contributed to poor morale and high desertion rates, but the inadequacy of training figured largely in a failure to develop esprit de corps. As one former ARVN soldier remembered, "We were demoralized the minute we joined the army. Not out of fear but because of the way we were treated and how poorly we were trained."[5] Diaries and memoirs of ARVN soldiers available to researchers suggest that this poor treatment started at the outset, with a new recruit's induction into the army.[6]

THE INDUCTION EXPERIENCE

Recruits began to suspect that the government was not properly organized for a war against the Communists from the minute they stepped into the induction and training centers. Overcrowded and underfunded facilities left most new recruits with the impression that the Saigon government and its army were no match for the Communists. "If the government could not organize our induction into the army any better than it did," one soldier explained, "how could we expect it to organize a war against a powerful and highly organized adversary?"[7] Another former ARVN soldier complained, "I slept on the floor in the training center my first three nights in the army. What kind of message does that send to troops?"[8]

To be sure, the government and army officers did not set out to create such an atmosphere. In fact, the government went to great lengths to convince the young men it forced to join the army that the nation supported their endeavors. Whenever a group of *truong dinh* (able-bodied men) received their induction orders, the provincial recruitment centers organized massive public ceremonies to honor those selected for military service. Public ceremonies were important in rural Vietnam. They provided families with the opportunity to bring prestige and status to the *xa* (village) and themselves. According to Neil Jamieson, an expert on Vietnamese social relations, villagers could determine themselves the scope of public ceremonies that they would sponsor, though peer pressure figured in the decision. "One could organize such events either cheaply or lavishly," Jamieson wrote in *Understanding Vietnam*, "but . . . for those with a reputation and social position to protect, or for those trying to rise in the status hierarchy, there was little choice."[9] Since the government sponsored these "welcoming parties," families had to work directly with Saigon's representatives. RVN political leaders hoped that public cooperation of this nature would build ties between villagers and the government, but—like most efforts to create harmony between Saigon and the countryside—the program failed miserably. Villagers who resented the government's draft policies naturally came to view the welcoming parties as "a farce covering a horrible policy."[10]

After the parades and speeches, each of the new recruits was given a khaki beret with a "badge of silver circle around a geometric shape superimposed with a flaming silver sword."[11] One new recruit, Nguyen van Khoi, remembered that his beret did not fit correctly; obviously it had been made for someone with a much larger head. The other new recruits laughed about the size and design of the beret, he recalled, until an officer told them to take great care of their hats because they must be turned over to military authorities at their induction. If he passed all of his tests, Khoi was told, he would be given a new hat.[12] "This whole business with the hat seemed absurd to me at the time," Khoi reported. "I remember thinking that my whole life had just been turned upside down by being drafted into the army, and all the officer cared about was that stupid hat. I did not know at the time that this experience would come to symbolize my year in the ARVN."[13]

In 1955 new recruits like Khoi reported to induction and training centers run by the joint U.S.-French Training Relations and Instruction Mission (TRIM). As the French withdrew from Vietnam after nearly one hundred years of colonial control, the U.S. Military Assistance and Advisory Group (MAAG) took over these operations. The MAAG then created the Combat Arms Training Organization (CATO) in April 1956 to bring nearly 150,000 new ARVN recruits into the army. Almost immediately CATO leaders saw tremendous problems in the system. "We could see clearly that the existing ARVN schools, induction and training centers, and instructors were inadequate for the job ahead," explained a former MAAG official. "We had to make major changes in every aspect of training."[14]

One of the most important changes was the centralization of national recruitment and training centers. From 1957 until 1961 all new ARVN recruits reported to the Quang Trung Training Center, a massive compound located 9.5 miles (15 km) from Saigon. When that facility became too overcrowded, the army established four new training centers: Dong Da in Phu Bai in Thua Thien Province for I Corps; Lam Son at Duc My for II Corps; Van Kiep at Phuoc Le in Phuoc Tuy Province, an extension of Quang Trung assigned to III and IV Corps; and Chi Lang at That Son in Chau Doc Province, also for IV Corps. Three more national training centers for new recruits were added in 1970 and 1971 at Da Nang, Phu Cat, and Kien Phong. By the end of the war more than thirty training centers existed in South Vietnam, each designed to bring new recruits into the ranks efficiently and effectively.

Effective orientation remained an elusive goal throughout the war. Like the "welcoming parades," induction at the national training centers gave new recruits a glimpse into the character of the ARVN and the nature of its relationship to the individual soldier. As one former infantryman reported after the war, "I had never seen such a mess in my life. The induction process was flawed from beginning to end."[15] Indeed, from its inception, the ARVN's induction program was terribly incoherent. Few officers paid attention to the details necessary to ensure proper operation. No one knew what was to take place in the induction centers and why. There was no regular activity or schedule. Officers herded new recruits in one direction and then another, with no apparent motive. "It was one of the most dysfunctional operations I have ever seen," said one American officer assigned to evaluate the Quang Trung center. "We made several recommendations to the ARVN leadership, but their only response seemed to be to add more recruitment and training centers without fixing any of the local problems. This meant, of course, that they were simply compounding a dreadful situation."[16]

One major problem facing ARVN recruits at induction was overcrowding. On average, inductees who were physically fit were scheduled to spend three or four days at the recruitment and induction center. The number of young men reporting daily to each center fluctuated greatly, however, making it impossible to properly staff each facility. Following national mobilization decrees, designed of course to increase ARVN ranks to meet the war's growing needs, young men waited until the last minute to report for induction. Thus, the recruitment center could be empty one day and extremely overcrowded the next. "It was impossible to predict how many young men would be processed at any given time," complained a former ARVN officer. "We always seemed to guess wrong at the Quang Trung center. On some days our staff had nothing to do; on others they could not process new recruits fast enough. This guessing game made the experience horrific for everyone involved."[17]

Adding to an already unpredictable situation were the uneven draft enforcement practices of the national police. It now seems clear that Saigon officials irregularly put pressure on the national police to track down draft resisters, without any consultation with the training centers.[18] This practice was usually initiated by a visit from a U.S. official or high-ranking military adviser. One former Saigon policy-maker claimed he could forecast when the government would take action: "Every time someone from MACV or Washington came over to the presidential palace, I knew that we would have to shut down the black markets, encourage more political debate, and round up draft resisters. I could predict the outcome of such visits, but no one else seemed to understand the ripple effect that such actions had on the country. This was especially true for the staff at the recruitment and training centers. Our actions simply made their impossible task even more ridiculous."[19]

According to official Saigon reports, draft resisters often accounted for 30 percent of the total number of new recruits at the induction centers.[20] At the peak of efficiency, for example, the Quang Trung center was equipped to process 8,000 new recruits at one time. Following sweeps by the national police, there might be more than 12,000 new recruits at the center.[21] At other times, the facility did not reach its optimal number of recruits. At the end of the year, in official reports, the centers seemed to be functioning well. "You could read the official Quang Trung annual reports," one former Saigon official recalled, "and it looked like everything was smooth sailing. They were handling roughly 25,000 new recruits each year, and that was near the target figure of 24,000. All seemed well, and no one raised any questions."[22] Of course, these reports masked the real problem, which was that this annual target figure was often condensed into a seven-month period at unsymmetrical weekly intervals. An official MACV report concluded that most ARVN training centers often operated at only 50 percent capacity.[23]

The large numbers made it impossible for the ARVN leadership to process individual soldiers in a timely fashion, and delays led to resentment among new recruits. One new recruit, Nguyen Dinh, described his bitterness in his memoir: "I could not believe that I had to wait for hours for the pleasure of being inducted into the army. I did not want to join, but those who had come to Quang Trung eager to fight the Communists soon lost their spirit when they saw how disorganized our army was. It created such an awful taste in my mouth. I never fully recovered from those first days in the army."[24] One young man, a third-generation anti-Communist soldier, complained that the war "would end before I got to it" because the wait at the induction center was so long. Another former soldier complained that the chaos and overcrowded induction facility was a metaphor for South Vietnam.[25] Yet another said, "It did not take a leap of imagination to see that the broken-down administration of the induction center mirrored the national government. During my first days in the army, I began to see the army as an extension of the problems of South Vietnam."[26]

Induction in most modern armies is measured in days, not weeks, as in the ARVN. The major problem for new recruits was that there seemed to be no purpose to their time at the centers. They spent days waiting for a doctor to show up for the physical exams. Weeks would go by before they could be administered the proper written tests. There was one delay after another.

As if this were not enough, the obvious fraud and corruption at the induction center also disgusted most new conscripts. When recruits first arrived, they were assembled in the reception area, where officers distributed cards and checked each soldier's national identification card. The men, divided into small teams, filled out these biographical data cards under the guidance of other soldiers.[27] According to Lieutenant General Dong van Khuyen, the level of false reporting at this initial step plagued the ARVN throughout its twenty-year history.[28] Those rounded up in police sweeps were always without proper identification, so assuming a new identity was easy. At the first opportunity, those who were forced to report for induction usually deserted. Only then did the ARVN command find out that they had filed false biographical data cards. Coordinated efforts to produce false identification papers, allowing new recruits to desert when given the chance, were prevalent in the countryside.[29] Some estimates place the level of false reporting at nearly 35 percent, an unheard-of figure for a modern army.[30]

Perhaps the most serious abuses occurred, however, at the physical examination. The ARVN divided new recruits into three categories: physically fit, physically unfit, and those requiring reexamination.[31] The physical consisted of a chest X-ray, bodily measurements, and a thorough doctor's examination.[32] Those who passed were immediately separated from the others. Each was given two uniforms, one belt, two undershirts, two pairs of shorts, one cap, one pair of canvas jungle shoes, one mess kit, one canteen, and one duffel bag.[33] They were rounded up, and escorted to the billeting area. Most knew that their numbers had shrunk dramatically. "I was rushed off to my bunk, but I had the sinking feeling that I was one of the few who had been selected to serve," recalled one former ARVN soldier.[34] Another complained that it "was so obvious that nearly half of the new recruits were being excused."[35] Official reports from Saigon support this anecdotal observation: nearly 30 percent of all new recruits failed their physical—not all for legitimate reasons.[36]

The physical exam process allowed for corruption at many levels. Not only could new recruits bribe some doctors at the induction center, but certain members of the review boards were also susceptible to cash payoffs.[37] When a conscript was determined to be "physically unfit," the induction center forwarded his file to the Central Draft Exemption Center. There a review board headed by a field-grade medical doctor examined the file for irregularities. The board required the young man in question to appear in person. In several reported cases board members accepted bribes to excuse able candidates; board members could also be swayed by paid substitutes.[38] "I made a living showing up before the review board for other young men who were listed as unfit," reported a former Saigon resident who was deaf.[39]

The psychological impact of such corrupt practices at induction was devastating. Most former ARVN soldiers interviewed for this book described the experience as akin to being on a sinking ship. "We felt completely helpless," was a familiar response to questions about corruption in the induction process. One highly decorated soldier reported that the arbitrary nature of the draft and induction procedures made him feel like a "victim."[40]

Indeed, victimization seems to have been an enduring state of mind for traumatized ARVN recruits. More important, many internalized their experience in the induction centers, making the fear of victimization a condition that they lived with daily. Over the twenty-year life span of the army, the weight of corruption and the dismal situation at the induction centers damaged any sense of esprit de corps. This damaged community remained so throughout the war because few ARVN officers understood the nature of the trauma and fewer politicians cared. It was, therefore, the condition of life in the army that began the process of alienation for most ARVN recruits.

The distancing recruits experienced during induction was only the first stage in a procedure that estranged soldiers from their government and its army. Following induction recruits were slated for infantry training to prepare them for battle. But this training fell far short of accepted military standards, an inadequacy that more than any other factor led to pervasive resentment and frustration among the troops.

FAILURES IN INFANTRY TRAINING

After making it through induction, every recruit had to undergo basic military training. The program, which lasted five to six weeks, was designed to provide new soldiers with a sense of duty and discipline, physical fitness, the ability to use weapons, and basic combat techniques. After basic training, recruits were selected for specialized instruction depending on their individual aptitude, as determined by psychological tests. Those who were to remain with the infantry continued on advanced individual training for another four to six weeks. Following the 1968 Tet Offensive, and again in 1972, the total training time was reduced for new recruits from twelve weeks to nine because of pressing replacement requirements.

By most accounts, the ARVN basic training was inadequate. Soldiers constantly complained to their American counterparts that they felt ill prepared for battle.[41] Nguyen van Dinh, a former ARVN infantry soldier, remembered "the awful feeling that filled the barracks each night. We knew we were not learning what we needed to know to survive on the battlefield. We felt helpless."[42] This theme is repeated in scores of ARVN memoirs. Nguyen Vu recalled in his memoir, *12 Nam Linh* (Twelve years of being a soldier), feeling out of control of the events that were shaping his life. The poor training he received left him incapable of responding to normal military situations, a condition that both frustrated and terrified him.[43] In another memoir, *Mau va Nuoc Mat* (Blood and tears), former ARVN infantry soldier Van Thanh Hao wrote that he felt like a pawn in a losing chess match.[44] He complained that his training had left him confused and frustrated.[45] This story is repeated in *Thang Ba Gay Sung* (The march of the broken rifles), Cao Xuan Huy's moving memoir. Huy recalled that he knew he was not adequately prepared for all that warfare can offer but that he had no idea how to remedy the situation.[46]

As these memoirs testify, the most significant problem in individual infantry training was poor instruction. Throughout the war, the quality of teachers was suspect. According to one MACV official, "The most highly qualified officers should have been placed in training positions; but too often these posts were filled by officers who were relieved of combat commands. Their superiors often reasoned that such officers could do less damage in these positions."[47] ARVN officers believed that they could not afford to send their competent cadres into the teaching ranks. The result was that most teachers were simply the "undesirables."[48] Many young officers were retained as instructors immediately after graduation; most had no combat experience. A majority of quality officers saw the instructor's job as "unrewarding" or a "downhill" slide for their career.[49] Compounding an already difficult situation was the fact that the army instituted no rotation policy for its instructors. "Bad instructors had a way of becoming lifelong teachers," complained one former ARVN officer.[50]

Basic training teaching techniques were also problematic. Throughout the war training programs were hampered by the lack of demonstrations or practical exercises, especially during tactical instruction periods. ARVN infantry and training centers never had a complete up-to-strength demonstration unit commensurate with the large number of students. When an operation required five experienced soldiers, most ARVN recruits saw it demonstrated with only two.[51] "We never had enough live demonstrations," reported one former officer, "and the ones we did have were never with the proper amount of personnel. I complained about the lack of both, but Saigon said spare troops for demonstrations were in short order."[52] Throughout the war demonstration units were often called away from their posts for defensive purposes.[53] According to one former ARVN officer, "You needed someone who knew how to use a rifle shooting it."[54] Several training centers used security protection units for demonstration purposes, but, lacking training, they made poor teachers.[55]

Training centers relied exclusively on teaching infantry techniques through lectures based on U.S. training manuals.[56] Teachers viewed the manuals as material that had to be covered quickly, not as a supplement to demonstrations and hands-on learning. To make matters worse, the manuals were often out-of-date, and sometimes the translations from English to Vietnamese were riddled with mistakes. Few ARVN officers informed their American counterparts of the problems with the manuals. Ngo van Nhan wrote home that he could not follow the manual. "I had trouble figuring out where we were at any given time," he explained.[57] Another former soldier reported that there were several pages missing from his training book, and that when he complained, he was reprimanded.[58] Ngo Ca Cong remembered being constantly bored during lectures. "It is hard to believe that a teacher could make such life-and-death issues boring, but mine sure did."[59] Another former ARVN soldier reported that his training manual was ten years old by the time he served in the army, and his instructor never looked up from the book when lecturing from it. "He stood at the front of the class and for six hours mumbled meaningless facts and figures into the book. In six weeks I never saw his eyes."[60]

The lackluster quality of instruction was a constant worry for the ARVN soldier. In a society where complaints about superiors were never made in public, many did complain about their instructors, at least to their own families.[61] In scores of letters sent home by ARVN troops, some reference to poor teaching occurs in most of those that mention basic training. An exasperated Hoang van Minh told his family that he had nightmares. "It is a strange world," Minh wrote, "when you fall asleep during the only training you get that shows you how to fire a rifle. How can this be? Surely, we will all die with bullets unfired."[62] Another ARVN soldier wrote to his mother that "if I die with bullets still in my gun, it will be the fault of my training instructor."[63] Ngo van Son's letter to his father concluded prophetically, "Surely we will die and the nation will die if the politicians and military leaders in Saigon do not do something about the quality of instruction at the training center. I know so little now. How will I survive? I believe that I will be killed with my rifle pointed into a dark jungle at nothing and the bullets still in the chamber."[64] Son died on patrol in April 1968.[65] According to the reporting officer, "his gun had not been fired."[66]

The motif of "the unfired weapon" dominates ARVN memoirs and memories. ARVN troops wanted to defend themselves against the enemy with their own bullets, but few felt capable. Only a handful of soldiers interviewed after the war reported satisfaction with their infantry training.

It now seems clear, however, that the unfired weapon was more than a metaphor for life in the ARVN. In one memorable training moment at Quang Trung, an instructor lectured for two hours on the fact that the M-16 round detonation created 50,000 pounds of pressure per square inch in each chamber. Yet only a handful of new soldiers hearing that lecture ever had a live demonstration showing how to clean that rifle.[67]

Most American advisers shared the ARVN infantry soldiers' concerns over poor training. According to Brigadier General James Lawton Collins, Jr., special assistant to MACV commander General William Westmoreland from 1965 to 1968, "poor training or its complete absence was a continual handicap for all South Vietnamese armed forces units."[68] Sadly, there was little that the Americans could do to change the culture in Saigon. Even though MACV had considerable power and influence in doctrine and strategy, it had little influence over training issues. Many MACV officials wanted to change the training program, or even force the ARVN command to accept change, but the RVN government refused to cooperate. This was one area in which American influence and desires were specifically neglected. "There seemed to be a belief among some ARVN officers," reported Colonel Herbert Schandler, "that battlefield experience was more important than basic training."[69] One American adviser remembered that he could not get his ARVN counterpart to take training seriously. "He looked me right in the eye and said, 'What can they learn in a class that they cannot learn in battle?'"[70] Official MACV reports confirm this view, highlighting the point that many ARVN units had "no formal training" and were expected to learn "by doing."[71]

This philosophy yielded uneven results. Even those units that were learning in the field experienced great hardship because new weapons systems and battle plans were constantly introduced without proper "conditioning."[72] In 1964, growing increasingly frustrated about their lack of influence on this issue, MACV leaders developed a plan that they thought would eventually remedy the situation. The formula called for the rotation of ARVN infantry battalions from the battlefield to rear-area training centers so that two infantry battalions from each corps would be undergoing training at all times. The thinking behind this program makes perfect sense: MACV leaders believed that most ARVN officers would welcome the rest and the replacement of their battalions and, therefore, would not object to training *after* their units had already experienced battle. "Our idea was to bring ARVN units back to the rear area, where American advisers could ensure that they were getting the training they needed. We knew that few ARVN officers would care what we did on a battalion's down time."[73]

In theory the plan worked well, but in practice it failed because of apathy in Saigon and a lack of support among ARVN officers. In just five months the number of battalions trained went from eight to four, and by September 1964 no ARVN infantry battalions were being released for formal training. Few ARVN officers would allow their units to be called back to a rear area for fear that the frontline situation in their country was too grave. "We could not afford to move our infantry battalions away from the strength of the enemy," explained Major Nguyen Hung. "Every bullet counted."[74] Other ARVN officers believed that the troops had earned the relief—not for retraining but for rest and relaxation. The result was that little ARVN unit training ever took place, despite the dictates of official policy.[75]

Sensing the problem in Saigon, MACV also introduced combined operations to compensate for insufficient ARVN training. With the complete breakdown of training at the unit level, combined operations became perhaps the most important training tool at the ARVN's disposal. The basic concept derived from the belief that by operating alongside U.S. units, ARVN personnel would be able to learn what they had missed during official army training sessions. When this program met with initial success, MACV leaders expanded it in 1968 to include what it called "the pair-off concept."[76] The new advising program was designed to improve the combat effectiveness of ARVN infantry units so that they could take over primary combat responsibility from U.S. units in the years ahead. Several combined operations were successively conducted under the pair-off program, such as Dan Thang McLain on August 1, 1968, and Dan Sinh Cochise conducted in Binh Dinh Province on August 22, 1968. Another MACV program, the Dong Tien (Progress together) Campaign, begun in mid-1969, also produced good results.

By most accounts, the combined operations made up for many, but not all, of the shortcomings in ARVN infantry training. Working closely with U.S. advisers, ARVN soldiers noticed a qualitative difference in their training compared to those who had not been trained by Americans. This difference led to improved morale and performance on the battlefield. It is interesting to note that many ARVN infantry soldiers believed that there was a significant difference in training by Americans.

Soldier Nghiem Tam Ngoc had three brothers who also served in the ARVN. Each had a different training experience. The two oldest, who had almost no contact with American advisers, were killed within their first month of combat. Ngoc's youngest brother, Thuy, was in the ARVN during the last year of the war, when training had been all but forgotten and few American troops remained in Vietnam. He too died in combat shortly after completing his training exercises. In sharp contrast, Ngoc was drafted into the ARVN in 1968 and went through all of his training with American advisers. As a result, he claimed, he knew what to expect and how to be an effective soldier. "Without the U.S. advisers," he said, "I surely would have died like my brothers."[77] As Ngoc suggested, at the core of the combined operations was the important relationship between U.S. advisers and ARVN soldiers, which many ARVN soldiers believed was the key to their survival.

Improvements in training through combined operations could never make up for the poor leadership and inferior instruction that were the cornerstones of the ARVN training experience. Try as they might, American advisers could never undo the damage that had already been done. Even when MACV officials noticed significant progress in ARVN unit training and performance, they knew that the success would be "short-lived" because there were fundamental problems in Saigon that could not be solved by Americans.[78] The most significant of these was the failure to train ARVN troops politically.

POLITICAL TRAINING

Unlike his successors in South Vietnam's presidential palace, Ngo Dinh Diem understood the importance of the political struggle in Vietnam's civil war. As a conservative nationalist, Diem had long championed an authentic Vietnamese blueprint for modernization that was, according to historian Philip Catton, a "third way between capitalism and communism."[79] Particularly intriguing to Diem was the notion of "cultural revisionism" that included a synthesis of the best political ideas from East and West.[80] For Ngo Dinh Nhu, Diem's brother, who served as Diem's political counselor from 1955 until his assassination in November 1963, "personalism" offered the best solution for South Vietnam.[81] The doctrine of personalism, which emphasized humanism and focused on the excesses and ills of modern industrial society, had once been a major political force in Europe. Adopted by the Catholic left in Europe specifically, personalism embraced the belief in a Supreme Being, the creative potential of humankind, and government's responsibility to provide a social safety net for the people.[82]

From 1955 until the November 1963 change of government, personalism had a dramatic impact on the army's political education program. Careful not to embrace a specific ideology, the personalists in Diem's cabinet sought to create a political system based on "communitarian socialism."[83] For Diem, personalism was attractive because it provided a "way to emerge from a state of underdevelopment" while also preserving Vietnam's "ancestral traditions."[84] The result for the ARVN was that political training would focus on proper ways to behave in Vietnam as it was on the path to modernity.

It did not take long for personalism to overwhelm all aspects of the ARVN's political training. One of the first requirements of all new recruits in their civics instruction was to memorize and recite the following personalist decree:

a. I pledge to accept every sacrifice and hardship in the fight for the survival of the nation, of my family, and of my own person;

b. I pledge to always obey and execute my commander's orders, and to be vigilant of the enemy's scheme to divide us;

c. I love my compatriots and will always endeavor to protect their lives and properties and respect their religious faith. I respect elders, love children, and behave correctly toward women;

d. I am aware that unpopular acts will push the people toward the Communist side, and this amounts to giving a hand to our enemy and destroying ourselves.[85]

Government officials insisted that the ARVN's political training take precedence over military training and that it focus on "how to behave" correctly. Accordingly, specific political training days were devoted exclusively to such topics as "learning how to drive politely" and "how to walk on the street full of ladies."[86]

Most soldiers accepted this kind of political training as routine. They understood that the business of nation-building required all South Vietnamese to reject some traditions and incorporate new ideas into patterns of life. Such cultural revisionism was not new to Vietnam. Vietnamese intellectuals, as historian Mark Bradley has explained, had long borrowed from other cultures and adopted foreign political ideas to meet national needs.[87] Diem's personalism promised to rid South Vietnam of the cultural straitjacket that had "kept Vietnam tied to the past and in poverty."[88] Soldiers and civilians would adapt to changing conditions, and all would prosper.

Not everyone embraced personalism, however, and Diem quickly found that his ideas did not resonate with the soldiers. Missing was a sense that the nation-building experiment in Vietnam was on the "correct path." Even the most committed anti-Communists worried that a "nation of opposition was no nation at all."[89] Other nations had been born in war, but for most soldiers, South Vietnam never moved beyond being the "bastard child of French colonialism and American anticommunism," as South Vietnamese writer Nguyen Trang eloquently put it.[90] The problem was that Diem and his successors never articulated a political vision of South Vietnam's future that made sense to the average soldier. The lack of any real political and ideological commitment to the government's abstract notions of nationalism and patriotism cost South Vietnam everything. Even in the early years of the war, from 1955 to 1959, when the Saigon government had considerable success against the Communists, most ARVN troops felt little ideological commitment to the conflict. "We had no idea why we were fighting other than to rid the nation of Communists," recalls Ngo Quynh. "I knew that simple anticommunism was not enough to defeat the Marxist-Leninists who had been indoctrinated for decades with the concept of *ai quoc* [patriotism]. We had no similar message."[91] Indeed, one of the keys to the Communists' success in Vietnam was the political motivation of People's Army of Viet Nam (PAVN) and People's Liberation Armed Forces (PLAF) troops.

In South Vietnam there was a general rejection of overt ideological political training. What training did occur emphasized the evils of communism. According to Lieutenant General Dong van Khuyen, Diem's original republican ideal was that the army not be made up of an all-volunteer and professional corps; rather, it should be composed of reserve elements politically motivated against communism. Diem believed that ideological awareness, once inculcated and "firmly held as a cause, would greatly enhance the effectiveness of weapons."[92] Following Diem's theory, most political training emphasized the aggressive nature of communism but never covered how to build a new nation and what it meant to serve that nation.[93] Nguyen van Chau, a former ARVN soldier, believed this approach was a serious mistake. "Most soldiers that I knew understood little about why we were fighting. Anticommunism was more abstract to us than scientific political theories. Not once did any of my instructors mention a proactive political agenda."[94]

In many respects the civil war in Vietnam revolved around modern interpretations of the old Sino-Vietnamese concept of *chinh nghia* (the just cause). Westerners generally refer to *chinh nghia* as "winning hearts and minds" or "gaining the mandate of heaven." Neither of these concepts goes far enough, however, in explaining the psychocultural power of *chinh nghia* or its impact on Vietnamese politics. *Chinh nghia* emphasized the collective view of what was right and proper. It was the body of public opinion that determined whether your cause had merit. Like all things in Vietnam, *chinh nghia* is not predetermined by elite individuals but rather is the collective expression of the will of Vietnam's small villages. A government that followed *chinh nghia*—and thus gained acceptance by collective will—could legitimately claim the devotion of the people and govern their behavior.

It was impossible, for instance, to simply claim the mandate of heaven, as Diem often did, and have it mean anything to the people of rural Vietnam. The will of the people was not something that could be demanded or forced. It had to come from the alchemy of social, supernatural, and psychological factors that had helped shape collective opinion in Vietnam's countryside for hundreds of years. According to sociologist Paul Mus, *chinh nghia* dominated Vietnamese village life—and therefore national life. "The major premise presents itself neither as a circle of things nor of persons but as the balanced total of opinions professed on the things that matter by the persons who count in the eyes of the community as a whole."[95] In other words, confirmation of *chinh nghia* brought moral and ideological power that transcended all individual power.

Much of Mus's work has been challenged in recent years, but it is clear that there was a feeling inside the ARVN that the Communists had history on their side because they paid attention to *chinh nghia*. "The Communists seemed to know why they were fighting, and we did not," remembered Nguyen van Ngo, a former ARVN soldier. "Our political training emphasized Diem's personalism but little else."[96] ARVN soldiers tended to idealize the Communists' political training, believing that they "had an ideological commitment to their cause that we simply did not share."[97] Such a romanticized view of the party's political training is commonplace in the literature.

Communist training manuals and political commissars made sure that PAVN and PLAF soldiers understood how the concepts of *dan toc* (nation, or the people) and *ai quoc* (patriotism, or love of country) merged to form a political ideology that put the cause of national liberation first. The PAVN and PLAF were organically connected to society, many ARVN soldiers believed, and their support came directly from people in liberated areas. The connection to the national cause had been underscored throughout the basic training of Communist cadres and was constantly reinforced by political officers. At the heart of this training was the notion that the PAVN and PLAF were armies "of the people" that supported national liberation—a common view shared by many ARVN soldiers.

Although the RVN government in Saigon supported limited political training, the PAVN and PLAF had an elaborate system for political training. Each company of PAVN or PLAF troops (a company equaled three platoons) had a political officer, *chinh tri chi dao*, who shared a dual command with the military leader.[98] The ARVN established no such system of political control or education. According to Lieutenant General Khuyen, the ARVN relied on staff officers summarily trained in psychological warfare techniques for its political training.[99] They "did not have the kind of protracted ideological training and experience that always inspired prestige and authority."[100] Many were young, inexperienced officers fresh out of Saigon's Political Warfare College, lacking the clout to influence troops.[101]

When ARVN troops received this kind of political training, it was usually ineffectual. Most soldiers considered their political training "reactive," "restrictive," and not "informative."[102] On those limited occasions when political training did take place, classes were held once a week, with lectures given by political "experts" or ranking members of the Can Lao Party. The classes had two primary purposes: to expose crimes and atrocities committed by the Communists and to warn ARVN troops about Communist propaganda.[103]

Another major problem with the ARVN's political training program up to 1963, limited as it was, is that it was run by an exclusive and decidedly antidemocratic political party—the Can Lao. Many ARVN officers felt "that in a free democracy, the military should stay away from party politics in order to be professionally active."[104] Of course, this notion had been a cornerstone of political thought in the United States since the founding of the American republic. The fear inside the ARVN was that the Can Lao would not be able to "differentiate between politics and ideology"—that political training under the Can Lao's leadership would be too narrow. "We feared that the Can Lao's political agenda was more important than our national ideological training," recalled one former ARVN soldier.[105] Another complained that he did not hear the words "nation" or "the people" during his entire political education lecture.[106] One more former ARVN cadre explained the problem this way: "We knew the difference between national ideological training and political indoctrination, but our teachers did not think we understood the difference. Sure, the Communists were training their troops the same way, but at the time, we thought that the Communists understood the national cause that they were fighting for; and we clearly did not."[107] Many ARVN soldiers thus believed that while their side received only political indoctrination, the Communists received proper ideological training that focused on the organic relationship between the army, the people, and the nation. As naïve as this charge may have been, it resonated loudly in ARVN circles.

Sensing a growing crisis in the early 1960s, American advisers repeatedly attempted to change RVN officials' minds about the need for organic political training. After Diem's assassination in 1963, successive Saigon governments had suspended political training altogether. Not until late 1965 was ideological training reinstated as a part of basic training, at least in principle. Eventually, however, MACV helped to create a General Political Warfare Department (GPWD) that periodically launched national education campaigns for the ARVN and citizens of the republic. For example, in 1966 MACV and the GPWD approved the creation of the New Horizon Campaign, designed to improve small-unit leadership and prevent desertions. The campaign's primary tools were informal troop education and programs to improve the material and moral welfare of ARVN soldiers. Casual discussions replaced large lectures, which had already proven ineffective.

For most in the ARVN, however, the discussions lacked the focus on the national question that all seemed to crave. The ARVN troops learned about the history of the Vietnamese struggle against the Chinese and the French. They also learned the fundamental principles of Marxist-Leninist thought and why the Communists had to be defeated. Instructors spent a significant amount of time explaining the role of the Americans in South Vietnam. "What was missing from the new training programs," suggested one former ARVN soldier, "was any notion of what our ideological program was. Anticommunism just seemed too reactive to us. We needed something that we stood for, not just notions of what we were against."[108] Another complained that the political talk of democracy and freedom never translated into meaningful action for the military. "When I first joined the army in 1962," explained Nguyen van Thanh, "I did so because I was patriotic. I loved my new country of South Vietnam and hated the Communists. Over time, however, I had a hard time explaining the political nature of my country. So many leadership changes in Saigon and dependence on the Americans made it impossible for me to talk about the nation."[109]

Many U.S. advisers sensed that the political aspects of the war were slipping away from the government in Saigon with each passing year. According to Colonel Richard Wyrough of the U.S. Army, a senior infantry adviser assigned to the ARVN, South Vietnamese officers constantly challenged the value of legitimate political education. Some balked when asked to include training sessions—outside the Can Lao's political realm—focusing on "the substantial role of the military in the political process of a developing nation." Others suggested that such training was "a waste of time."[110]

In May 1969, to remedy that situation and impress upon Saigon that it was serious about political training, MACV initiated a "For the People" campaign. American military and political leaders designed the program to achieve three objectives: to remind servicemen of all ranks that the ARVN was responsible for protecting the people; to promote civic action; and to improve military deportment and discipline. During another political training exercise sponsored by MACV and the GPWD, ARVN units competed against each other in civic action programs. They dug irrigation ditches, gave medical care, built schools, and taught English to young students. Each of these actions, it was thought, would link the ARVN to the people and the people to the ARVN.

According to official ARVN reports, however, such a relationship rarely developed.[111] The main problem was that political training in general "usually took place after political and military events had occurred, and almost never in anticipation."[112] Rightly or wrongly, many ARVN troops believed that when their own political training stopped, that of the Communists had just begun. ARVN soldiers developed this elevated sense of the Communists' cause and political training from their own experiences in the villages of South Vietnam.

Given the nature of the war, this perception of meaningful ideological commitment among Communist cadres should have been expected. Lacking a sophisticated understanding of the ideological underpinnings of the war for South Vietnam, few ARVN troops believed that their cause was just. Because so many peasants associated the ARVN with the successors of the French Union forces, more should have been done to link the army to the countryside and to bring the soldiers and the people together in the national cause. A basic breakdown in political training meant that soldiers never fully understood why they should be motivated to surrender themselves to commonwealth goals. Because political training failed to instill an ideological commitment to the struggle inside the armed forces, it was almost impossible for officers to rally men to the cause. Even more devastating for the South Vietnamese army, however, was the lack of camaraderie between individual soldiers; this too was a failure in training.

WHY SOLDIERS FIGHT

Since Herodotus and Thucydides, military historians have wondered why individuals will endure combat and eventually throw themselves before the weapons of their enemies. Most conclude that bravery in battle has little to do with idealism, patriotism, or treasure. Instead, they suggest that "soldiers fight to protect their comrades at their side."[113] Historian Victor Davis Hanson suggested that the "ideal of the brave man" has led soldiers to combat throughout the history of warfare. The "brave man" cannot bear the thought of watching his comrades die or the shame of playing the coward before their eyes. In the battles of ancient Greece, Hanson explained, men who did not have blood ties to one another and "who had no common experience under fire were hardly willing to form up together into the dense ranks of the phalanx."[114]

In George Washington's revolutionary army, patriotism was not a great motivating factor for the continental soldier. Washington urged the Continental Congress to increase pay for soldiers to encourage longer enlistments, but he too recognized that men under arms eventually fight to protect one another.[115] Writing of his World War II experience in the Pacific, William Manchester put it this way: "Those men on the line were my family, my home. They were closer to me than I can say, closer than any friends had been or would ever be. They had never let me down; and I couldn't do it to them. I had to be with them rather than let them die and let me live with the knowledge that I might have saved them. Men, I know now, do not fight for flag, country, for the Marine Corps, or glory or any other abstraction. They fight for one another."[116]

Indeed, based on soldiers' experiences in World War II, several military historians concluded that men fight because of a "matter of fact adjustment to combat, with a minimum of idealism or heroics, in which the elements which come closest to the conventional stereotype of soldier heroism enter through the close solidarity of the immediate combat group."[117] In other words, the "band of brothers" is a proven reality.

Fighting for one's comrades has always been associated with morale and motivation. True, some armies have marched for treasure and others for revenge, but the willingness to die is usually allied with esprit de corps. On the field of battle, war is always about small groups of people banded together by common experience. The ARVN soldiers had plenty of common experiences, most of them unpleasant. No effort was made, however, to link the men to each other in any meaningful way.

American advisers recognized the problem throughout the war, but they had little leverage in Saigon on this issue. For most Americans in Vietnam, training was the period in a soldier's life where the army replaced the family as the basic social unit and where individuals became a unit. This never happened in the ARVN. There was no systematic training that explained the soldiers' connection to each other or to the nation. In the end, the absence of such training meant that the ARVN soldiers did not fight for each other.

John Keegan told us that inside every army is "a crowd struggling to get out."[118] This dictum certainly held true for the ARVN. Nguyen van Thanh remembered that he lacked "any empathy with my fellow soldiers."[119] Thanh, a five-year ARVN veteran, embarrassingly recalled that he saw fellow infantry soldiers as "adversaries" competing with him for the army's limited resources. "I did not see others as countrymen or comrades, but rather as people looking out for themselves."[120] Another former soldier suggested that few in the ARVN were drawn to each other. "We did not bond as an army," reported Ngo van Son. "I felt little connection to anyone in my unit, and no officer made any attempt to bring us together. I hardly knew the names of people I fought with."[121]

In 1967 MACV tried desperately to convince Saigon to "do something" to increase morale and motivation among ARVN troops.[122] Outlined in several official reports was MACV's desire to "link troops to one another," to foster an understanding of "why they were fighting," and to address fundamental issues of warfare such as "comradeship."[123] American military leaders correctly worried that ARVN troops felt little attachment to each other and that their alienation would in turn lead to disaster on the battlefield. In a 1967 report titled "Increasing the Effectiveness of RVNAF," MACV urged Saigon to consider "altering basic training and unit training" to include the development of esprit de corps.[124] At the root of the problem, MACV had determined, were the training officers themselves. The report lamented that they were "lacking in the application of the basic fundamentals of leadership" and that they were "apathetic towards training requirements."[125] For some reason, the report concluded, ARVN training officers were reluctant to discuss the bonds between men under arms and the role of unit morale in battle.

There are several explanations for this behavior. Most have to do with how the government treated its officer corps. Several political leaders in Saigon saw the ARVN as protection against possible coups and insurance for their personal security. The intrigue that filled the streets of Saigon was made even more pervasive by the thinking that each politician had his or her "own officers."[126] Under these conditions, it was difficult if not impossible for officers to train troops politically. "We served at the behest of the politicians, and they feared the army," remembered one former ARVN officer.[127] "They forbade us to do much political training because they did not want an army of nationalists. That would have placed their own precarious political careers in constant jeopardy." Another former ARVN officer agreed, adding, "It was impossible for us to train the troops for the political struggle at all given the political mess in Saigon. We were on a very, very short leash."[128]

Problems in training never seemed to go away. With each passing year, the ARVN education program grew increasingly moribund. In the end, the absence of meaningful political education programs coupled with the ARVN's own experience at induction and training centers left a bitter taste in the mouths of most troops. Over time soldiers began to drift away from the national cause. "We felt unconnected to our mission," one former soldier reported. "After the meager political training we received, it is no wonder that so few of us felt any connection to the Saigon government and to our fellow soldiers. For us, the war was a matter of survival."[129] Ironically, few in the ARVN saw their lives as tied to the fate of their comrades. This disconnection helps explain the failure of the ARVN.

It now seems clear that the ARVN was also locked into a narrow reading of the political situation in Vietnam because of its own meager infantry and political training. Every setback or defeat reinforced the feeling among the troops that they were on the losing side of history. Most ARVN troops left their training for the battlefield convinced that the Communists went to that same place better prepared. It was not fear of dying that paralyzed the troops but rather the fear that they were not ready for combat and an awareness that they were not as committed to the national cause. Both feelings would have a dramatic impact on the battlefield. More important, however, poor training further damaged the ARVN's declining morale. Other social factors contributed significantly to a failure of confidence among the ARVN that figured largely in its eventual defeat.

THREE

MORALE

In his official 1975 postmortem on the Vietnam war, General Hamilton Howze of the U.S. Army declared that the greatest unanswered question of the war was why "the enemy apparently fought so much better than the South Vietnamese."[1] Howze suggested that the answer is simple: Communist forces had superior morale and motivation. This view is shared by a number of experts on the Vietnam war, including Jeffrey Race. In his classic study of the village war, *War Comes to Long An*, Race argued: "Victory of the revolutionary movement . . . could be stated as the communist leadership's comprehensive view of revolution as a stage-by-stage social process."[2] At the heart of that process, Race contended, was the understanding that the revolution was about replacing one social system with another. Once that idea was communicated properly, the Communist Party's success came about "through the development of social policies that led to superior motivation."[3] That motivation, according to Howze, "decisively defeated a South Vietnamese Army . . . numerically stronger and equipped with billions of dollars in U.S. arms."[4]

In the midst of the war, Americans in Vietnam never grew tired of trying to explain poor ARVN morale. MACV leaders were particularly interested in morale studies. Frances FitzGerald suggested that these studies "had their own scientific curiosity" and that they were examples of "perfectly circular logic."[5] Poor ARVN morale could be traced to improper training and poor leadership, which could be traced to motivational problems. What was the cause of the motivational problems? Most MACV studies concluded that it was poor political leadership in Saigon. Few government officials could tell the ARVN soldiers what they were fighting for or why the war mattered.

The most tangible result of this morale problem was an alarming desertion rate. According to one official U.S. report, the ARVN desertion rate for 1968 was an average of 17.7 per 1,000 assigned.[6] If these figures are accurate, ARVN desertions are among the highest in the history of modern warfare. For example, the U.S. desertion rate in 1944 during World War II was 3.2 per 1,000.[7] Like all statistics, however, ARVN desertion figures call for explanation. On the surface it appears that the ARVN did have "an institutionalized unwillingness to fight," as one critic claimed.[8] Beneath the surface, however, there are more complicated and more interesting explanations for such alarming numbers. Idiosyncrasies in reporting—for instance, what conditions were counted as "desertion"—is one. The ARVN had one of the most stringent active-duty classification systems in history. Fearful that the United States would not take its army seriously or believe its leaders were capable, the government in Saigon took a "get tough" stance with deserters. President Diem believed that he had to show resolve in order to impress the Americans. Beginning in 1957, at Diem's orders, the ARVN command listed as "absent without leave" any infantry soldier who failed to answer the morning muster.[9] Classification as a "deserter" usually came in about two weeks. Using this standard, Saigon routinely listed annual desertion figures at over 100,000. Such practice was highly unusual and probably added to the public relations and morale problems the ARVN already faced. Still, Saigon thought this tough stance would show the Americans that the South Vietnamese were serious about fielding an army.

Further blurring the picture, many Vietnamese deserters soon returned to their units.[10] Still others—over 60 percent in one 1967 study—did not return to their units but were later found serving in other units closer to home.[11] Although exact figures are not available, U.S. military advisers estimated that only 20 to 30 percent of the soldiers listed as deserters actually were.[12]

Still, desertion accounted for 77 percent of the ARVN's total manpower losses, and the Saigon government thought it had to respond somehow.[13] Typically, it used a carrot-and-stick approach that often created more problems than it solved. After 1966 ARVN soldiers found a new and improved award and decoration policy and a more liberal leave program. To discourage desertions, however, the government introduced a new fingerprinting identification system and established a desertion control board with unprecedented authority to make decisions on a soldier's status.[14] In addition, the United States agreed to provide $200,000VND per quarter for a deserter apprehension program.[15] In August 1966 RVN officials authorized long prison terms and the death sentence for desertion. South Vietnamese civil-military courts tried more than 12,000 deserters in the first two years of this tightened policy. A common sentence for an ARVN enlisted man convicted of desertion was five years' imprisonment at hard labor.[16]

Another way to look at desertion figures is to examine the underlying causes. Official U.S. reports and ARVN documents confirm that soldiers often left their assignments because of social concerns. Oral-history interviews support this thesis, suggesting that the soldiers did not fear contact with the enemy. The ARVN's military performance from 1973 through 1975 demonstrates that it was not an army "filled with cowards."[17] Casualty figures—five times the rate of U.S. forces—also indicate that fear was not the basic cause of ARVN desertions.[18] Overwhelmingly, the leading causes were inadequate leave, pay, food, housing, and medical care, all contributing factors to low morale.

Deficiencies in basic requirements were highlighted by the belief among ARVN troops that American soldiers seemed to "have things so much better."[19] "There were serious shortcomings in some very fundamental areas of life," complained Nguyen Hue, an ARVN infantry soldier from II Corps.[20] ARVN captain Tram Buu protested late in the war:

> U.S. soldiers are leaving, and you want the Vietnamese soldiers to take their place. But look at the U.S. soldier: he is well-paid, well-fed, well-supported, gets good housing, doesn't have to worry about the safety of his wife and family while he's away, gets R&R trip and sometimes a trip home, and he can leave for good in one year. The average ARVN soldier is not well-supported, makes very little money, and may live in squalor even when he is on leave, and knows he will be in the army for many years to come.[21]

Most ARVN enlisted men shared Captain Buu's concerns. In a MACV survey conducted in 1966, improvement in quality-of-life issues ranked as the highest priority for ARVN infantry soldiers.[22]

LEAVE

Of all the issues facing those concerned with the ARVN's welfare, none was more difficult than that of annual leave. Official policy permitted the infantry soldier only fifteen days of leave per year, taken in separate seven-to-eight-day periods. Such a short sabbatical hardly met the needs of men who had to return home to help harvest crops.[23] The leave system was also alien to Vietnamese culture. For centuries Vietnam had had a standing army that routinely went home to help plant and harvest crops, support parents, and assist in rituals of venerating ancestors. The government ignored this tradition, however, developing a very restrictive leave system that set aside Vietnamese customs and traditions known as *on* (a high moral debt) and *hieu* (filial piety).

The idea of *on* was instilled in Vietnamese at a young age. Children were taught that they owed their parents a moral debt of immense proportions. The debt could never be fully repaid, but children were expected to try to please their parents constantly and to obey them faithfully. A child's greatest comfort would come from the knowledge that he had reduced the burden of work on his parents. The debt did not diminish with age. As parents grew older, responsibility for their care rested more heavily on the children's shoulders. A person who chose to dismiss the moral debt and live according to his or her own aspirations and desires was ostracized in a society where social standing within the family determined everything, even what a person called him- or herself and others. Repaying the debt also extended to the ancestors and the generations to come. To show gratitude for the accumulated merit and social standing that his or her ancestors had provided, each person owed the next generation his or her best effort not to diminish the family's position within the *xa* (village).

According to Gerald Hickey, there was homogeneity in the social expectation of the *on*. "It was the desire of most villagers to improve their lot," Hickey wrote in his classic work, *The Village in Vietnam*, but only because wealth allowed for the proper veneration of ancestors and kept the family together.[24] Young people rarely left the confines of the family. If they did leave the village, it was usually to earn income to satisfy family obligations, not for independence or self-improvement. Obviously, the *on* carried tremendous responsibility, and it also limited one's actions in life. No wonder ARVN enlisted men believed that their parents' wishes came before those of the army and the nation.

Most ARVN infantry soldiers were responsible for the care of the ancestral house and family graves. In traditional Vietnam, peace and happiness in the afterlife could be achieved only through proper ancestor veneration—a duty that fell to all members of the family, but especially to the *truong toc* (eldest male), who was at the top of the patrilineage. The *truong toc* relied heavily upon his oldest sons to carry out family rituals. Neglect in any one of these areas meant great disrespect to the ancestors and the perception of damage to the family's good fortune.

When war came to Vietnam, young men did not dismiss their social responsibility to the family. "We thought of life in terms of generations and centuries," explained Le van Duong, an ARVN enlisted man from Tay Ninh province. "We saw the French and the Americans as temporary, but our family stretched out in front of us and stood solidly behind us. Our longer-term responsibility was not to a nationalistic cause but to our ancestors and family."[25] The government in Saigon, which could never link the two, appeared distant to peasants.

In addition to repaying the moral debt, most ARVN enlisted men took the concept of *hieu* seriously. "My primary role in life is to provide for my family and to venerate my ancestors," explained Nguyen Tang. "It was very difficult to leave the village . . . even if it was under threat . . . to fight. I would rather have died with my family at home than leave them and not be able to care for them."[26] *Hieu* was the center of Vietnamese family life. Children were taught from a young age that they were to obey, honor, and respect their parents. It would have been unthinkable for a young man to go off to war without satisfying his parents' wishes and needs first. Thousands of ARVN soldiers felt this family obligation, and when the contradiction between the concept of *hieu* and ARVN regulations became too great, they simply deserted to be closer to their families and responsibilities.

The Saigon government faced this manpower drain back to home villages within the first five years of war, yet its response to the desertions did not indicate that policy-makers or military leaders understood the cultural and social traditions of their countrymen. Instead of developing a policy more consistent with the needs of the peasants, as the Communists had done, Saigon's top officials helped create high desertion rates.

Some U.S. officials recognized the contradictions between peasant life and soldiering in the ARVN. In a special 1971 Rand Report titled "A People's Army for South Vietnam: A Vietnamese Solution," Brian Jenkins suggested that ARVN desertions would decrease significantly if the men were deployed in their home provinces and had a flexible service policy that took into account family obligations. Furthermore, Jenkins suggested that a new deployment strategy would help integrate the ARVN more fully into the overall allied military strategy:

> Almost one-half of South Vietnam's able-bodied men are already soldiers, not counting those who serve part-time in the People's Self-Defense Force. Because of the high casualty rate and even higher desertion rate, the annual net loss to the armed forces exceeds the potential influx of young men who reach draft age each year. The armed forces maintain their present size only by not allowing the release of any soldiers and by dipping deeper into the manpower pool of 18 to 38 year olds who have not already served. . . . Desertion rate of Regional Forces who serve in their home provinces is considerably lower than that of the regular army, and the desertion rate of Popular Forces who serve in their own villages, is lower yet.[27]

The Saigon government refused to reform its practices, however, claiming that the security needs in the urban areas were too great to release ARVN enlisted men to units in their home provinces.[28] In reality, successive Saigon governments had grown dependent on the ARVN as coup protection. RVN political leaders kept the army within arm's length for cover but also to watch for signs of intrigue. They routinely promoted officers based on loyalty, not battlefield performance, and these officers treated the ARVN like a private security force. Lacking proper ideological training and suffering from poor morale, the ARVN was no match for the People's Army of Viet Nam (PAVN) and the People's Liberation Armed Forces (PLAF).

THE PEOPLE'S ARMY

Although the Communist Party was never as successful as it claimed in building PAVN morale, it did not face the same desertion problems.[29] PAVN forces were often hundreds of miles from their homes too, and for long stretches of time, and were just as firmly tied to traditional culture, but the party's political training by and large had successfully linked peasant customs with its nationalistic and patriotic cause. By promoting the concepts of *dan toc* (the people) and *quoc gia* (the nation), the party had extended family obligations to the larger community and state. Ho Chi Minh and his followers realized that they could force the Saigon regime into a static and reactive position by linking Vietnam's past with its future. In fact, as historian Philip Catton has explained, Diem's vision for modern Vietnam purposefully rejected the traditions and mores of village life.[30] His distaste for the countryside was legendary, and the party thought it could exploit this obvious weakness. Furthermore, strategists in Hanoi and the National Liberation Front (NLF) believed that Diem's U.S. allies "were not at all interested in the people they were supposed to be defending."[31]

The party borrowed heavily from Marx, Lenin, and Mao, but the theories and strategies were adapted to local conditions. Ho Chi Minh had realized early in his struggle that Confucianism and Marxism were compatible in Vietnam and that this combination would serve the revolution well. Both stressed social order; both believed there were laws governing historical forces; and both emphasized duty and obligation to society, as opposed to individual rights. These Confucian values were at the core of political education, even if their place in society has been overstated.

Ho also understood that revolutionary success depended upon his cadres' training in two areas: revolutionary virtues and revolutionary patriotism. By revolutionary virtues, Ho accentuated the need for cadres to exhibit generosity, courage, respect, uprightness, and fidelity to learning. These Confucian values were at the core of military education. Revolutionary patriotism implied that the people of Vietnam shared a geographic past and a strong attachment to the land. The mythic land tied all Vietnamese together in a narrative that led Ho Chi Minh to state repeatedly that "Vietnam is one people, one land, with four thousand years of history." When the land came under attack, therefore, cadres mobilized the general population by promoting the concept of the fatherland. Accordingly, the Vietnam war is referred to by Marxist scholars in Vietnam as *Cuoc khang chien chong My, cuu nuoc* (the great anti-American resistance war for national salvation of the fatherland).[32]

The fatherland concept developed in Vietnam after the party promoted the idea that the land was sacred and that all Vietnamese had an obligation, similar to *on,* to save the country from foreign invaders. Perhaps the term *long ai quoc* (love the country) represents this notion best. It arrived in Vietnamese discourses on patriotism and anticolonialism in the early-twentieth-century poems of Phan Boi Chau, a leading anticolonial activist. Chau's poems encouraged Vietnamese to "love the country" and "love the race."[33]

The poems reverberated throughout Vietnam at the time when the monarchy and the old political order fell apart under the weight of French colonization. On the ashes of the old regime, Chau urged his countrymen to develop political loyalty and a sense of national obligation to the new patriotic cause. The party appropriated Chau's ideas and developed them into the belief in partisanship known in Vietnam as *cu nghia ai quoc* (patriotism). One of Ho Chi Minh's aliases, Nguyen Ai Quoc (Nguyen the patriot), drew on this very formulation. The party also encouraged the veneration of past heroes in the same manner in which Vietnamese paid tribute to their ancestors. Cadre training manuals stressed the need to "venerate our heroes" and "repay our heroes for past sacrifices."[34] In this way—and many more, according to historian Greg Lockhart—the party extended family loyalty and obligation to the nation.[35]

As romantic and idealized as cadre training about patriotism and nationalism was, it served its purpose. Thousands of young Vietnamese men and women from the North marched south thinking that they were fighting for the future of the race and the fatherland. They willingly left family and friends to make the dangerous journey down the Ho Chi Minh Trail without regard for leaves or any of the social obligations that consumed the ARVN.

The party's success in mobilizing the peasantry to its cause contrasted sharply with the RVN's, a telling difference between life in the ARVN and soldiering in the PAVN. The party was also able to build esprit de corps through its national message, something the RVN government refused to do. According to Bui Diem, former South Vietnamese ambassador to the United States, Ngo Dinh Diem's own policies specifically forbade the development of any patriotic attitudes.[36] Fearing that a rival might harness nationalist sentiment, Diem demoted anyone caught trying to rally the troops. Members of the ARVN consequently felt unconnected to anything larger than themselves, a concept alien to Vietnamese culture. As journalist Frances FitzGerald correctly reported at the time, the ARVN was never more than a collection of individuals.[37]

FOOD

As the saying goes, an army travels on its stomach. Ancient armies fought relatively short battles at short distances from their food supply because a soldier had to eat at least one meal per day to remain effective. In the nineteenth century railroads and canned goods released the army to farther fields of combat, but it was still dependent on complicated logistics for resupply.[38] Air drops changed all of that in the twentieth century, but the nature of wars for liberation created its own special problems with regard to food delivery.

During the Vietnam war the Communists gained a legendary reputation for their ability to move quickly and deeply into the jungles and highlands, and away from enemy forces, by "living off the land."[39] What this phrase usually meant was that Communist cadres secured food locally from sympathetic villagers or took food and supplies by force. For long journeys soldiers took rice balls stuffed inside the inner tubes of bicycle tires. One rice ball per day was often the only meal for those traveling at high speed under adverse conditions.[40]

In his memoir, former NLF leader Truong Nhu Tang described life on the run: "In addition to rice, each man's personal larder was rounded out by a small hunk of salt, a piece of monosodium glutamate, and perhaps a little dried fish or meat. The rice ration for both leaders and fighters was twenty kilos a month."[41] Bui Tin, a PAVN colonel, made the long journey down the Ho Chi Minh Trail on several occasions. Each time, he reported, food was found locally:

We woke every morning at 4 o'clock to cook rice, which we ate with roasted sesame mixed with salt. Sometimes we were able to catch fish in streams. We dried and salted them, although there was often more salt than fish. Then when we ran out of salt, we licked the banana leaves used to wrap the dried fish. What we really lacked was vegetables and fruit. Occasionally, we would find an orange tree close to a deserted house and really treasured its fruit. In the same way, whenever we saw any edible leaves we stopped to pick them to make a soup for the evening meal.[42]

Despite these hardships, Communist officers claim that food shortages never led their cadres to suffer from serious morale problems. "We always knew that we could find food if we needed it," reported General Nguyen Dinh Uoc of the PAVN. "Local villagers were always willing to give us what they had, and the diet was familiar to us. We never ate food outside the normal Vietnamese diet and this helped us keep our strength and good spirits."[43] Even if General Uoc understated the amount of looting that took place and overstated PAVN morale, he was correct in saying that Communist soldiers did not share ARVN troops' concerns about food. Nor did PLAF and PAVN field hospitals often report malnutrition.[44]

For the ARVN, however, food was always a problem. Throughout the war, deficient field rations weakened the army's ability to conduct sustained combat operations. According to one MACV report, the number of non-combat-related illnesses was unusually high in the ARVN because of poor nutrition in the field.[45] Although rations changed over time and according to each unit's position in the field, most South Vietnamese infantry soldiers consistently complained of poor food quality and quantity. "We never had enough to eat," said Nguyen van Hieu, and the distribution system "forced us to spend much of our time searching for food."[46]

Several U.S. "After Action Reports" confirmed this problem. According to a December 1967 statement, ARVN battalions often supplemented their Vietnamese rations with U.S. rations acquired through the "buddy system." Apparently U.S. infantry units often gave ARVN soldiers extra food rations "in the interests of harmony and in the spirit of the combined operation."[47] However, this type of sharing and cooperation was not official U.S. policy; it depended on the varying inclinations of American units. "If it were not for the kindness of our American friends . . . , the enlisted men," one former ARVN soldier told me recently, "we would have been in a terrible fix."[48] Sharing U.S. rations also meant that the ARVN soldiers did not venture into the local market to supplement their own food supply—handily denying the enemy intelligence on troop movements based on food purchase patterns and making more ARVN infantry soldiers available for duty.

When ARVN units were forced to rely on their own rations, they habitually used Class A rations—fresh local products purchased by a supply officer in the Vietnamese market—instead of operational rations (canned goods). "The ARVN soldier does not like the operational ration," concluded a U.S. report, "because it is not palatable to him, does not contain fresh meat and vegetables which he considers essential to his diet, and he loses his advance ration allowance (36 Vietnamese dollars per day) when this ration is issued."[49] The daily diet was extremely important to southern Vietnamese, who had always had an abundant food supply, even during the French war. "The South has traditionally been the bread basket of Vietnam," a former ARVN officer explained after the war, "and we had always considered our diet part of what made us Vietnamese. We were used to the high-protein foods like *bun thit heo nung* [rice vermicelli with grilled pork] and *tom xao xa ot* [shrimp with lemon grass on rice], but then we were forced to eat meat from a can made in the United States. It made me sick."[50]

In his memoir, *Doi Quan Ngu* (Life in the army), Tran Ngoc Nhuan reported that rice made available for ARVN troops was "stored too long, eaten by rice worms" and that it "turned into powder when pressed hard."[51] Another former ARVN soldier complained, "We could see our traditional foods all around us, but we were forced to eat imported food in the field. It made no sense to me or my friends. We would have been better off without the ration system."[52] To combat this problem, many U.S. advisers simply allowed the ARVN to buy and use Class A rations to replace the standard operational ration, despite the security risks of large purchases in local markets.

Another difficulty facing the ARVN was food rations for attachment forces. When extra military personnel—Kit Carson Scouts, interpreters, local guides—were attached to regular ARVN units, official food rations for them were rarely authorized in advance; not until late 1970 was there an attempt to rectify the problem.[53] Nguyen Hue, an ARVN volunteer, discussed the problem in a recent interview: "Because of my skills as an interpreter of mountain people languages, I was often moved from unit to unit. My food ration never seemed to find me, and I often had to buy food from local villagers."[54] Nguyen Co Huong, a Kit Carson Scout in II Corps, also reported problems receiving his food ration while in the field. "For most of 1968 my ration of food goods was never quite right. I also had problems with the ration tickets."[55]

One of the most astonishing aspects of the ARVN food program was that the cost of meals was deducted from the pay of infantry soldiers.[56] "We had such limited access to food during the war," complained an ARVN veteran, "but we still had to pay for what little we ate with our units."[57] The requirement to pay for food was an enormous burden on ARVN soldiers already struggling with rampant inflation, and the cost of food seemed excessive to most. For example, in 1964 all single privates and corporals were required to eat meals at the unit's mess hall. A supply officer deducted the cost of all meals at a fixed daily rate of $26.50VND in rural areas and $33.00VND in cities.[58] When an ARVN soldier was away from his home base, he received combat rations that were subject to pay deductions at the prevailing rates of the daily food allowance. The problem, of course, was that the enlisted man's pay could not cover his food expenses. In 1964 the typical ARVN private's pay was $36,122.00VND.[59] On average, then, an ARVN private eating with his unit in 1964 was forced to spend nearly one-third of his entire annual salary on food. Since most ARVN soldiers were supporting their entire extended family, this was a system designed to fail and to leave the ARVN searching for alternative food sources.

Food supply problems became so serious that one former ARVN enlisted man remembered habitually searching the bodies of Communist soldiers for food.[60] Others bought food locally, stole from nearby villages, or returned to their villages for resupply. "I went home at least twice per month without official leave," remarked Thinh Pham. "There was no way I was going to pay for rations at the rate we were charged, and I did not want to steal food from my fellow countrymen. I know that it was wrong to leave my unit, but even my commander knew that we were faced with an impossible situation, so he never reported me as missing."[61]

Corruption made a bad situation worse. Graft in the rationing system often led ARVN soldiers to work outside established protocol, creating severe tensions between the South Vietnamese and their American advisers. "We had to make sure that the ARVN weren't alienating the local population by stealing their food," explained one U.S. adviser.[62] Another concern was that assigned food rations were not making their way to ARVN soldiers. To fight corruption, MACV introduced in July 1967 a system of supported supplies during combat operations. These rations consisted of an A-Pack of 800 grams of dehydrated rice and a B-Pack consisting of canned meat, pork, or fish, plus an accessory package of salt, pepper, and candy. Indications were, however, "that rations were not reaching the troops. Most were being held at corps level where administrative red tape made it improbable that the units in combat operations were able to obtain them when required."[63]

Perhaps most infuriating to the ARVN enlisted man was the careless disregard that some U.S. advisers and the Saigon government showed for traditional Vietnamese food culture. Food has always occupied a special place in the customs and rituals of rural Vietnam. It is the centerpiece of all family and village ceremonies, and some dishes are the basic offerings at temples and shrines. In traditional Vietnam—the Red River Delta and along the coast—rice determined (and still does to some extent) the rhythm of life. Almost all villagers were caught up in the seasonal round of planting and harvesting, and most public ceremonies revolved around rice production. Peasants made offerings to begin the rice season and celebrate the harvest. The emperor maintained a special temple to the gods of soil and grain. At the beginning of each lunar New Year, Tet, he presented a ritual offering to the gods and planted the first paddy seed. In the colonial period, the French knew enough to allow these celebrations to continue.

During the American war, few in Washington or Saigon paid much attention to such customs. Modernizing ideologies originating in Washington and Saigon spared little room for something as culturally fixed as cuisine. Food was important to the ARVN, however, and most soldiers noticed the lack of care and attention.

Particularly troublesome was the decline of rice culture in the RVN. For centuries an exporter of rice, during the war the RVN was forced to feed its soldiers imported rice. In fact, as the war dragged on the only food aid supplement given by the U.S. to ARVN soldiers was rice grown in the United States, Japan, Thailand, and South Korea. Washington's Commercial Import Program provided urban Vietnamese with access to rice at reasonable prices, but only by flooding the market with imported rice.[64] That South Vietnam had to import rice at the same time that North Vietnam was exporting rice was not lost on the average ARVN soldier.[65] Throughout the war there was a feeling in the ARVN that the war was already lost because the country was not feeding itself. "When we had to import rice," reported Nguyen van Pham, a former ARVN corporal, "I knew the war was over. That Washington or Saigon did not understand this problem just shows how out of touch they were with the people of Vietnam. Their lack of understanding of rural Vietnamese culture made me sick every day."[66]

A vivid example of this cultural insensitivity was the replacement of Vietnamese *nuoc mam* (fermented fish sauce) with imported soy sauce. *Nuoc mam*, a staple of the Vietnamese diet, is high in protein. Together with rice, it provided Vietnamese soldiers with the perfect mixture of protein and carbohydrates. And it was readily available. The move to replace *nuoc mam* with soy sauce came about because U.S. supply officers attached to ARVN units believed that the foul-smelling *nuoc mam* spoiled too easily. Matters of diet and taste aside, ARVN soldiers also resented importing soy sauce. "We were treated as if it did not matter that the war was taking place in our country," reported one ARVN vet, "or that we were Vietnamese and had a unique diet. We were given what all Asians should eat, according to the Americans . . . soy sauce."[67]

Worse still, according to several former ARVN soldiers, most of the imported soy sauce came from South Korea.[68] During the war South Korea sent nearly 10 percent of its entire armed forces to Vietnam and suffered a casualty rate equal to that of the United States.[69] More important, South Korean troops were given substantial offensive missions inside Vietnam, while the ARVN was reduced to mainly a security force. "We hated that the Americans gave the South Koreans such significance in our country," commented Cao van Ngia, a former ARVN corporal.[70] "They went on offensive missions alone from an early date, while we sat and waited for our orders. That we then imported our food from them convinced me and most of my friends that the Americans would never view us as a legitimate nation."[71] Another former ARVN soldier put it this way: "How could the U.S. bring South Korean troops to our country and unleash them? How could the U.S. then make us eat their food? What sense does any of this make? Is that any way to build a nation or care for its soldiers?"[72] Most ARVN troops thought that their American counterparts favored Koreans over Vietnamese. Importing food from South Korea was simply an outward manifestation of deeper racial and political feelings.

Many ARVN veterans complained that aspects of their daily diet had a dramatic impact on morale. According to Nguyen van Thien, food was a constant worry. "We needed to eat in order to fight, but we could not bring ourselves to eat those imported rations."[73] Another explained, "I know I was listed as a deserter, but actually I left to get food from some cousins in a nearby village. I eventually came back to my unit, but it took me weeks to clear my name with my commanding officer."[74] If an army does travel on its stomach, clearly the ARVN did not want to stray too far from its home or its home diet.

PAY

Equally troubling to the ARVN soldier was inadequate pay. Throughout the war, U.S. advisers complained to officials in Washington and Saigon that pay and allowances for the ARVN had not kept pace with the cost of living.[75] By 1969 an army private made half as much as a common laborer.[76] Part of the problem, of course, was that pay increases did not keep up with inflation. The cost of basic foodstuffs and household supplies continued to rise in the 1960s as the arrival of Americans and their money had an inflationary impact on the South Vietnamese economy. Attempts to rectify the situation always involved increasing pay, but little was done to control costs, and this too meant that ARVN salaries remained inadequate. "We could never buy the basic goods we needed because the prices for everything kept going up," complained the wife of an ARVN soldier.[77]

U.S. attempts to create a new pay and allowance system met with disaster. On June 1, 1967, MACV authorized a "rice allowance" of $200VND for each ARVN soldier and each dependent. Under this new policy an ARVN private with three years of service and five dependents (defined only as immediate family) earned a base pay of $1,680VND per month, a family allowance of $1,012VND per month, a cost-of-living allowance of $2,212VND per month, a rice allocation of $1,200VND per month, and a temporary pay raise of $1,471VND per month, for a total of $7,575VND per month.[78] The problems of introducing pay increases into an inflationary economy soon became apparent, however, as prices continued to soar. Worse still, price supports and pay increases created a certain dependency on the United States that the Saigon government and its soldiers found hard to shake. "We used to be an exporter of many agricultural products," explained one former Saigon official, "but the Americans introduced a system that made us buy what we used to grow ourselves. Our soldiers' pay could never keep up with the rising costs of imported goods. I don't buy the argument that the war made it necessary to import goods. The Vietcong didn't import food and clothing."[79]

Throughout the war the Saigon government routinely spent 50 percent of its budget on non-defense-related items. The United States supported these expenditures directly but never provided enough maintenance to meet rising needs or costs. By 1965 the South Vietnamese deficit had mushroomed to unmanageable proportions, and the inflation rate approached unprecedented levels. According to Jeffrey Clarke, consumer prices in South Vietnam rose 900 percent between 1964 and 1972. The cost of rice during this period rose an unbelievable 1,400 percent.[80] Military personnel on fixed salaries felt these economic strains intensely. During that same period salaries of enlisted men rose only 500 percent, despite fifty redress actions.[81]

With rising prices and lower salaries, many ARVN supplemented their incomes with part-time jobs or returned to their families for food, clothing, and shelter. Those near large cities could earn extra money driving taxis, teaching school, or moonlighting in construction jobs created by the war. Soldiers stationed in rural areas had fewer opportunities. Still, they were allowed to cultivate gardens to feed themselves and make extra money. By 1966 the government had actually organized a program to coordinate such activity, creating new opportunities for ARVN soldiers to grow their own rice and sell pigs and chickens they raised to the government. The surplus meat would then be turned over to local villagers at reduced prices. This subsidy program worked well at first, but the government simply ran out of money to sustain it.

The official exchange rate between the U.S. dollar and the Vietnamese piaster also created inflationary pressures that had a devastating impact on ARVN morale. From 1964 to 1972 the exchange rate rose from $35VND to $420VND per $1USD, decreasing the actual value of ARVN pay. For example, an ARVN private saw his pay in real terms drop from $77USD to $30USD per month.[82] Nguyen Tin Thanh, a private from Da Lat, reported that he had to sell family possessions just to keep pace with his devalued salary and expenses. "I was losing money every year. I remember going to my commander to ask what the latest exchange rate was. He told me it did not matter because it would be higher in five minutes anyway. It was devastating to watch my pay buy less and less for my family."[83] Another ARVN private complained that he made less in the army than his younger brother was earning parking cars in Saigon. "Can you imagine? I was putting my life on the line every day, and my fourteen-year-old brother was making twice as much money each month. I was disgusted."[84]

Facing these financial pressures, many ARVN soldiers simply left their units. "I felt like I could not do anything but return to my family," Nguyen van Hieu explained. "I was forced to go home for food and work to support my wife and three kids. No one told us how we were supposed to fight the Communists and take care of our families at the same time."[85]

Inflation was just part of the problem. ARVN enlisted men felt further demoralized by the discrepancy between their pay and officers' salaries, often four times higher. In most modern armies, that spread is below average, but the ARVN was unique in several respects. First, the educational discrepancy between officers and enlisted men in the ARVN was not as dramatic as is usually the case. Second, many officers had obtained their posts based on connections rather than qualifications. It was well known that the ARVN created much of its officer corps through family ties, personal loyalties, and bribes.[86] Finally, the difference in experience level between an ARVN private and an officer was not as great as in other modern armies. Most ARVN privates lacked a year or two of formal educational and training to qualify as an officer. However, because of the army's growing needs, few were given the opportunity for advancement. One requirement, that all officers had to hold a bachelor's degree, seemed particularly outrageous to enlisted men living on low wages.[87] The government created further distance between officers and enlisted men by offering "special allowances" for selected officers, including housekeeping, clothing, and entertainment.

One of the few "special allowances" available to ARVN enlisted men was an enlistment or reenlistment bonus. To be eligible, a soldier had to reenlist for a minimum of two years. The government prorated the bonus for additional years of service. The bonus was paid out over time: the first installment was included with the soldier's first month of pay under the new enlistment from the central government. The second came with the first month's pay from the soldier's unit, and the final payment came after three months of service. Of course the government saved money when a soldier was killed within the first three months of his new tour of duty. After the government drastically altered its conscription policies in 1965 and again in 1967, bonuses became a privilege of the past.

Enlisted men were sometimes encouraged to undergo further technical training, and ARVN officers often enticed them with increased pay. Beginning in 1962, the government promised a technical bonus to all enlisted men holding a B1 or B2 diploma. This raise was extended to all privates who had completed a CC1 or CC2 training certification course.[88] The problems with this system became evident early in the war. Of the 2,000 enlisted men in I Corps who requested further technical training in 1964, only thirty were allowed time away from their home units to attend classes. "We had a system for advancement," remembered one ARVN private, "but we could never use it. The irony was that the officers we so wanted to become made the decisions that kept us where we were . . . as enlisted men."[89]

One unusual attempt to create equity in the pay system actually caused more problems than it solved. In 1964 the government announced that it would add a cost-of-living allowance to ARVN pay based on rank and location. Officials in Saigon divided the country into two economic zones, a "high" cost-of-living area—Phuoc Long, Phuoc Thanh, Binh Long, Hue, Da Nang, Da Lat, Saigon, Gia Dinh, Cho Lon, and Cam Ranh—and a "low" cost-of-living zone that covered most of the highlands and the Mekong Delta. The difference in pay was so substantial that it provided another reason for the ARVN to "hug the coastline and ignore the village war in rural provinces."[90] Many ARVN officers complained bitterly during the war that the United States handled all offensive military operations and that the ARVN had been reduced to little more than a security force along coastal enclaves.[91] According to Clarke, the official U.S. policy, begun in 1965 with the introduction of American ground troops, "gave the bulk of the South Vietnamese regular army area security missions and left only eleven reserve battalions to participate in mobile offensive operations with U.S. ground units."[92] Supporting this policy, however, was the ARVN's own pay scale. More than one frustrated RVN analyst in Saigon noted the problem, but the decision to create pay "zones" was never revoked.

Low pay and inflation wreaked havoc on ARVN morale. Instead of caring for their families, as custom dictated, many ARVN enlisted men became dependent on them, a position that took its toll over time. "We know that the government and our superiors have done many things to help us and our families to alleviate miseries," one soldier remarked, "but that was not enough. We have been tightening our belts to make ends meet but there is only a limit to what we can do. How can we fight with an empty stomach? As our centuries-old wisdom has it: To be able to practice the 'correct way,' one must have enough to eat first."[93]

One U.S. officer explained, however, that what the Vietnamese wanted was an American standard—they wanted to live, eat, and get paid like Americans—and that was precisely what the war was about. Only victory would bring about that change.[94]

HOUSING

Soldiers struggling to make ends meet, to find food, and to fulfill their obligation to family too often lived in shacks. The lack of suitable housing for the ARVN soldiers and their dependents became one of the war's most embarrassing lapses and contributed significantly to desertions and low morale. Throughout the war there never seemed to be enough housing, especially for ARVN dependents; the quality and upkeep of troop quarters was especially dismal. Ngo Ca Cong, a former ARVN soldier, confessed that he often left his unit to take care of his family and search for food but that he also left when housing "was just too crowded or there was an outbreak of some illness."[95] Ironically, the soldiers would have preferred to be closer to home "sleeping in hammocks hung from the trees"[96] than tied to remote, overcrowded bases.

From the beginning of the war, the lack of suitable ARVN housing plagued American commanders and political leaders in Washington. "It was clear," reported former secretary of defense Robert S. McNamara, "that Saigon would do little for ARVN housing."[97] MACV commanders routinely conducted ARVN housing surveys. In 1965, for example, MACV estimated that the ARVN needed 200,000 family units for regular forces. By the end of 1966 fewer than 60,000 had been built, and budget figures from 1967 suggest that fewer than 4,000 were added to the total figure that year.[98] By the Tet Offensive in 1968, therefore, less than 30 percent of the 1965 needs had been met. Of course the ARVN continued to increase its overall troop strength annually, far outstripping the 1965 housing needs within one year.

Several problems plagued ARVN housing: graft, corruption, budgeting procedures, and short supplies. The government's inability to solve these problems kept it from earning the full confidence of the South Vietnamese people. "If we could not meet our most basic requirements," remarked Nguyen van Hieu, "how could we mobilize our entire society for the war effort?"[99]

A look at some of the schemes for dependent housing illustrates the difficulties faced by MACV and the ARVN. The first, initiated in 1962 and implemented by the Social Welfare Directorate of South Vietnam (SWD), created two construction programs to build military villages for officers. Over four years the office for dependent housing supplied construction materials to individual ARVN units, allowing them to build shelters at a rate of fifty buildings (with ten units in each building) per year.[100] Unit commanders were given the authority to build wherever they saw fit. If private land was involved, the United States would reimburse the landholder at the local market rate. On the surface the plan had merit. Unlike many other joint U.S.-RVN ventures, the first dependent housing plan gave resources and control to the ARVN. It was also free from the bureaucratic nightmares evident in other army programs.

From the start, however, there were serious shortcomings. Some were caused by the archaic political system in Saigon, but others were more endemic and pointed to significant levels of corruption in most areas of ARVN life. The local control promised at the beginning soon gave way to unprecedented infighting and stagnation. The first official report by SWD revealed far too many irregularities in the buildings and the construction timetables.[101] An inventory taken after several housing units were completed revealed that the number of buildings did not match the total of materials issued, suggesting to Saigon officials what they probably already knew: corruption.[102] Newly constructed buildings lacked toilets, many had deteriorated beyond repair in only a few months, and most needed major repairs after one year. In a special SWD subcommittee report, investigators revealed that many of the housing units had been left vacant or unfinished because troops had been reassigned. SWD suggested that the government create a new housing authority that dealt directly with the Americans to secure needed funds and materials.[103]

The government responded to the SWD report with its usual deftness. It ordered SWD "to clean up the problems in dependent housing"[104] and

to create a special committee to deal specifically with ARVN housing issues. As was their custom, Saigon officials simply moved the problem to
another level of bureaucracy. The new SWD committee issued a bold report
early in its tenure that claimed a "new day had come to the ARVN housing puzzle."[105] To improve the quality of housing units, the SWD initiated
a new construction plan requiring that all ARVN housing include cement
floors, ceilings, plumbing, and toilets. The idea, SWD officials claimed, was
to make ARVN housing "permanent."[106] The rub was that all new building
was to be done by local contractors and that land purchases were no longer
tied to market conditions.

No one in MACV was surprised when its own initial reports of the SWD's
new housing plan revealed that only 1,000 new housing units had been built
each year.[107] The level of graft was unprecedented. According to Ngo van
Chuong, a former Saigon official attached to the attorney general's office,
"there were more complaints about corruption in the SWD-controlled program than in any other ARVN initiative in the early years of the American
war."[108] The problems were not with SWD officials, who by and large
were honest, but with the system they had created. "There were simply too
many areas where the undisciplined could make good money," remembered
Nguyen van Mui, a reporter for one of Saigon's daily newspapers who covered the housing story early in 1964. "There were at least four ways to
make money on building ARVN dependent housing: selling land, selling
materials, providing construction, and granting permits. Each had a built-in
guarantee of big money."[109]

To document SWD's ineptness, MACV ordered its own study of ARVN
dependent housing in IV Corps. The results, as most MACV officials had
predicted, showed that corruption had destroyed all that SWD had hoped
to build. In 1965 IV Corps received a $10 million grant from the United
States to construct housing for ARVN enlisted dependents. Not one unit
was built.[110] Local commanders and South Vietnamese officials siphoned
off money and supplies to rent-seeking construction projects that promised
them personal rewards.[111] Further investigation by MACV officials revealed
that IV Corps may, in fact, have had the most efficient program in the SWD
housing plan. According to one former MACV official, "Construction projects offered anyone interested a real estate bonanza. Anyone could make
money off the housing program."[112]

When General William Westmoreland took command of MACV in June
1964, one of his first agenda items was to "fix" the dependent housing
problem. He correctly pointed out that ARVN morale was tied directly to
proper housing and other material conditions.[113] To combat corruption,

Westmoreland used U.S. funds to support a self-help housing system that bypassed the Saigon government and ARVN command. The plan required enlisted men to use U.S. supplies to build their own temporary housing. U.S. advisers and construction engineers would monitor the progress.[114] This self-help program was first established in base areas near Saigon; if successful, it would spread to other provinces.

But the program quickly failed.[115] Land purchases from the Saigon government proved troublesome, and individual soldiers were never given the time to construct the units. In 1967 a frustrated Westmoreland announced the transfer of responsibility for ARVN dependent housing construction to the Engineer's Office with MACV's Central Logistics Command. According to the general's new plan, MACV would directly purchase all of the land and pay private contractors to construct nearly 200,000 housing units at a cost of $7.6 million.[116]

Westmoreland's revised plan for dependent housing also failed. By the end of 1968 his successor, General Creighton Abrams, complained bitterly that the self-help and dependent housing programs were a complete failure. He suggested that at the current construction rate, it would take fourteen years to finish the limited self-help program near Saigon.[117] For two years the dependent housing program languished while MACV tried to find a solution. In early 1969 the new secretary of defense, Melvin Laird, approved $8 million in funds to provide supplies and materials for construction of 1,160 additional family shelters in fiscal year 1969.[118] Laird also announced an eight-year plan to house 40,000 ARVN soldiers and their dependents in vacated American facilities and construct an additional 200,000 new housing units. The United States would provide $6 million per year for new ARVN housing and cost-share with the RVN government at an annual level of $13.2 million.[119]

Despite good intentions, Laird's plan also failed to meet the ARVN's increasing needs. Saigon's archaic annual budgeting procedures prevented funds from being available when needed to purchase building materials. As a result, by the end of 1970 less than half of the anticipated shelters had been built. By 1972 only 1,690 units had been constructed as military conflicts took precedence over housing.[120] Corruption continued to plague the housing program during Laird's tenure, and eventually the Nixon administration abandoned most of its housing programs.

According to Nguyen van Dinh, a former Saigon official who worked closely with MACV on housing issues, overcrowded barracks and bases led to a host of social problems.[121] Improper sanitation, most significantly, led to a number of serious health concerns. During the war ARVN soldiers were more likely to be infected with malaria or cholera than to die in combat. Overcrowded housing exacerbated both of these conditions. The anopheles mosquito that spread malaria was common in southern Vietnam. To prevent malaria, each ARVN enlisted man was required to sleep under a mosquito net in camp or with a headnet and insect repellent when in the field. Sadly, at some camps these items were not given to individual soldiers but rather allocated by the standard number of beds.[122] Overcrowding led enlisted men to add beds without including proper netting. Moreover, the weekly dose of chloroquine-primaquine assigned to all ARVN servicemen, a prophylactic against malaria, assumed housing stability that simply did not exist. Because of overcrowded housing conditions, many soldiers simply fell through the health care safety net.

Cholera, an acute bacterial infection of the intestine caused by ingestion of food or water contaminated with the *Vibrio cholerae* bacillus, was also often attributed to poor sanitation in overcrowded ARVN housing. The incubation period is short, usually one to five days. Cholera tends to occur under conditions of unhygienic disposal of human feces, an inadequate supply of safe drinking water, and unsanitary facilities for food storage and preparation. Overcrowded ARVN housing units provided the perfect environment for cholera to develop and spread rapidly. Symptoms of the disease include vomiting and watery diarrhea, which can result in severe dehydration. If left untreated, death can occur rapidly; fatality rates in Vietnam during the war were often near 50 percent.[123]

When cholera outbreaks hit ARVN camps, many enlisted men simply returned to their families. Some commanding officers even encouraged these "medical desertions" because they knew from their own experience that mass chemoprophylaxis (antibiotics) did little to control the spread of the disease. According to Huynh van Cuong, a former ARVN officer, "there was little point in keeping my men in the very conditions that had helped create the cholera outbreak to begin with. At the first sign of the disease, I encouraged them to leave camp for a few days if they showed no signs of illness. Of course, we often tried to go out on maneuvers when outbreaks did occur, but the men were so demoralized that they were not very effective."[124]

Disease associated with poor housing conditions had a devastating impact on morale. Some ARVN encampments entered the war's mythology as "death camps," more dangerous than the Communists. "If you got sent to Long Khanh or Duc My, you were sure to die of some disease," claimed an ARVN veteran.[125] On some level, troops prepared themselves mentally for combat deaths and casualties. It was difficult, however, to come to terms with perhaps the fiercest horseman of the Apocalypse: pestilence. Some illnesses were natural by-products of war, but most ARVN soldiers considered malaria and cholera "domestic diseases."[126] These two ailments were part of everyday life in the rural villages of Vietnam, but villagers had learned how to cope with disease on their own terms. Once in the army, ARVN soldiers were removed from their traditional domestic reference points, a severely dislocating and demoralizing experience.

MEDICAL CARE

Soldiers' fears of domestic diseases were compounded by their belief that their medical care in the field was substandard. Although the United States spent millions of dollars on medical aid in Vietnam, ARVN enlisted men often complained about the quality of their care. Nguyen van Thanh, an ARVN captain, remembered that "men in my unit died in the field because of poor treatment."[127] Another ARVN officer reported that conditions in the hospitals "were pitiful," especially when "compared to the Americans."[128] One former Saigon official agreed, stating that "the ARVN's concerns about their medical treatment were justified. It seemed clear to me that there were two systems of care: one for the Americans and one for the South Vietnamese. Because of this obvious discrepancy, I think ARVN morale suffered tremendously."[129]

ARVN soldiers generally complained about two aspects of their medical care: evacuation from the field of battle and treatment in hospitals. When soldiers were wounded, they were usually first treated in field hospitals. According to Lieutenant General Dong van Khuyen, resources were so limited toward the end of the war at ARVN field hospitals that staff sometimes washed and reused disposable supplies such as bandages, syringes, needles, surgical gloves, and intravenous sets.[130] Personnel shortages often forced recovering patients to clean wards and toilet facilities.[131] Lack of running water and proper sanitation were constant problems facing those who treated the ARVN soldier, and most field hospitals needed repair. When soldiers were successfully evacuated to military hospitals in large towns and cities, they often had to wait days for treatment and sleep on cots in the hallways because bed occupancy was always near 98 percent of total capacity. The Republic of Vietnam Armed Forces (all those under arms for South Vietnam) had a high of 24,547 hospital beds at its disposal in 1973, far short of the estimated need of 35,000.[132]

Perhaps the most serious shortcoming, however, was lack of medical personnel. In 1966 South Vietnam had only 1,000 qualified doctors, and of these 700 had already been forced into the armed forces. This shortfall put a tremendous burden on the general population but also meant that a growing number of ARVN casualties failed to get the attention they deserved. The supply of doctors was further reduced by the number who served hospitals as chief administrators to fulfill an RVN policy that only medical doctors could serve in that position. Little information is available to explain the requirement.[133] Perhaps leaders in Saigon feared that military or political administration would leave hospitals vulnerable to corruption. In any event, medical doctors needed to treat the growing patient list were siphoned off to administer ARVN hospitals. Because the RVN never instituted a professional corps of nurse supervisors, doctors were also required to supervise the training of nurses.[134] Ward physicians trained nurses "on the job" and usually as medical attention demanded. This haphazard system led many soldiers to criticize their care and others to suffer because of it.

The shortage of nurses and doctors jeopardized all areas of medical care. There were never enough nurses to properly order and control medicine. MACV allowed the ARVN a thirty-day supply of medicine for the field and sixty days' worth of provisions for most hospitals. Difficulties in procurement and storage, however, meant significant lag time between placing new orders and receiving the needed goods. The Port of Saigon, where most medical supplies were delivered, had grown overcrowded and inefficient shortly after the American escalation of the war in 1965.[135] Direct shipment from overseas depots in Japan or Guam alleviated some of the congestion, but the new system only resulted in confusion over code addresses of ports and field depots, worsening the situation. One former ARVN corporal, Thinh Pham, remembered spending an entire week in Saigon looking for a pallet of medicine, only to discover that it had been delivered accidentally to Da Nang.[136]

Almost all ARVN pharmaceutical supplies came from U.S. Army medical depots worldwide—top-quality goods—but the supply was subject to funding discussions in Washington. Ironically, at times of the heaviest ARVN casualties—the Tet Offensive (1968), the Easter Offensive (1972), and the Ho Chi Minh Campaign (1973–1975)—debates in Washington led to significant delays if not outright reductions in ARVN supplies. For example, in January 1975, as the Ho Chi Minh Campaign began, the ARVN had a $9.1 million shortfall in medical supplies, or nearly 70 percent of its total requisition objectives. Had the war lasted just one week beyond April 30, 1975, the best ARVN estimates predicted that 548 of the 865 medical supply items used by the army would have been completely depleted.[137]

Troop morale was likewise affected by a widespread perception that American wounded received priority in battlefield evacuation. ARVN enlisted men often described a two-tiered evacuation system favoring Americans.[138] In one account a former ARVN corporal claimed that his friend died "on the ground because an American helicopter refused to take him to the hospital." Instead the pilot "picked up a less wounded American because that was official policy . . . Americans first."[139] This is one of the war's most enduring rumors, and many ARVN officers spent a great deal of time trying to convince their men that it was a myth.

The documentary record seems clear on this issue. Only a handful of sources tell of Americans receiving preferential treatment. Beginning in 1962, the U.S. Army's 57th Medical Detachment unit was responsible for evacuating wounded ARVN by helicopter when possible. In late 1964 the 82nd Medical Detachment unit joined the 57th, operating mainly in the Mekong Delta. Aeromedical evacuation cut the transportation time from the field to a permanent medical treatment facility from six to two hours, significantly improving morale among soldiers. Problems occurred, however, when the number of wounded began to increase in 1965. On occasion, field commanders had to make difficult decisions regarding the use of limited medical resources. As a result of some of these decisions, there were occasional incidents when U.S. Army officials favored medical evacuation and treatment for Americans over ARVN soldiers.

For example, a February 1965 "After Action Report" claimed that on three separate occasions a request was submitted from the field for medevac for several seriously wounded ARVN soldiers. The call came back by radio that only American soldiers would be evacuated from the field.[140] During the 1968 Tet Offensive, ARVN soldiers were again denied aeromedical evacuation from Bao Vinh, and the 3rd Medical Battalion "indicated that it could no longer receive VN casualties because of the U.S. patient load."[141] In a routine exit interview a former U.S. Army staff sergeant claimed that he had been ordered to treat only Americans even though there were several empty beds at his medical facility.[142] Though these episodes were rare, it did not take long for them to take hold in the soldiers' lore.

One of the constant problems facing committed ARVN officers was how to combat these rumors. Some officers routinely told their soldiers that U.S. helicopters performed most of the medical evacuation missions for ARVN soldiers. According to official ARVN sources, U.S. helicopters accounted for nearly 80 percent of all daytime evacuations and 100 percent of all nighttime missions.[143] Still, the rumors persisted. One former ARVN colonel, Phan van Thuy, declared that he spent much of his time with new recruits trying to convince them that they would be cared for properly if wounded in battle. In a 1999 interview he reported:

Most new recruits came to me with so little understanding of the war, including how they would be treated if wounded. Most believed it was better to be killed by the bullet that hit you than suffer from the lack of medical treatment. I tried in vain to tell them that our field medical care and evacuation was the best in the history of warfare. I told them about Operation Dustoff [ARVN soldiers evacuated by American helicopters], but few believed me. It was one of the great myths about the war that had infested our training centers.[144]

Other ARVN officers agreed with Colonel Thuy's assessment of the problem in training centers. "I wanted to train my troops to fight," reported Sergeant Pham van Cao, "but I spent most of my time at the training center in Gia Dinh dealing with all the lies new recruits heard from others about airlifts. Overcrowding in the training centers meant that it was impossible to stop rumors from circulating."[145]

Throughout the war, both damaging legends and real shortages contributed to soldiers' views of their medical care. These perceptions lowered morale among ARVN troops and psychologically paralyzed many soldiers before their first taste of battle. The psychology of fear that developed within the ARVN is understandable. No soldier wanted to go to battle facing the prospect of dying from a wound that could have been treated with proper medical care.

Medical care issues, whether anticipated or actual, fostered desertion. Some ARVN deserters did leave the army because of anxiety over this issue. According to Nguyen van Ngo, a former ARVN private, many men in his unit left the army in 1972 because they worried that they would not be properly cared for if they were wounded.[146] More significantly, Saigon reported that in 1972 more than 10,000 soldiers went home when wounded rather than go to overcrowded and poorly supplied RVN hospitals.[147] The return of disabled men—who not only were unable to work or care for others but who themselves required care and attention—placed a tremendous burden on family members, deepening the distrust that peasants felt toward the army and the government.

Poor ARVN morale obviously had a devastating impact on the conduct and outcome of the war. The government was out of touch with the cadence of peasant life, developing military policies that ran counter to Vietnamese traditions. This largely peasant army had needs that neither American nor Saigon officials fully understood. From the establishment of the ARVN in 1955, its leadership failed to recognize that this army of the people needed to keep rural customs alive. More frequent contact with families and villages should have been the cornerstone of any manpower plan. In the absence of proper ideological training, periodic contact with home was even more important. The government's failure to respond to ARVN demands for a more congenial leave system is typical of the reasons why South Vietnamese peasants considered RVN political leaders incapable of governing a new nation south of the seventeenth parallel. In the battle for hearts and minds in South Vietnam, the RVN lost because it treated its own army with contempt.

The RVN never fully recognized the role of sons in rural Vietnam's patrilineal system. These young men were the caretakers of their families, yet once drafted into the army they became dependent on their families because of low pay, poor food, inadequate housing, and medical shortages. This dependency threatened to destroy the social fabric of rural South Vietnam. At the time when the RVN should have been reaching out to peasant families to try to make their lives better, it actually contributed to their misery. Not only did the government drag away peasant families' most significant source of security, labor, and income, it also reduced these young men to "marauding cowards."[148] For this, rural Vietnamese never forgave and never trusted the RVN.

FOUR

BATTLES

Military historian John Keegan claimed that the battle piece is at the heart of all military writing. "For it is not through what armies are," wrote Keegan, "but what they do that the lives of nations and of individuals are changed."[1] What, precisely, the ARVN did in Vietnam is one of the most controversial chapters in the history of the war. Often portrayed as fearful and incompetent, the real ARVN infantry soldier has simply disappeared behind these negative stereotypes. In most historical accounts, the ARVN is to blame for losing the war.[2] Poor political leaders and cowardly, self-interested soldiers were no match for the Communists, historians claim, and that is why the United States suffered its first defeat.

Like most stereotypes, the picture of the ARVN in battle needs further investigation. Close inspection reveals that ARVN troops were not trained properly and did not fight well at times. But more significant is the fact that the ARVN simply reflected U.S. Army doctrinal thinking in Vietnam—and that doctrine was flawed. As one former American adviser recently commented, "You cannot blame the ARVN for every failure in Vietnam. Military leaders in Saigon and in Washington share the blame. They developed the tactics and the strategy that were defeated in Vietnam."[3] In other words, many of the ARVN's military shortcomings were the result of flawed doctrines.

Another way to understand the ARVN in battle is to examine how missions changed over time and how troops responded to that change. Such examination helps show why the ARVN did what it did. It also helps put its actions into proper context. For example, as U.S. tactics and strategy changed in Vietnam, so too did the ARVN's role in the war—from the types of battles its troops fought in, to the equipment they used, to what they thought about their battlefield performance, and, ultimately, to how they viewed the relationship between the battlefield and the nation. To understand battle from the perspective of ARVN soldiers, it is best to look at representative periods over the war's twenty-year history. In each instance, ARVN soldiers were deeply affected by doctrinal thinking outside their control.

THE SPECIAL WAR: AP BAC, 1963

By now the story of Ap Bac is familiar to most students of the Vietnam war.[4] On January 2, 1963, ARVN forces from the 7th Division attacked the 261st Main Force Battalion of the People's Liberation Armed Forces (PLAF) at the tiny hamlets of Bac and Tan Thoi ("Ap" means "hamlet" and "Bac" means "northern"), located 37 miles (60 km) southwest of Saigon. Though outnumbered and outgunned, the PLAF stood its ground. It shot down five U.S. helicopters and retreated under cover of darkness without suffering high casualties. The ARVN, in embarrassing contrast, refused to advance under fire and lost eighty men. This pivotal battle gave the guerrillas confidence that they could overcome the technological superiority of their adversaries and proved a harbinger of things to come.

The Battle of Ap Bac began innocently enough. In late December 1962 the Radio Research Unit at Ton Son Nhut Airport near Saigon detected a PLAF radio transmitter in Tan Thoi, on the eastern border of the Plain of Reeds. Intelligence experts also predicted that the PLAF was using Tan Thoi as a regional headquarters, a threat that made an attack on the site a priority. When orders came down to attack Tan Thoi, Lieutenant Colonel John Paul Vann, the senior American adviser to the ARVN's 7th Division, welcomed the news. Vann believed that Communist victories over an ARVN ranger platoon in October 1962 had strengthened the Communists' resolve and heightened recruiting by the National Liberation Front (NLF) in the important northern delta region. He looked forward to taking the offensive and hoped that the Communists would finally show themselves in a set-piece battle. According to journalist Neil Sheehan, Vann's most important biographer, no American officer, Vann included, expected the PLAF to change its tactics.[5] In October the guerrillas had attacked the ARVN rangers by surprise, withdrawing before they could be detected. This was their mode of operation in the delta.

Vann's job was to design an attack plan that would destroy the transmitter and the forces protecting it. His intelligence showed that the PLAF had 120 guerrillas guarding the radio transmitter. As was often the case, however, intelligence estimates were considerably off. More than three hundred PLAF regular guerrillas were near Bac and Tan Thoi, and another thirty irregular forces were in reserve. The NLF's own intelligence indicated that an attack was imminent, but the precise details were unknown.[6] However, the commander of the PLAF's 261st battalion believed that the attack would come near Ap Bac because the ARVN command had long targeted a string of villages controlled by the NLF. The 261st first learned of the attack from a scout in My Tho who reported the arrival of over seventy truckloads of ammunition. By New Year's Day 1963, the PLAF commander could deduce that the attack was scheduled for the next morning.[7]

Since the NLF's founding in December 1960 the party had relied on a combined political and military struggle; Communist forces in the South had operated under cover and along classic guerrilla lines. They had never engaged the ARVN in a set-piece battle, instead favoring sneak attacks and strategic withdrawal. By late 1962, however, the commander of the 261st had determined to stand and fight at Bac and Tan Thoi. Sheehan suggested that the PLAF decided to change its course of battle "to restore the confidence of their troops and the peasantry who supported them."[8] Vann had inflicted a serious blow to the PLAF in the northern parts of the delta the previous fall, and many cadres had begun to question the NLF's leadership and the war effort in the South. Furthermore, Tan Thoi and Bac were among the most important PLAF strongholds in the northern delta. The best way to discourage ARVN forays into the liberated zones was to make the South's army pay a high price for any offensive actions. The NLF's own documents support Sheehan's claims, emphasizing the importance of the northern delta towns to the revolution.[9]

On the morning of January 2, 1963, most of the region was covered by ground fog that delayed the ARVN offensive and, as a result, changed the location and scope of the battle. Vann had been promised thirty helicopters to take the three infantry companies of the 321st into the northern delta. General Paul Harkins, Vann's immediate superior, changed this order at the last minute, saving Vann's helicopters for Operation Burning Arrow, an offensive against the suspected Communist headquarters in Tay Ninh Province. The change in plans meant that Vann had to take in one company at a time. The first arrived in Tan Thoi a little after 7:00 A.M. The next two drops were delayed by increasing fog, causing a lag of nearly two hours before all three infantry companies were on the ground. From the moment the first infantry company landed, it experienced heavy machine-gun fire from PLAF guerrillas in advance positions. The attack stalled, with the ARVN infantry bogged down in Tan Thoi.[10]

When Vann spotted the firefight in Tan Thoi from his command plane, he knew that the battle was already getting out of his control. He could tell this was not the place to fight the PLAF. He searched the area for a place to land ARVN reserve infantry units and, in the process, redirect the battle. Eventually he decided that he wanted the reserves to land at Bac, fearing that the PLAF there might be part of a larger force. He also had concluded that the guerrillas in Tan Thoi were irregulars assigned to harass the ARVN infantry companies. Accordingly, he ordered ten H-21 "Huey" helicopters to drop the reserve infantry companies to the west and south of Bac.[11]

Landing the giant Hueys amid enemy fire was not so easy. The first helicopter took repeated hits in its aluminum fuselage, and another was downed immediately. The initial rescue attempt resulted in another downed Huey. In a brave and daring recovery effort, two more Hueys attempted to land in the paddy fields near Bac. They too were shot down. In a few short minutes the PLAF had brought down four of the most important aircraft that the ARVN and its U.S. advisers could place on the battlefield. Although the odds were against them, the PLAF guerrillas took great pride in their accomplishments, cheering the news of each downed aircraft. "We knew that the war was changing on that day," reported one NLF cadre after the war, "and that we were a part of history."[12] Indeed, Ap Bac was to change the character of the war.

After the first two hours at Tan Thoi, Vann and others realized that the PLAF regulars had probably withdrawn from there to focus on the reserves being flown in at Bac. It was an opportune time to redirect the ARVN infantry companies away from Tan Thoi and toward Bac, but Vann understood all too well that the ARVN would never launch a frontal assault against dug-in PLAF regular forces. He decided instead to use the ARVN's unwillingness to fight to his own advantage. He would use the ARVN at Tan Thoi to block one of the PLAF's obvious escape routes while he attacked Bac with M-113s, the ARVN's most impressive armored personnel carrier. The M-113 had a .50-caliber heavy machine gun mounted in front of the command hatch; some also carried a flamethrower. A combat unit of twelve men carrying M-1 machine guns fit inside. (The M-113 was rarely pressed into battle, however, because President Diem liked to keep his armored personnel carriers nearby for coup protection.)[13] Vann thought a frontal assault by the M-113s would clear the tree line at Bac and frighten the PLAF troops. Facing such a menacing opponent, the PLAF forces would leave their entrenched positions, exposing themselves to air attack and ground fire.

Vann's coordinated assault did not go as planned. The commander of the M-113s delayed his attack on Bac for nearly an hour—a deliberate and typical ploy, according to most U.S. sources, to postpone offensive action in the hope of avoiding contact with the enemy altogether.[14] A difficult canal crossing cost the attack another hour. When the attack on Bac finally came, the PLAF surprisingly stood its ground to take on the powerful M-113s with hand grenades and small-arms fire.

The set-piece battle that Vann had longed for was under way, but it was not going as planned. When the M-113s launched their attack, they did not mass their firepower. They came at Bac in uncoordinated waves rather than in the usual lineup for an assault. Furthermore, the .50-caliber guns were ineffective against the PLAF in the tree line outside Bac. The .50-caliber was a particularly troublesome machine gun to control because the recoil often sent the gun straight up into the air. It was extremely difficult for the ARVN gunners to keep the fire aimed at the trenches and low in the tree line. Many of their blasts soared into the sky over the treetops.[15] Conversely, PLAF infantry forces could easily direct their fire against the carriers' gunners and commanders, who were continually exposed to enemy fire. (It was only after the Battle of Ap Bac that the M-113 had armor added to protect the gunner.)[16]

After nearly an hour the PLAF had repulsed the M-113 frontal assault. Vann's last hope rested with a paratrooper drop near Bac by the experienced and battle-hardened ARVN airborne forces. The drop did not start until 6:00 P.M., an hour before dark. The airborne troops missed their target, landing too close to Tan Thoi and the fresh PLAF troops there, and within a matter of minutes they experienced heavy casualties.[17] The coordinated attack against the PLAF never transpired, and darkness fell over Tan Thoi and Bac.

In the final act of humiliation for Vann, the ARVN troops refused to use night flares and artillery to stop the anticipated PLAF retreat. In the past the guerrillas had always used the cover of darkness to withdraw from the battlefield. Vann was hoping that he could rescue victory from defeat by attacking the PLAF as it made its getaway. Again ARVN commanders refused Vann's advice, allowing the PLAF a safe retreat into the nearby jungles.

In the end the ARVN had lost eighty men, with another one hundred wounded. Three U.S. advisers had been killed, bringing the total for Americans killed in Vietnam to that date to thirty. Eight more Americans had been wounded. The Hueys had fired 8,400 rounds of machine-gun fire and had used one hundred rockets.[18] But the PLAF had suffered only eighteen casualties, with another thirty-nine wounded. The guerrillas had used only 5,000 rounds of ammunition, most of it previously captured. Particularly impressive were the captured Browning automatic rifles used by PLAF machine gunners dug into foxholes. Using machine guns and grenades, the PLAF had shot down five Hueys and changed the course of the war. No longer afraid of the giant U.S. helicopters or the M-113s, the PLAF had scored an important psychological and morale-boosting victory at Ap Bac. For their outstanding performance, the 514th regionals who held off the ARVN infantry companies at Tan Thoi were renamed the "Ap Bac Battalion."[19]

Several PAVN officers called the victory at Ap Bac "the most important of the early days of the revolution in the South."[20] One of Hanoi's official postwar histories described the Battle of Ap Bac as essential because the ARVN and its U.S. allies were "causing . . . many difficulties and losses," so defeating the ARVN and its "armored vehicle mobility" and "helicopter mobility" in the northern delta became an "urgent requirement of our armed forces."[21] The victory at Ap Bac, according to this official source, "had an important historical significance. It signified the coming of age of the new revolutionary armed forces in the South."[22]

Le Duan, the Communist Party's secretary general, also believed that Ap Bac had changed the course of the war. In a letter to the leaders of the Central Office for South Vietnam (COSVN), the party's southern headquarters, he explained, "After the Ap Bac battle, the enemy realized that it would be difficult to defeat us."[23] Few could disagree with the importance of the Battle of Ap Bac or with its outcome, even though MACV leaders tried to put the best face on a grim situation.

In the days following the battle, readers of English-language wire services and newspapers were given their first solid indication that MACV reports on Vietnam had been overly optimistic and that something had gone terribly wrong. Reporting for the United Press International, Sheehan first heard about the debacle in the early afternoon of January 2, just as the M-113s were meeting their match in the tree lines near Bac. That evening he and Nick Turner of Reuters took a motorcycle to Tan Hiep, a command post in the northern delta. There, in the darkness and away from the ARVN, Vann described the battle scene at Bac. He told reporters that a number of mistakes had been made and that the PLAF "were brave men" who gave a "good account of themselves today." The next day David Halberstam, writing for the *New York Times,* joined Sheehan and Turner at the Tan Hiep command post. The young reporter asked Vann, "What the hell happened?" Vann replied candidly, "A miserable damn performance, just like always."[24] Sheehan and Halberstam filed their reports and changed the nature of the relationship between the press and the high military command in Vietnam forever.

Sheehan's account was the most detailed, suggesting that Ap Bac was a "major defeat" and symptomatic of larger problems in Vietnam.[25] On January 7 the *Washington Post* ran one of Sheehan's stories on the front page: "Angry United States military advisers charged today that Vietnamese infantrymen refused direct orders to advance during Wednesday's battle at Ap Bac and that an American Army captain was killed while out front pleading for them to attack."[26] For five consecutive days Halberstam's stories appeared on page 1 or 2 of the *New York Times.* The headlines told the story: "Vietcong Downs Five U.S. Copters, Hits Nine Others";[27]

"Vietnamese Reds Win Major Clash";[28] and "Vietnam Defeat Shocks U.S. Aides."[29] Sheehan's and Halberstam's reports contradicted the most optimistic predictions from the Kennedy White House and suggested that the public was not "getting the facts on Viet-nam, even at this time when American casualties are mounting."[30]

Before the March 1965 introduction of U.S. marines, reporters provided the public with the most significant and realistic view of the war and the ARVN's performance. The Kennedy administration understood this clearly, but it could do little to shape a countervailing view of the ARVN. The ARVN's public image in the early years of the war came from the pens of young reporters sent to Vietnam to cover a new kind of warfare. No amount of spin from the White House could change what reporters were seeing and writing about.

A few days after the negative press reports, Admiral Harry Felt, the commander in chief of the U.S. Pacific Command (CINCPAC), flew from Hawaii to Saigon for an inspection tour. He met with reporters his first night in Vietnam and suggested that he did not believe "what he had been reading in the papers."[31] Instead he insisted that Ap Bac "was a Vietnamese victory—not a defeat, as the papers say."[32] Felt called Ap Bac a victory, he later reported, because the NLF had abandoned the area to the ARVN's 7th Division.[33] General Harkins supported Felt's assertions, claiming that the ARVN had "taken the objective."[34] Savvy journalists questioned the logic of these statements: most knew that this was not a war about territory.

Halberstam, recounting the surreal experience some months later, wrote, "We were all stunned at these new rules for guerrilla warfare—evidently the objective now was terrain, not the enemy."[35] Malcome Browne of the Associated Press was so infuriated by Felt's comments that he challenged the military leader's understanding of the guerrilla war. Felt's angry response was, "Why don't you get on the team?"[36]

In Washington, policy-makers were deeply concerned over the press reports on Ap Bac. On January 3 Roswell Gilpatric, the deputy secretary of defense, presented President Kennedy with a memo from the Joint Chiefs of Staff that suggested the press was purposefully misleading the public on the events in the delta: "It appears that the initial press reports have distorted both the importance of the action and the damage suffered by the US/GVN forces."[37] On January 7, the day Sheehan's key article appeared on the front page of the *Washington Post,* Kennedy expressed his own uneasiness over the press reports. In response Harkins sent the president a long cable suggesting that the ARVN had made a number of errors, but "this day they got a bear by the tail and they didn't let go of it. At least they got most of it."[38] Felt later added that it was important "to realize that bad news about American casualties was filed immediately by young reporters representing the wire services without careful checking of facts" and that "along with the bad news of damage to helicopters and three Americans lost, there is some good news which you may not read about in *The Washington Post*."[39] Felt and Harkins claimed there had been a number of successful ARVN operations in the delta but that the inexperience of the reporters had caused them to miss the real story.[40]

Despite the early reports about the ARVN's poor performance at Ap Bac, most Western reporters were sympathetic to the plight of the ARVN enlisted men. Andy Krepinevich, an expert on the army in Vietnam, suggested that ARVN troops were not "the target of press criticism." Instead, he argued, the press "focused their unsettling questions on South Vietnamese military leadership and, by implication, their American counterparts in MACV."[41] On January 11 Halberstam suggested that field command was the problem at Ap Bac, not the courage or ability of the ARVN privates and corporals. "In general," he wrote, "Americans here feel respect for the Vietnamese private."[42] In his book *The Making of a Quagmire*, written shortly after Ap Bac, Halberstam confirmed that it was not "the courage of the individual soldier that was being questioned, but the way he was led and the basis of the advisory relationship."[43] He went on to suggest that most Americans in Vietnam felt that the "Vietnamese was about as good a soldier as his leaders wanted him to be."[44] For Halberstam the problem rested with the ARVN's leaders and their counterparts in MACV.

Vann shared Halberstam's view of the ARVN. He once told the young reporter, "The first thing you'll learn is that these people may be the world's greatest lovers, but they are not the world's greatest fighters. But they're good people, and they can win a war if someone shows them how."[45] In his official after-action report, Vann's comments were directed at the officers, not the enlisted men. He attributed the defeat to the "poor state of training of the South Vietnamese units," a "poor system of command," a "reluctance to incur casualties," an "inability to take effective advantage of air superiority," and a "lack of discipline in battle."[46] Vann had always believed that the ARVN was being misused and that if MACV changed its strategy, the ARVN could hold its own against the guerrillas. He believed this political war had to be fought in the countryside by Vietnamese peasants. The ARVN had its share of motivated peasants, but the MACV strategy stripped them of their connection to the political objectives of the war.

Not surprisingly, most of the memoirs and diaries from ARVN enlisted men who were at Ap Bac support Vann's views regarding the problems in the South Vietnamese army.[47] "We had corrupt officers," one ARVN private in the 7th Division wrote, "who owed their positions to Diem. Since he was most interested in staying in power, he gave military command to his friends and not necessarily to the most deserving. This practice always showed it-self in battle."[48] Diem was known to use officer assignments as rewards for personal loyalty and to reserve some of his most powerful troops and weap-ons for his personal and political protection.[49] Furthermore, Diem feared that large battle losses would attract too much negative attention from the Americans, his own loyal officers, and the enlisted men.

At Ap Bac several of the officers in charge appeared unwilling to take the initiative for fear of reprisals. "I was in one of the units dropped by the helicopters," Nguyen Co Huong reported. "My commanding officer refused to move us from behind the protection of the rice paddies, fearing that high casualty numbers would embarrass those he reported to and reflect badly on his command."[50] Dug into the sides of the paddies, the reserves instead died one by one from gunshot wounds in the back. During the initial phase of the battle, ARVN civil guards at Tan Thoi were dug deeply into the side of a dike to protect themselves from the first volleys. After the ARVN com-pany commander and his lieutenant fell, the infantry followed the orders of a captain. "Our captain was brave," explained one ARVN soldier, "but it was clear to me that he was not going to risk his career on clearing out the Viet Cong at Tan Thoi. He just did not know what to expect from his com-manders."[51] For the rest of the day, these civil guard soldiers did not move, exchanging only sporadic fire with the irregular guerrillas in Tan Thoi. An infantry soldier with the M-113s had a similar experience: "It was clear to me that Captain Ba did not want to engage the enemy. I was not a coward. . . . I wanted to move forward on the Viet Cong, but we were not allowed to."[52] After the battle Ba was severely reprimanded by his commanding of-ficer for his failure to move the M-113s and attack the PLAF in the tree line at Ap Bac.[53] Such a strong reaction was an unusual occurrence, by all accounts.

In several postwar Vietnamese-language accounts of the Battle of Ap Bac, it is clear that ARVN enlisted men believed they had been trained for the wrong war. "The battle near Bac and Tan Thoi showed the problems in our approach to combat," wrote Nguyen van Huong. "We emphasized fire-power when this was a war about politics. The Communists understood that better than we did."[54] Another ARVN soldier connected with the M-113s complained, "All our officers understood was bombs and artillery. They knew nothing of men and maneuvers. Firepower . . . that was all they knew."[55]

Most experts on the military in Vietnam agree with these sentiments. Colonel Herbert S. Schandler, who teaches grand strategy at the U.S. Army's National Defense University and who served two tours of duty in Vietnam, suggested that the ARVN "was trained for the wrong mission." Instead of concentrating its efforts on the guerrilla war, the ARVN was prepared to fight a conventional war with enormous firepower. "Ultimately," Schandler wrote, "U.S. strategy forced the South Vietnamese forces to the road, making them dependent on a motorized offensive force that was hard to resupply and totally inappropriate for the people's war in the countryside."[56] Furthermore, Schandler added, few ARVN officers or enlisted men were trained for the political war. The ARVN, in sum, was incapable "of directing a complex political and military struggle."[57]

In the days and months before Ap Bac, Vann too had complained about the ARVN's complete reliance on firepower. He often criticized MACV's counterinsurgency plans, protesting that Washington only sent in "more artillery, more fighter planes, more napalm."[58] He also feared that the enormous American material commitment to the ARVN posed a significant hazard. According to Halberstam, Vann often expressed his own credo for the needs of a guerrilla war: "This is a political war and it calls for discrimination in killing. The best weapon for killing would be a knife . . . the worst is the airplane. The next worst is artillery. Barring a knife, the best is a rifle—you know who you are killing. By giving them too much gear—airplanes and helicopters—we may be helping them to pick up bad habits instead of teaching them to spend more time in the swamps than the enemy."[59] Most military experts agree with Vann's assessment and suggest that the ARVN often used its borrowed firepower as a substitute for more direct military action.[60] At Ap Bac it now seems clear that overwhelming firepower did little but warn the PLAF that the ARVN was approaching. As was often its practice in response, the ARVN later unleashed a torrent of artillery to reclaim Ap Bac, but by that time the PLAF had left the area.

The use of firepower to fight a guerrilla war demoralized ARVN troops and put them in a compromised position. "I understand that to many American reporters and to the outside world we appeared to be cowardly and afraid at Ap Bac," one former ARVN private explained, "but we were really angry and upset over the way battles were being fought. We understood better than our leaders that we needed to be on the ground . . . in the villages . . . providing local security and explaining our political positions without bombs. The problem was that we lacked the political training and our leaders did not understand the nature of a guerrilla war."[61] Another ARVN infantry soldier at Ap Bac reported, "No . . . I didn't want to die for these rotten people using these tactics. What did this have to do with the needs of people in my village? I was ashamed and disgusted . . . so yes, I hid my head and fired my weapon at random."[62]

Perhaps these attitudes help explain why ARVN soldiers admired John Paul Vann. According to Sheehan, the feeling was mutual. "Vann took a particular liking to the common soldiers," he wrote, "who were peasants like their guerrilla opponents."[63] Vann believed that they were "potentially good soldiers who deserved to win their war and not have their lives wasted."[64] However, that was precisely what many ARVN enlisted men thought was happening at Ap Bac and other battles throughout the South. This belief fostered low morale and a strong aversion to dying in a battle waged by reluctant officers. That feeling would intensify over the course of the conflict, especially after the Johnson administration introduced U.S. ground troops and changed the character of the war.

THE LIMITED WAR: 1965 OFFENSIVES

In the spring of 1965 General William Westmoreland, the MACV commander, became convinced that the ARVN was incapable of winning the war on its own. The United States would have to increase its military presence in Vietnam to prevent a total collapse in Saigon. Westmoreland had replaced Harkins as MACV commander in June 1964, and since that time he had supported an American takeover of most military operations.

When the president finally accepted the Joint Chiefs' recommendation to begin the sustained bombing of North Vietnam in February 1965, known as Operation Rolling Thunder, Westmoreland asked for two U.S. Marine Corps battalions to protect the American air base at Da Nang.[65] He feared that the base was vulnerable to Communist reprisal attacks. He also initiated a lengthy study of ARVN troop levels and their mission in South Vietnam. He concluded that a massive ARVN buildup was needed and that there was no alternative to greater American participation in the war. If the United States did not act soon, South Vietnam could be lost by the year's end. The president accepted Westmoreland's report and approved the general's request.

The limited introduction of U.S. ground troops in March 1965 did little to change the course of the war. By early spring 1965 the situation in South Vietnam had deteriorated significantly. The ARVN performed poorly in a number of battles with the PLAF, and morale was at an all-time low. Desertion rates had increased dramatically, even though the air war over

North Vietnam had been designed in part to strengthen the ARVN's resolve. Furthermore, Westmoreland's optimistic ARVN troop-level goals remained well out of reach. Johnson had approved crucial U.S. troop increases, but the mission remained primarily defensive and had little impact on events in the South. By May Westmoreland had realized that the limited American commitment was not enough to stem the tide of Communist advances. He routinely informed the president that "more of everything" was needed in Vietnam or the situation could get out of control.[66] Just as Westmoreland was reaching his fateful conclusions, events seemed to confirm his most dire predictions.

On the overcast evening of May 10, 1965, near the village of Song Be, the capital of Phuoc Long Province, four PLAF battalions attacked the ARVN's 36th Ranger Battalion. ARVN regulars stationed with the rangers repulsed an initial surge by PLAF guerrillas, but within minutes the rebels were inside the ARVN compound. Low cloud cover made it impossible for U.S. forces to provide the usual air support. As a result the PLAF troops made their way into the center of the camp and engaged the ARVN soldiers in hand-to-hand combat that lasted for more than three hours.[67]

As dawn broke the PLAF forces withdrew to Song Be village, located 44 miles (70 km) north of Saigon and entrenched themselves in the town market and temple area. The ARVN followed closely but was unable to uproot the guerrillas. The next day two ARVN battalions launched an attack on the PLAF in Song Be, but a 2.5-mile-long (4 km) guerrilla ambush dissipated the intensity of the raid. This time U.S. forces were able to make repeated air strikes on PLAF positions, but enemy troops were so well entrenched that airpower could do little. The ARVN suffered heavy losses, and its leaders were "devastated by the new direction of the war," according to Nguyen van Hieu, an ARVN infantry soldier.[68]

"I was at Song Be," reported former ARVN corporal Nguyen van Vinh. "It was awful. We knew that the Communists were going to launch attacks that spring, but this came out of nowhere. In the middle of the night they attacked us with mortars and rockets. Before the sun came up the Communists were in our camp fighting us with small knives and pistols. I saw one group attack our medics who were taking care of the wounded. It was awful."[69] Another ARVN soldier who was at Song Be confessed that he spent much of the battle shooting at shadows and hiding: "I couldn't believe what was happening. I could see nothing but smoke and people running. I couldn't tell who was who. The Viet Cong came out of nowhere. They seemed to come with the fog. It was the worst night of my life."[70]

Song Be was another important turning point in the war, and it now seems clear that the ARVN infantry soldier understood this better than most. "I knew that the attack on Song Be meant that the Communists were going on the offensive," Dinh Phuong explained. "We had not met their full strength until Song Be, and it was clear that they wanted to end the war quickly by crushing us."[71]

Official postwar histories from Hanoi seem to confirm this view.[72] In 1980 a special committee established by the People's Army Publishing House wrote a three-volume history of the American war in Vietnam. They reported that the attack on Song Be was the beginning of large-unit offensives designed to "annihilate an important part of the enemy's elite main-force manpower," to attack and interdict strategic east-west roads and the railroad, and to step up military and political struggle movements.[73] A postwar collection of Communist Party secretary general Le Duan's letters reveals a communication with COSVN director Nguyen Chi Thanh shortly before the attack on Song Be explaining that the spring offensives were designed to "destroy thirty to forty thousand" of the ARVN's main force.[74] Add the projected desertions, the letter concluded, and the ARVN could lose up to sixty thousand of its infantry soldiers.

The spring attacks would also show the Americans that the nature of the war in the South had changed and that the government in Hanoi and the PLAF had little difficulty choosing where and when to fight. The combination of these factors, the secretary general concluded, would "convince the United States to withdraw from Vietnam in a face-saving defeat."[75] General Thanh, who had long advocated a more offensive-minded strategy in the South, welcomed Le Duan's predictions and the Song Be attacks.

In Saigon and Washington, policy-makers feared that Song Be was indeed the beginning of a new phase in the war. According to one *Pentagon Papers* analyst, American officials believed that the attack on Song Be indicated that the Communist "storm broke in earnest."[76] For months Central Intelligence Agency reports had predicted that the Communists were planning a major buildup in South Vietnam.[77] In April dispatches had reached Saigon claiming that the PAVN 325th Infantry Division was in Kontom Province and planning to attack the ARVN in the highlands. Captured Communist documents had also revealed that a major policy shift had taken place at the party's Ninth Plenum in December 1963.[78] After years of supporting the political struggle alone in the South, the party had approved the formation of the NLF and its military arm, the PLAF, in 1960. By 1963 southern revolutionaries believed the time was right to increase the military struggle in the South and convinced their northern counterparts to support such measures. Accordingly, at the Ninth Plenum party officials adopted a resolution approving the increased shipment of men and supplies down the Ho Chi

Minh Trail.[79] Party leaders had hoped to take advantage of the chaos caused by Ngo Dinh Diem's assassination in November. These initial efforts were checked by American airpower, but by mid-1965 the first of the large PLAF divisions had reached the South.[80] The attack on Song Be was the initial sign that the ground war was about to change drastically.

Two weeks after the attack on Song Be, PLAF regulars of the 1st Regiment attacked a battalion of ARVN infantry, this time near Ba Gia, a small village in Quang Ngai Province. American intelligence reports had suggested that the PLAF operating there were "a bunch of ragtag guerrillas incapable of sophisticated military action."[81] Once again the intelligence proved wrong. PLAF commanders had skillfully established a series of strategically placed ambush zones designed to catch the 1st Battalion of the ARVN's 51st Regiment and any reinforcements in a deadly crossfire. On the morning of May 26, 1965, the lead ARVN company unknowingly walked into a hailstorm of rifle and machine-gun fire and was wiped out before the ARVN commander could get a second company to the scene of the attack. On its way this company too experienced the deadly accuracy of the PLAF's strategic crossfire. Eventually the commander of the 1st Battalion sent what remained of his five-hundred-man battalion to rescue the few remaining survivors. According to the official ARVN report, it took less than twenty minutes for the PLAF to destroy most of the 1st Battalion.[82] Shelby Stanton, a historian and former soldier, wrote that only sixty-five ARVN soldiers and three American advisers survived the initial attack at Ba Gia.[83]

The battle at Ba Gia dragged on for four days before a three-battalion relief force rescued the ARVN. To save what was left of the 1st Battalion, the 2nd Battalion commander ordered a three-pronged infantry attack supported by M-113s. Before the counterattack could take shape the PLAF unleashed a torrent of artillery fire, isolating the three ARVN battalions and forcing them to fight alone. Detached and confused, the 2nd Battalion used the M-113s for cover and retreated back toward Ba Gia. The other two battalions, the 3rd ARVN Marines and the 39th ARVN Rangers, did not fare as well. Surrounded by the enemy, they grouped in a circle, making it easier for the PLAF's 75-mm howitzers to strike. Near dusk the PLAF discovered that by shelling the small trees behind the 39th Rangers it could create a natural barrier, pinning the ARVN down. After two hours of shelling, rebel guerrillas stormed the ARVN's battalion headquarters and headed toward the provincial capital of Quang Ngai and its airport. Finally, as the sun rose on the fifth day of the battle, the PLAF retreated into the countryside. Only American airpower (some reports suggest as many as 450 sorties) saved three ARVN battalions from annihilation.[84]

Shortly after the Battle of Ba Gia, the Intelligence Committee of the U.S. Mission in Saigon, with Westmoreland's support, cabled Washington indicating that ARVN losses at Song Be and Ba Gia were "dangerously high."[85] The reports also suggested that the psychological toll of these defeats could lead to the "collapse . . . of the will to fight" on the part of the South Vietnamese forces and that U.S. troops would probably have to be used to avert such a disaster.[86] On June 7 Westmoreland sent a long telegram to CINCPAC headquarters for relay to Washington outlining the difficulties in Vietnam. "In pressing their campaign," the general wrote, "the Viet Cong are capable of mounting regimental-size operations in all four ARVN corps areas, and at least battalion-sized attack in virtually all provinces. . . . ARVN forces on the other hand are already experiencing difficulty in coping with this increased VC capability. Desertion rates are inordinately high. Battle losses have been higher than expected; in fact, four ARVN battalions have been rendered ineffective by VC action in the I and II Corps zones."[87] Westmoreland saw "no course of action open to us except to reinforce our efforts in SVN with additional U.S. or Third Country forces as rapidly as practicable during the critical weeks ahead."[88]

Consequently, on June 7, 1965, Westmoreland requested an additional forty-four battalions (roughly 150,000 men) for Vietnam, and permission to go on the offensive.[89] He believed that he could halt Communist advances by deploying U.S. troops along the coast and near the major southern cities. He would then send units into the Central Highlands to block any Communist attempt to control Highway 9 (a major east-west road) and sweep to the sea in an effort to divide the country. After securing the coastal areas, the cities, and the highlands, Westmoreland believed he could launch "search and destroy" missions with U.S. forces that would eventually grind down the enemy and diminish the Communists' will to continue the fight. The general would also rely on massive American firepower, including the bombing of the North. Finally, the pacification effort in the countryside would provide enough local security for the government's programs to take hold.

As the Johnson administration considered Westmoreland's request, another PLAF assault against the ARVN illustrated the gravity of the situation in Vietnam. On June 9, 1965, PLAF forces attacked ARVN military headquarters near the city of Dong Xoai in Phuoc Vinh Province, northwest of Saigon. In four days the ARVN lost a total of 743 men as the PLAF attacked some of its most important mobile battalions.[90] Once again the rebels hit at night, using mortars to soften the defensive enclave and a ground assault to break through the perimeter. Hundreds of PLAF irregulars served as sappers, crashing through the barbed wire. At 2:30 A.M. the insurgents overran the command post under a deluge of automatic-weapons fire. In the morning U.S. Army helicopters were brought in to rescue the ARVN command and to drop the 1st Battalion of the ARVN's 7th Regiment near Dong Xoai. Within minutes the PLAF's machine guns had mauled the ARVN infantrymen. Trying to salvage victory from defeat, the helicopters then attempted to drop the remainder of the battalion a few miles north at the Thuan Loi rubber plantation. Only eight men made it to the ground, the PLAF once again using heavy fire against men and machines. Eventually ARVN commanders decided against any further rescue attempts for the 7th Regiment. The following day, after a heavy U.S. air assault directed at the PLAF stronghold inside Dong Xoai, the ARVN's 7th Airborne Battalion, joined by a battalion of American paratroopers, landed by helicopter to reclaim the command headquarters.[91] They met little resistance, rebel forces having once again escaped under cover of darkness.

The Battles of Song Be, Ba Gia, and Dong Xoai were important for several reasons. They made clear that the PLAF had changed its tactics and that it now was able to take and hold key district and province towns using massive force and automatic weapons. The village war of the first decade of the conflict, 1955–1965, had given way to more conventional fighting. The attacks also signaled that the United States had underestimated the strength of the PLAF and overestimated the ARVN's ability to go it alone in conventional battles. Furthermore, at Dong Xoai, the largest battle in the war to date, American soldiers had joined in direct combat to help save the ARVN. This was the beginning of the changing role for U.S. servicemen in Vietnam. After the ARVN defeat at Dong Xoai, Westmoreland was given the authority for the first time to commit U.S. ground forces anywhere in the country to strengthen the South Vietnamese army.[92] This license released the general from merely defending U.S. installations and, in theory, allowed him to better coordinate U.S. troops with the ARVN. It also paved the way for U.S. troop increases.

According to Colonel Schandler, Westmoreland's troop recommendations "stirred up a hornet's nest in Washington."[93] Few U.S. policy-makers wanted to commit the nation to a ground war in Asia, and most understood that Westmoreland's recommendations "did not contain any of the comfortable restrictions and safeguards which had been part of every strategy debated to date."[94] Nonetheless, Johnson and his closest aides declared that a change in policy was necessary to save South Vietnam. Johnson did not want to "lose Vietnam" the way that Truman had "lost China."[95] Accordingly, on July 28, in what historian George C. Herring has called one of the most important decisions in the war, Johnson approved the deployment of 175,000

U.S. ground forces to Vietnam (later raised to 219,000) and a new offensive strategy.[96] A relieved Westmoreland reported that a new course had been taken: "Explicit in my forty-four battalion proposal and President Johnson's approval of it was a proviso for free maneuver of American and allied units throughout South Vietnam. Thus the restrictive enclave strategy with which I had disagreed from the first was finally rejected."[97] In his postwar memoir Johnson concurred, stating that the July 1965 decisions committed the United States to "major combat in Vietnam."[98]

With a change in mission and a significant increase in the number of U.S. troops in Vietnam, the most important problem facing Westmoreland was how to integrate the ARVN into his new strategy. He did not want the Americans, in their new role, to appear as if they had taken over the war completely. He worried that the United States might be "cast in the role of the French," fighting an antinationalist colonial war, but he saw no alternative to greater American participation.[99] John McNaughton, the assistant secretary of defense for international security affairs, suggested that the ARVN be given responsibility for "control over areas now held" and for "pacification operations and area control where possible."[100] Offensive operations, however, would be handed over to "U.S. and Allied forces, in conjunction with the GVN [ARVN] national reserve."[101] This concept, according to Jeffrey Clarke, "gave the bulk of the South Vietnamese regular army area security missions and left only eleven reserve battalions to participate in mobile offensive operations with U.S. ground units."[102] As the United States and the Communists escalated the conflict, the ARVN was being pushed aside.

Observers in South Vietnam understood the shift immediately. "Instead of leading offensives," one ARVN enlisted man complained, "we were little more than security police. It may have pleased some, but it made me sick."[103] Another infantry soldier wondered, "Why are we fighting at all? If the Americans are going to make all the decisions . . . what kind of country will we be left with?"[104] Saigon's newspapers offered mixed reviews of the increased American commitment, but many intellectuals complained that the people of South Vietnam and their army were becoming "colonial subjects" once again.[105] "A foreign army has entered our land to tell us what we are fighting for and who will do the fighting," declared Nguyen Phuong, a writer from Saigon. "There is little good that can come of this."[106]

From a military standpoint, some ARVN officers believed that although the entire system in South Vietnam needed a massive overhaul, the war against the Communists must always be a "Vietnamese problem."[107] "We had not fared well," explained Nguyen Dinh, an ARVN captain, "but we needed to clean up our own house and fight our own war. The dependency that the U.S. policy created was as dangerous to the future of South Vietnam as the Communists."[108]

By November the ARVN's limited participation in offensive actions had been further reduced. The Joint Chiefs of Staff had grown increasingly frustrated over the ARVN's inability to execute "complex, detailed U.S. conceived programs" and thus strongly recommended that a revised concept of operations be approved.[109] Under the new plan the "bulk of operations against the VC forces and bases outside the secure areas will be undertaken by US/Third Country and RVNAF general reserve forces, while the bulk of RVN forces will be committed to the defense of GVN installations and securing operations."[110]

Westmoreland strongly supported the change, but former U.S. ambassador to South Vietnam Maxwell Taylor, now the president's special military adviser, complained that the new concept would result in the United States taking over the war completely and reducing the ARVN to a static, defensive force. Taylor also predicted that an increased role for American ground troops would lead to high U.S. casualties, threatening public support for the war. Finally, he concluded that "giving the primary combat role to U.S. forces and reserving the ARVN for secondary combat missions . . . was a mistake from the point of view of GVN psychology and U.S. domestic opinion."[111] Taylor's objections were overruled. By the end of 1965 the ARVN had reduced to a passive actor in its own counterrevolution.

Unknown to Westmoreland and most other U.S. military leaders at the time, events taking place in Hanoi would further reduce the ARVN's participation in offensive military actions. By the summer of 1965 policy-makers in Hanoi had concluded that earlier predictions of a military victory in a "relatively short period of time" had been overly optimistic.[112] The PLAF now faced the awesome firepower of the world's most powerful military force, and it was clear to most in Hanoi that a change in tactics was drastically needed. In December 1965, at the Twelfth Party Plenum, policy-makers in Hanoi made further commitments to the southern battlefield. In a compromise that angered many in the Political Bureau, the party approved a resolution that increased the number of PAVN regulars shipped south and at the same time heightened the political and diplomatic struggle.[113] In his own calculations, Westmoreland had always believed that an increased presence of PAVN regulars in the South meant that the United States would have to match that escalation, increasing MACV's dependence on U.S. ground troops and further reducing the ARVN's combat role. According to party leaders, PAVN escalation was determined by the U.S. response. If the U.S.

expanded its bombing raids over the Democratic Republic of Vietnam (DRV) or substantially augmented the number of ground troops in Vietnam, the Military Commission of the Political Bureau would respond by approving an increase in the number of PAVN regulars heading South. In this way, party officials later claimed, the Johnson administration actually controlled the flow of men and supplies to the South by its own actions.[114]

Whatever the cause of PAVN infiltration, it is now clear that the presence of the PAVN 325th Division near Kontom in mid-1965 and three PAVN infantry regiments at the Battle of the Ia Drang Valley in November 1965 further reduced the primary combat role for ARVN regular infantrymen. Rather than participate in large-scale offensive operations, the ARVN had first been relegated to a coastal and urban security force. Now, with the infiltration of large numbers of PAVN regulars, it was pushed further to the sidelines. Most ARVN troops saw the shift as a clear indication that the United States and the Saigon government had little confidence in their abilities. "It was demoralizing," remembered one former ARVN soldier. "Once the PAVN regulars showed up in the Central Highlands, we were thrown aside like rotten fruit. How can you build a nation without a well-trained army that knows why it is fighting and then gets to fight?"[115] Another former soldier likewise complained that life in the army had become "unbearable." To begin with, troops "were not properly trained," he said. "Then, our role in the battles kept getting reduced. We felt like the worst kind of soldier, the pathetic one."[116]

STALEMATE, TET, AND VIETNAMIZATION, 1967–1975

Following the Battle for the Ia Drang Valley in November 1965, the ARVN rarely participated in offensive operations. Instead it joined American military units in search-and-destroy missions. In February 1966 MACV introduced a review and analysis program to establish objectives and measure the ARVN's progress under the new combat operations plan.[117] After two years U.S. military officials in Saigon were pleased to announce that by every measurable indicator the ARVN had dramatically improved its performance.[118] The number of operations conducted had nearly doubled, as had the number of days each battalion was in combat. In addition, the number of company-size or smaller unit actions had risen remarkably.[119] There were several "bright spots," according to MACV leaders, but most impressive were ARVN search-and-destroy and "sweeping" missions in 1967. These were limited actions for which there was a clear objective and little use of air support. In combined operations they involved close association with U.S. forces, but these were generally light infantry brigades.

In Saigon U.S. ambassador Ellsworth Bunker was extremely optimistic about the ARVN's increased effectiveness. In his weekly report to the president in June 1967 he suggested that it had "responded well" to challenges "throughout the country."[120] He was particularly impressed with the performance of I Corps, which had "accounted for 1,400 enemy killed in action."[121] Bunker, who had replaced Henry Cabot Lodge, Jr., as ambassador in early 1967, believed that the ARVN was capable of defending South Vietnam if given enough time to develop into the kind of fighting force that MACV and the embassy envisioned. With the proper training and the correct system of command and control, Bunker told his subordinates, the ARVN "could match the Viet Cong" on any battlefield.[122] Bunker worried that ARVN successes were not receiving the attention they deserved and that many in Washington simply did not understand the progress that was being made. According to one intelligence expert stationed in Saigon during Bunker's tenure as ambassador, "the embassy had an unshakable faith in the ARVN's ability."[123]

It is interesting to note that ARVN successes in the field actually came from operations in which the number of U.S. advisers had been purposefully reduced.[124] According to several U.S. advisers' after-action reports, even the weakest of the ARVN's infantry divisions were performing satisfactorily on their own.[125] In July 1967 the 141st PAVN regiment attacked the ARVN's 5th Division in Binh Long Province. Most U.S. advisers considered the 5th Division one of the weakest in III Corps.[126] The PAVN attacked from two directions, employing small arms, automatic weapons, and mortar and rocket-launcher fire and penetrating the ARVN position at two points. In the past, U.S. advisers claimed, the ARVN would "have cut and run."[127] This time, however, "ARVN forces launched an aggressive counterattack."[128] Eventually the PAVN abandoned the battlefield and, uncharacteristically, left many of its dead and nearly a hundred weapons behind. Even better, the ARVN captured ten prisoners, including a PAVN captain.[129]

Throughout 1967 the ARVN experienced similar successes, but nowhere was it more impressive than in Chuong Thien Province in the delta. During the late fall and into December 1967, the 21st Division had made sweeps against Communist forces from Khanh Hung and the southernmost reaches of the Ca Mau peninsula deep into Chuong Thien Province. In the early morning hours of December 8, elements of the 21st were on a search-and-destroy mission when they discovered two battalions of enemy forces. Using a classic "pincer and anvil" maneuver, they trapped the Communists between a canal and two infantry companies. By midafternoon, the cavalry troops had moved up the east side of the canal and "all elements began to tighten the noose."[130] For three days the ARVN attacked relentlessly, using small arms and infantry tactics. Ambushes were set up along potential enemy escape routes, and ARVN rangers served admirably as reinforcements. By daylight at the beginning of the fourth day, an unusually long time for the ARVN to engage the enemy, the Communists had retreated into the countryside, leaving behind weapons and thirty-one prisoners of war. All told, Communist losses exceeded four hundred, while the ARVN had only sixty-seven casualties. Interestingly, no Americans were killed in this major engagement in the delta.

MACV leaders were impressed with the end-of-the-year rally, calling it a "brilliant performance" for the ARVN's 21st Division.[131] According to the ARVN's own reports, "the infantry is coming alive. After fighting the enemy alone for ten years, the Americans took over the war. But in the last year, we have reasserted our units into the battles . . . and they have done well. We are now fighting the war on our terms again."[132] In his annual command history, Westmoreland described the overall improvement in the ARVN this way:

> I have worked with the Vietnamese military for more than three years, and I have learned to understand and admire them. A look at their record in combat . . . reveals an exceptional performance when all is considered.
>
> During the last three years I have seen them literally hold their country together. . . . They fought the enemy guerrilla and main forces alone, until we arrived, and, during that time, they were expanding their forces to the limit that their manpower and economy could support. Except for the Continental Army of our earliest years, never before in history has a young military force been subjected to such a challenge.
>
> In my book, the Republic of Vietnam Armed Forces have conducted themselves with credit. As I tour the country several times each week, I am encouraged by the obvious improvement in the morale, proficiency and quality of their fighting.[133]

Still, the ARVN was weak in several areas, and the nature of the war in 1967 probably masked the military realities in Vietnam.

By 1967 the war had reached a stalemate, and there was growing opposition in the United States to further escalation. Secretary of Defense Robert S. McNamara was increasingly hostile to an escalation of the air war over North Vietnam, a policy supported by the Joint Chiefs of Staff. In August

1967 he appeared before the Stennis Committee, a special Senate Armed Forces subcommittee, and testified that the air war over the North could not be a substitute for the ground war in the South.[134] "You cannot win the war on the cheap by bombing," McNamara told the committee.[135] In late October, during a presidential review of Vietnam military policy, McNamara told Johnson that he believed the United States had to change its course in Vietnam. He suggested that the United States should announce an indefinite bombing halt, publicly fix a ceiling on force levels, and turn more of the war over to the ARVN.[136]

The Joint Chiefs, in sharp contrast, argued that the United States should drastically expand the war in Vietnam, ending Johnson's policy of gradual escalation. Specifically, they urged the president to consider expanding the air war over North Vietnam, mining the harbors and deepwater ports, widening the war into Laos and Cambodia to attack Communist supply routes, and increasing covert operations in the North.[137] The president rejected these proposals and instead as always took a middle road between McNamara's radical plan and the Joint Chiefs' desire to expand the war. According to Herring, the president was "unwilling to admit that the policy he had pursued was bankrupt" and therefore urged Westmoreland to rely more heavily upon airpower in the South so that he would not have to attack the enemy in the North.[138] U.S. troop levels in Vietnam continued to increase, and in November 1967 Westmoreland asked for an additional 200,000 troops, most of them for combat operations in Vietnam.[139]

The gradual escalation of the war, and the increased reliance on airpower, shielded the ARVN from the most dramatic military action in the Central Highlands in 1967 and gave the impression that the ARVN had "turned the corner."[140] The ARVN had performed well in low-intensity conflict in the villages, but in these confrontations it was generally facing irregular guerrillas and not the regular PLAF guerrillas or the PAVN's main force units. As the North began to take over more and more of the fighting, the real story was in the highlands, where the Communists were preparing for their massive 1968 military offensives. Nonetheless, the ARVN had acquitted itself well in 1967, getting back to what it called the "small war,"[141] that is, localized fighting with small units. When released from its overreliance on airpower and mechanization, it performed satisfactorily. Few in Saigon could have predicted that the "small war" was about to become a thing of the past, as Hanoi was making plans in the fall of 1967 to break the military stalemate with a bold offensive.

In October 1967 the Communist Party's Central Committee approved Resolution 14, or the Quang Trung Resolution, named for the emperor who had defeated the Chinese invaders during Tet of 1789. The party's new strategy combined a protracted war of attrition with morale-shattering attacks on southern urban centers. Its centerpiece was a projected three-phase offensive in South Vietnam, known in the West as the Tet Offensive. The Political Bureau reasoned that widespread attacks against southern cities would compel the United States to pull back its firepower to defend the urban areas and thereby deescalate the war against the North.[142] The offensive would show the Americans that they had to choose one of two alternatives: to step up the war substantially—difficult to do in an election year—or go to the negotiating table. In either case, the party was committed to continue the war until the United States withdrew from Vietnam under terms favorable to the North.

Plans for the Tet Offensive had circulated at the highest levels of the Communist Party since the early spring of 1967, during the military stalemate. In most reports the party predicted that "the upcoming general offensive/general uprising will be a period, a process, of intense and complicated strategic offensives by military, political, and diplomatic means. . . . It is a process in which we will attack and advance on the enemy continuously both militarily and politically as well as a process in which the enemy will counterattack ferociously in order to wrest back and to reoccupy important positions that will have been lost."[143] When the full scope of the three-phase offensive reached the PLAF, many southern military leaders thought it played into the strengths of the ARVN and their Americans allies.

For years COSVN director General Nguyen Chi Thanh had advocated a more forceful party policy that would fully utilize the party's resources behind military offensives in the South. His role in the planning of the Tet Offensive, however, remains unclear, since he died on July 6, 1967, of an apparent heart attack. Some Vietnamese sources suggest that Thanh was in favor of the military action and that he in fact died from a heart attack in Hanoi after celebrating the decision. According to Bui Tin, a former PAVN colonel and editor of the party's official newspaper, *Nhan Dan,* General Thanh "drank heavily" after reviewing plans for the offensive and then "went back to his home in Ly Nam De Street," where he "took a bath" and, having suffered previously from a weak heart, "collapsed and died."[144] Other sources suggest that Thanh joined General Tran van Tra in his opposition to the proposed offensive, understanding full well that it placed southerners in the PLAF in great jeopardy.[145]

Throughout the war the PLAF had used the tactic of *tien cong va noi day, noi day va tan cong* (attack and uprise, uprise and attack). This tactic required the support of the local population, and once this support was guaranteed and sustained, future attacks could take place. As the war progressed the PLAF modified the tactic to include *noi day dong loat* (simultaneous uprisings), a series of military attacks with logistical support by the local population over a large area to avoid concentrated counterattacks by the ARVN and its American allies. This tactic had allowed the ARVN to score its victories in the delta in the limited engagements of 1967, but it had been part of a larger Communist strategy preparing the way for the Tet Offensive. According to many southern Communists, plans for the Tet Offensive relied too heavily on the notion of *dut diem* (to take over a target completely),[146] a concept that opened the door for reprisal attacks and exposed the PLAF to the full power of the American armed forces. Johnson's policy of increasing the air war in the South to avoid the political problems associated with expanding the bombings over North Vietnam also meant that the PLAF was overexposed.

Despite voices of concern within the PLAF, party leaders in Hanoi decided to go ahead with the Tet Offensive. On January 30, 1968, in the early-morning hours, combined PLAF and PAVN forces launched a series of attacks on key district and provincial cities throughout South Vietnam. The Communists also attacked five of South Vietnam's major cities; in Saigon, the attacks specifically targeted the U.S. Embassy. Over the next ten months the Communists initiated two more massive raids on southern urban areas, leading to some of the war's bloodiest fighting and ending the military and psychological stalemate that had marked 1967.

In Hue, the Nguyen dynasty's imperial capital, ARVN and PLAF forces fought hand to hand and from house to house, a clear indication that the war had changed dramatically. Early press reports exaggerated Communist military advances, and even the venerable newscaster Walter Cronkite, an early supporter of American intervention, exclaimed, "What the hell is going on here! . . . I thought we were winning the war."[147] What was going on was a new phase of the war, conceived by Hanoi but felt strongly by the ARVN.

Surprisingly, the ARVN performed quite well under enormous pressure. According to Westmoreland, the ARVN "in most cities . . . threw back the enemy attacks within two to three days—in some cases, within hours."[148] Westmoreland's military strategy had left the ARVN defending the cities while U.S. troops roamed the countryside. The ARVN held its own and was instrumental during the second and third phases of the offensive, when Communist troops were pushed out of the cities. It is now evident from more detailed reports that the PLAF took exceptionally high losses, many of them at the hands of the ARVN.[149]

What the ARVN did not know at the time, however, was that the Johnson administration would pay a high price for Hanoi's gamble. In the immediate aftermath of Tet, Lyndon Johnson asked his new secretary of defense, Clark Clifford, to examine Westmoreland's latest request for additional troops. Johnson ultimately rejected Westmoreland's appeal, granting only about 10 percent of the troops requested for Vietnam.[150] Clifford then suggested to Johnson that the ARVN assume more combat responsibility while the United States slowed the increase in troop levels. Johnson accepted Clifford's recommendations, marking the first serious policy shift since the fateful decisions of 1965.

Domestic politics intervened in the 1968 U.S. election year. When Senator Eugene McCarthy fared better than expected in the New Hampshire primary, Johnson announced that he would not accept his party's nomination for another term as president. Instead, Johnson told a television audience on March 31, 1968, that he would focus all his energy on finding a solution to the war in Vietnam. That solution would be a policy known as "Vietnamization" (regrettably implying that the Vietnamese had not been fighting and dying all along).

The new approach to the war called for plans to expand and upgrade the ARVN and gradually shift primary responsibility for military operations to them. It made good sense "to bring American boys home" and "let the Vietnamese do more of the fighting," Johnson argued in the summer of 1968.[151] The consummate politician, Johnson also believed that a combination of peace talks and Vietnamization might sway public opinion in favor of his vice president, Hubert Humphrey, who was in a dead heat for the presidency with Richard Nixon. Johnson went one step further on October 31, 1968, announcing a bombing halt over North Vietnam, hoping again that this move would push Humphrey over the top. Johnson's usually reliable political antenna was wrong about the impact of Vietnamization, the peace talks, and the bombing halt, however, as Nixon won the presidency by a narrow margin.

Within weeks of his inauguration Nixon announced that he was extending Johnson's policy of "Vietnamization" with a few modifications. Under his new doctrine the president would slowly withdraw American troops but strengthen the ARVN to "withstand the North Vietnamese."[152] The combination of a phased American withdrawal and renewed commitment to the ARVN provided the best chance for security in the countryside, the new president argued, and security was the "most important element of the war in 1969."[153] General Creighton Abrams, Westmoreland's successor, advised, however, that Vietnamization could not hide ARVN weaknesses. Abrams candidly admitted that the ARVN was not ready to take on this burden and that it would be a significant amount of time before it was. "If you took out all the United States . . . forces now," he warned, "the Government (RVN) would have to settle for a piece of Vietnam."[154] Still, the Nixon administration pressed forward with Vietnamization.

Inside the ARVN the new strategy of Vietnamization was met with both cheerful anticipation and outright condemnation. Some ARVN infantry troops welcomed the opportunity to "fight the Communists on our own terms."[155] Many believed that U.S. advisers had been pushing an American-style war and that it was finally time "to do things the Vietnamese way."[156] Others thought that the ARVN could now return to the "rice war" and get rid of its reliance on American firepower.[157] "I thought that the problem in Vietnam had been the Americans and their war plan," remembered Ngo Quynh, a former ARVN infantry soldier. "I applauded the news that we would be able to take over more and more offensive military operations. After all, what good is a national army if it cannot determine its own fate and that of the country it is trying to defend?"[158] Many others also welcomed the change in strategy and waited anxiously for the ARVN command to quickly change tactics.

Others were not so naïve. They clearly understood that the ARVN was no match for the Communists, and by 1969, the "die had been cast."[159] According to Nguyen van Linh, a former ARVN soldier drafted in 1968, "the Communists were already dictating the terms of battle by 1969, and this meant that we could not simply return to the village war."[160] Indeed, large-unit warfare would stay the key element of battle for the rest of the war, despite the Nixon administration's efforts to focus on South Vietnamese village security through its pacification program.

Pacification focused on key PLAF strongholds and included military attacks, assassinations, and arrests. The goal was to destroy the NLF infrastructure and regain control of vast territory in the South in case negotiations in Paris produced a cease-fire. Combined with Vietnamization, the pacification program relied upon the ARVN to "do much of the dirty work,"[161] a job that many were not prepared to undertake. "The change in tactics, so welcomed by many, simply meant that we were more exposed than we were before Vietnamization and pacification," argued Nguyen van Hieu. "It did not change the fact that we were poorly trained, poorly led, and suffering from low morale."[162] Indeed, ARVN desertions were at an all-time high in 1969.[163]

Others viewed Vietnamization as the ultimate sellout. "Many of us believed that the U.S. was simply giving up, that Washington had set us on this course and was now abandoning us in our hour of greatest need," reported one former ARVN soldier.[164] Some in Saigon called Vietnamization the "U.S. Dollar and Vietnamese Blood Sharing Plan."[165] The Saigon government condemned the plan, thinking it was a "fig leaf to cover U.S. abandonment."[166]

Likewise, in scores of memoirs, the Vietnamization policy has been condemned for its assumption that ARVN soldiers had not been fighting and dying all along. "We lost nearly five times as many men as the United States," explained one former ARVN soldier after the war, "yet the Nixon administration had the nerve to say it was time for us to pick up the burden of military operations."[167] Many ARVN complained that the United States had changed course too late and that Vietnamization was "tantamount to surrender."[168]

Another common complaint among the ARVN was that American leaders really never intended for the South Vietnamese army to stand "toe to toe against the Communists."[169] Many feared that the Nixon administration had little faith in the ARVN's ability and that the new policy was a way to shift "to an air war and to withdraw U.S. troops for domestic political consumption."[170] Indeed, Vietnamization did mean a dramatic increase in the air war over the DRV. From 1969 until 1973 the Nixon administration launched one of the most massive air campaigns in history.[171] But this strategy did not mask the feeling among many senior American military officials that the ARVN would never be "an army with the offensive and aggressive spirit that will be necessary to counter either the VC [PLAF] or the NVA [PAVN]."[172] The ARVN felt this lack of trust daily, and it stung. "How could we be expected to fight well when our major benefactor and ally doubted our capabilities?" asked one former infantryman.[173]

MACV leaders were right to constantly ask the question: Could the ARVN go it alone? That was the key to an independent South Vietnam. The problem was that by 1969 U.S. doctrinal thinking had already relegated the ARVN to a secondary role, and it was nearly impossible to reverse course so late. Years of neglect could not be corrected through pacification programs, an intensification of the air war, or even combined operations such as Lam Son 719, a joint effort launched in February 1971 to disrupt PAVN supply lines in Laos. The ARVN could not turn itself into an effective army overnight, and Vietnamization only highlighted that problem. Furthermore, leaders in Hanoi correctly understood that domestic political pressures made it impossible for the Nixon administration to stop the phased withdrawal of American troops or come to the ARVN's rescue. Congress was also growing increasingly reluctant to fund the ARVN, its hesitation suggesting that political shortcomings in Saigon made the war "unwinnable."[174]

Sensing the ARVN's precarious situation, the PAVN and PLAF launched an all-out military offensive in the spring of 1972 that eventually paved the way for further Communist advances. Known in the West as the Easter

Offensive, the Communist attacks highlighted the ARVN's weaknesses. Beginning in March 1972, the PAVN launched conventional military attacks against the ARVN to destroy key elements of the army. The Military Commission of the Political Bureau in Hanoi believed that the combined assaults, much like the Tet Offensive of 1968, would lead to a knockout blow against the Saigon government.

These predictions proved overly optimistic, but the offensive did expose the fragility of the ARVN. The offensive relied on new tactics and weaponry, creating difficulty for the ARVN command. The first phase was a strike across the Demilitarized Zone by three PAVN infantry divisions, reinforced by T-54 tanks. Three days later three additional divisions struck from inside Cambodia, laying siege to the strategically important provincial capital An Loc. Ultimately only American air power saved An Loc from being overrun by the PAVN. PAVN forces also attacked Kontom in the Central Highlands, and two more PAVN divisions took control of several key district towns in Binh Dinh Province along the central coast of South Vietnam.

Although some reports suggest that the ARVN held up well against the PAVN, it was clear to everyone in Vietnam that the Communists held more territory after the attacks than before. With the Paris peace talks gaining increased importance in a U.S. election year, many South Vietnamese feared that the Easter Offensive signaled the beginning of the end of the ARVN and the Republic of Vietnam. "I thought that Vietnamization was a bad idea. I believed that it was the end of the army and my country," recalled Nguyen van Phuoc. "The Nguyen Hue Campaign [Easter Offensive] of 1972 convinced most of us that the war was over."[175] Indeed, even though the Nixon administration increased the air war over the DRV and mined the harbor at Hai Phong and other key ports, the Easter Offensive signaled things to come. Despite estimated Communist losses of over 100,000, and optimistic reports that the ARVN had held its own against the PAVN, especially in Quang Tri Province, most in the ARVN knew that it was only a matter of time until a Communist victory.

One former ARVN soldier remembered that most of the men in his unit felt "impending doom" following the Easter Offensive. "We all believed that we had fought heroically in Quang Tri," he recalled, "but that our best was not good enough. The Communists simply replaced their losses and continued to march on."[176] Others believed that history was conspiring against the ARVN. It had been given full latitude to fight on its own only when the Communists were at their strongest and the Americans could no longer stay the course. "We came into our own exactly when the Americans were leaving and the world was ready to forget about the fate of South Vietnam," explained Nguyen van Thien.[177] Another former soldier suggested that if Vietnamization had "happened in 1955," then the ARVN "might have had a chance against the Communists. By 1972 it was too late."[178] One former soldier reported that most of his comrades believed that if the ARVN had been allowed to develop more independently and organically, it would have been a more viable fighting force. "We became completely dependent upon the United States for everything," he confessed, and that "led to our defeat."[179]

The end came soon enough. Saigon surrendered on April 30, 1975.

Local citizens provide water to ARVN soldiers on a Saigon street during or just after the coup that deposed President Ngo Dinh Diem, 1963. (Douglas Pike Photography Collection, The Vietnam Archive, Texas Tech University)

ARVN barracks near U.S. Army "Davis Station," 1964. (John Klawitter, Vietnam veteran)

ARVN soldier preparing a duck for dinner at Ly Vanh Manh Outpost. (Photographer Lt. Charles Conn, National Archives)

ARVN soldiers get their uniforms, May 26, 1968, Camp Evans, First Cavalry Division, U.S. Army. (Photographer PFC Robert Fromm, National Archives)

ARVN retraining program at Camp Evans. (Photographer PFC Robert Fromm, National Archives)

ARVN basic trainees attend map reading class at ARVN infantry school in Thu Duc, September 30, 1967. (Photographer PFC J. E. Brotherton, National Archives)

ARVN basic trainees attack
an obstacle course, July 6,
1969. (Photographer SP4
Pearson, National Archives)

ARVN trainees at Quang Trung Training Center undergo a field exercise on squad
attack, June 26, 1970. (Photographer SP4 Hinton, National Archives)

South Vietnamese soldiers stand near a captured 12.7-mm antiaircraft gun, similar to enemy antiaircraft weapons that surrounded An Loc and made aerial resupply of the town very dangerous. (Dale Andrade Collection)

The slow South Vietnamese push toward Quang Tri City resulted in the capture of enemy heavy weapons, such as this 130-mm howitzer. (U.S. Army)

Soldiers from the ARVN 25th Division with weapons captured during the Cambodian incursion, June 1970. (Douglas Pike Photography Collection, The Vietnam Archive, Texas Tech University)

South Vietnamese marines and an unidentified U.S. adviser (left) stand victorious near the ruins of the Quang Tri citadel. It was recaptured on September 16, 1972. (U.S. Marine Corps)

FIVE

FAMILIES

Exhausted, demoralized, and continually defeated, ARVN troops struggled to find meaning in the war. For many, anticommunism was enough. For most the lack of a viable government in Saigon meant that a free and independent South Vietnam "was a dream that simply would never come true."[1] Compounding that depressing reality was the feeling among many ARVN regulars that the officer corps was corrupt and that the government had mistreated its soldiers. One former ARVN infantryman asked rhetorically, "How can we put faith in a government that treated its citizens and military so badly? They mishandled every aspect of the war. It did not take long for us to develop a sense that the army was at odds with Saigon."[2]

Indeed, one theme that surfaces in hundreds of ARVN memoirs is the notion that the army itself represented "a third way," something quite separate from the Saigon government or the Communists. This notion of a third force manifested itself in unique ways among the ARVN, most notably in the notion that the war was no longer about the freedom and independence of South Vietnam but rather about the long-term stability of families.

ARVN soldiers came to this view through their experiences in the army. Starting with the conscription and induction process, men in the ARVN were slowly alienated from the government and its policies. Soldiers viewed their dismal treatment as proof that Saigon's political leaders were incapable of running a country. With each coup and each fixed election, the ARVN grew more distanced from Saigon. When inflation reached nearly 500 percent on key household items while soldiers' salaries remained stagnant, ARVN families lost more hope. The lack of food and proper medical care further alienated the troops, as did changing conscription laws and length of service requirements. By 1968 most young South Vietnamese men were doing anything they could to avoid the draft. Even the most committed anticommunists who had volunteered for military service thought the government "was lacking in some fundamental ways."[3] When officials in Saigon turned their backs and allowed the Americans to dictate the conditions of the war, most soldiers looked inward to find something worth defending.

They found it in their families. Even during the radical upheavals created by the Vietnam war, the family remained the most important institution in Vietnamese society. The young men who served in the ARVN had been socialized to be family members first and foremost. No talk of personalism or modernity could change the fact that most ARVN soldiers' primary loyalty was to their families. War did not alter this truth, except to intensify it among many. When things went badly—and they did early in the army's history—most soldiers resorted to doing all they could to protect their families and ensure their stability. The absence of training programs designed to cultivate this same intense loyalty to fellow soldiers and the nation was just one of the many shortcomings of South Vietnam's leaders. Interestingly, it was this loyalty to family and not to the government and its policies that kept soldiers in the army at all.

Over time the ARVN created a subnational culture that focused the war's meaning on family survival. Servicemen arrived at a shared understanding that the war was no longer about "the national question" but about something more elemental. Drawing on cultural and historical traditions, the ARVN redefined the meaning of the war. What held it together in the face of enormous difficulties was a growing belief among soldiers that military service was actually a way to increase the odds that their individual families would survive intact. Of course, this shared subnational culture meant that few soldiers saw the war as the Saigon government and its American allies did. It further alienated the ARVN from U.S. policy-makers and contributed to many of the stereotypes that persist today. Still, most soldiers accepted (and continue to accept) an unfavorable reputation as a small price to pay for accomplishing their main objective: saving their families.

BARRACKS LIFE

The most obvious and direct way that an ARVN soldier could protect his family was to bring them with him into base camps. In contrast to most other cold war–era conflicts, the Vietnam war included camp families and camp followers. Most nonmilitary occupants of the camps were immediate family members, but prostitutes and others also set up near ARVN bases. Families joined their young men for several reasons—most obviously for their own security and protection but for other economic, cultural, and social factors as well. ARVN officers encouraged this practice, viewing it as a partial solution to the burden of caring for so many men and a hedge against desertion.

Camp followers were not new to army life, even if they were a rare exception during the cold war. Throughout history women had followed armies both as wives and as workers. From the fourteenth through the nineteenth centuries, for example, women were a vital part of army life in Europe. According to historian Barton C. Hacker, "Armies could not have functioned as well, perhaps could not have functioned at all, without the services of women."[4] In early modern Europe, women performed a variety of essential tasks, including cooking, cleaning gear, and tending to the sick. "The most striking fact about women's activities in the army," claimed Hacker, "is how little they differed from the ordinary run of women's work outside it."[5] During the Napoleonic wars, the state assumed more control over camp followers, whose duties did not change greatly as a result.

An army and its followers was "like a vast moving city with its own community life," according to historians Geoffrey and Angela Parker.[6] Women and other camp followers often doubled the number of mouths to feed and added significantly to the cargo burden.[7] Still, most military officers understood the importance of keeping the base camp clean and rationalized that women performed many such thankless duties.

During the American Revolution, the Continental Army took on thousands of camp followers who had personal (as opposed to official) ties to the army. Sutlers and wagoners served a dual purpose: to attend to the needs of the nascent army but also to help form a sense of community within the army. For a new republic concerned about the impact of a standing army on a virtuous nation, a community of camp followers helped foster a sense that the army was serving the people. As the founding fathers wrote of the nature of a moral commonwealth, the army and its followers lived it. According to historian Holly Mayer, there was a symbiotic relationship between the Continental Army and the camp followers. It was essential that noncombatants accept the military's "superintendence" and promote "the military mission," but it was equally important that the army have camp followers to attend to the soldiers' needs.[8]

By the late nineteenth century, most armies had incorporated the work performed by camp followers into their daily support and supply teams. As European armies became more professional and bureaucratic, they also became exclusively male. As a result women almost disappeared from base camps. The Crimean war in 1854 saw large numbers of camp followers— including pioneer nurse Florence Nightingale—and the American civil war also saw large numbers of women near camps, but by and large women had returned to home villages while men marched off to war. Of course industrialization brought with it new opportunities for working-class women, and soon the work of war was replaced by piecework in factories. For many women, wages earned by following armies had been one of the few economic options available. Although the line between prostitutes and army sutlers has not always been distinct, it is evident that many camp followers performed essential functions for the army that did not require sexual favors.

Throughout Vietnam's own history women had performed vital functions within and alongside the military. From its beginnings Vietnam had relied on women warriors to help repel invaders and to aid in its "long march South" against the Cham.[9] Two of Vietnam's most famous warriors were female: the sisters Trung Trac and Trung Nhi (known in Vietnam as *Hai Ba Trung*). In A.D. 40, Trung Trac's husband, a minor feudal lord, was killed by a small group of Chinese from the occupying army. In response the Trung sisters raised an army and led a revolt against the Chinese that delivered Vietnam's first victory over its imperial neighbor. A new and independent country was established, over which the Trung sisters became queens. Three years later, however, the Chinese counterattacked under the famous General Ma Vien and defeated the Vietnamese. Rather than surrender, the Trung sisters committed suicide by drowning in the Hat Giang River. To this day, images of the Trung sisters atop elephants can be found in every hamlet, village, and city in Vietnam. One of Hanoi's most important city streets carries the name Hai Ba Trung.[10]

Women also served the Vietnamese army in other ways. Historically, Vietnam had always relied on wives and camp followers as cooks, laundresses, and, most importantly, nurses. During Vietnam's long battles against the Cham, Mongols, and Chinese, wounded soldiers found their way to makeshift care centers, if they were lucky, where the wives of officers and other camp followers nursed them back to health or comforted them in their last days. According to Vietnamese legend, in 1419 a nurse saved a key battle against the Ming armies in Thanh Hoa Province by "getting the wounded officers on their feet and back into battle."[11] When Le Thai To, also known as Binh Dinh Vuong (as well as the pacification king and Le Loi), led the Lam Son uprising against the Chinese in 1418, female sutlers accounted for nearly a third of his total army.[12] Nurses were an essential part of this entourage. In the late 1400s Emperor Le Thanh Tong battled the Cham in Quang Nam Province and the Lao along the shared border. According to some Vietnamese historians, the ability of Emperor Tong's army to travel great distances at great speed was actually "enhanced by camp followers," ensuring victory.[13]

One interesting aspect of the role of women in Vietnam's military past is that legend and history have accorded them the status of national heroes.

According to historian Keith Taylor, the cult of women warriors, especially the Trung sisters, carries with it the message that if they had not resisted the Chinese there would be "no Vietnamese nation today."[14] Women who served the army were historically treated no differently than men. In many of Vietnam's state histories, women sutlers are mentioned as an essential element in "saving the army and the nation."[15] For example, in one text, female camp followers were applauded for "keeping the army fit and prepared for battle" against the invading Mongols.[16] Women who served the army in the fifteenth century were called "salvation sisters of the nation."[17]

In contemporary Vietnam women in the People's Army also served the national cause. Bui Tin, a colonel in the People's Army of Viet Nam (PAVN), recalled that women were essential to the widening of the Ho Chi Minh Trail. In 1961 Colonel Tin led a small unit of PAVN soldiers, women among them, down the trail to assess "the nature of the terrain . . . the logistical ability of the enemy and the feeling of the people."[18] All along the way women within the army and camp followers helped blaze the trail. Some camp followers from the Quang Ngai region achieved immortal status within the army by carrying up to 200 pounds (90 kilos) on their backs or pushing Chinese-made "Phoenix" bicycles carrying 550 pounds (250 kilos).[19] In the South, the National Liberation Front (NLF) leadership included several women—including Nguyen thi Binh, its most important diplomat, and Nguyen thi Dinh, one of the most successful generals of the People's Liberation Armed Forces (PLAF).[20] Women also played an integral role in the guerrilla movement in the South, living underground in tunnels and in mangrove swamps as nurses, cooks, cleaners, warriors, wives, and mothers.[21] In each instance women and camp followers performed necessary functions for the regular and irregular armies.

The ARVN also enjoyed the presence of wives and companions in camp. As in the American Revolution, women played a dual function in ARVN camps. First, they undertook domestic duties for ARVN families and single soldiers. Second and more important, they served as the living inspiration for the war.

ARVN troops may have deserted to be with their families during the first ten years of the war, 1955–1965, but during the last ten years (1965–1975) they tended to bring their spouses, children, and parents with them to base camp or to live nearby. Increasing security concerns in the countryside also played an important role in delivering ARVN families to the barracks doorstep. As shown earlier, housing was always a problem for the ARVN. There never seemed to be adequate shelter for ARVN troops, and housing for dependents was almost nonexistent near most base camps. As a result, clusters of makeshift housing surrounded almost every military base. A typical example, according to Jeffrey Clarke, was the base camp at Tan Hung, home to the ARVN's 2nd Battalion, 9th Regiment, an infantry unit of the 5th Division.[22] Like most other ARVN camps, Tan Hung was a square enclosure, several hundred yards long on each side, formed by interlocking bunkers, barbed wire, and fence posts. Most families set up house in separate bunkers, although there were some communal shelters as well. In each of these bunkers wives and children spent their days preparing meals, doing laundry, sewing, and cleaning. To supplement poor ARVN pay, many women took in laundry or performed other household chores for soldiers without families.

As the war dragged on and Americans began to leave Vietnam under Nixon's Vietnamization policy, ARVN families established more permanent settlements near base camps. Using corrugated fiberglass and plywood found at U.S. installations, ARVN wives set up shantytowns all over South Vietnam. These makeshift "villages" served as the vital link between the soldier and his community. For many ARVN troops the shantytowns soon replaced traditional villages as the center of social and cultural life. "Everything that was important to me was near the base camp," reported Nguyen van Hieu. "My wife brought the family altar with her and pictures of my aunts and uncles. Everything was there except the graves of my ancestors."[23] Indeed, much like the now famous NLF tunnels west of Saigon, ARVN shantytowns witnessed births, weddings, burials, and other ceremonies. In every respect shantytowns replaced the village as the nexus of life for the soldier.

For many family members life in the camp was not that different from life in the village, and this similarity added to the sense that the war was not about the national question. "I got up every morning to prepare *pho ga* [hot chicken soup] for my husband," remembered Nguyen thi Mai. "After breakfast I would do laundry, mend clothes, and take care of my children. It was a solitary life, but more secure than life in the countryside."[24] Another ARVN wife remembered that she took "great pleasure in being able to feed my husband. His rations were so meager and expensive. We got by with help from our families and friends, and I was lucky to be able to prepare his meals. This brought us closer together than we ever had been."[25]

Diaries of ARVN wives are rare, but the few that do exist share similar themes. One is the ordinary nature of life in the camps. In one diary a young ARVN wife wrote with pride, "Our lives are exactly as we would have lived in the village, but without the rice harvest. My husband enjoys the warmth and comfort of home-cooked meals and my care."[26] In another a wife and mother recalled that she "made my husband feel at home" even though he was "trapped inside the army."[27] One young newlywed "nursed her husband back to strong health" following a serious shrapnel wound in the leg. "I was so thankful to be near him, to protect him, to make him well," Ton Nu Mai recalled.[28]

Most ARVN wives took great pleasure in serving their husbands in this manner. They understood that their primary role "was keeping their husbands fit and healthy."[29] The modern Vietnamese revolution and South Vietnam's counterrevolution had promised to end the suffocating paternalism associated with Vietnam's past and "liberate women" throughout the country.[30] Both had promised that the patriarchal traditions associated with *che do gia ding* (the family system) would be wiped out of Vietnamese life forever. This system had denied women educational or professional opportunities and made them second-class citizens in their own homes. For a brief period the Marxists had purposefully asked women to subsume their fight for sexual equality to the fight for national independence, but by the late 1930s most of that language had disappeared from political discourses regarding the struggle against the French. The Saigon government had gone out of its way to show that the old family system, along with other outmoded Vietnamese traditions, had slowed Vietnam's natural political development. Some of the early literature on women and the counterrevolution in South Vietnam used terms familiar to those with knowledge of the various radical groups of the 1920s who saw Vietnam as a backward society in need of modernization.[31] Many Saigon political leaders had family ties to these radicals and shared their views on modernization and the place of women in a modern country.

Most ARVN women gladly accepted that their primary role remained in the domestic sphere. According to historian Holly Mayer, such behavior should have been expected. Much like other women near base camps throughout history, ARVN wives and mothers may have "clung all the more tenaciously to an image of peaceful domesticity" rather than focus on the realities of the war.[32] Given the helplessness felt by so many soldiers and their families, it was natural for women and men to romanticize domesticity. Furthermore, the social and cultural revolution promised by Diem and subsequent Saigon governments had never really taken root. It was unlikely that women would abandon familiar practices in a war that had created such unfamiliar terror.

The government in Saigon even made a halfhearted effort to take advantage of women in the base camps. Starting in early 1960, Diem's government supported several programs designed specifically to foster the relationship between "the work of women at our military camps" and "patriotism."[33] The goal was to convince ARVN wives and mothers that they could best help serve the national cause by supporting their husbands. A woman could display her patriotism, the government contended, through her actions as caretaker and household manager for her husband, son, or father or by taking on extra chores for single soldiers at base camps. In one pamphlet distributed at many base camps, the government applauded "the patriotic work of the Republic's women who take care of the men in the army."[34] Even though official Saigon policy encouraged families to remain in their home villages or in strategic hamlets, government leaders hoped to capitalize on the migration to the base camps. "We wanted to create programs that promoted patriotism through the traditional family way of life," remembered one former Saigon official.[35]

Diem's sister-in-law, Madame Ngo Dinh Nhu (born Tran Le Xuan in Hanoi in 1924), supervised several of these patriotic campaigns.[36] With now famous fanfare, Madame Nhu urged the wives of soldiers to care for their husbands "with all of your heart."[37] To strengthen the family, she supported national laws that abolished divorce, made adultery a crime, banned abortions, and prohibited any form of birth control. She outlawed dancing, beauty contests, and boxing, all of which she thought were a moral affront to the family.[38] Most importantly, however, she spoke frequently in public of the "patriotic work women were doing at army bases" to care for their husbands.[39] In the mid-1960s, RVN premier Nguyen Cao Ky's wife would continue to emphasize the connection between domestic work and patriotism.[40] She often praised the "women of South Vietnam" for their sacrifices to the republic and urged them to continue to "support your husbands and sons by caring for them in the camps."[41] She added that patriotic Southern women could also strike at the enemy by "praising [their] men for their hard work and sacrifice" in the "name of the nation."[42]

This modern Vietnamese version of republican motherhood promoted domestic work and national sacrifice. However, for most ARVN wives, daughters, and mothers, their actions had little to do with patriotism. Instead they followed their husbands, fathers, and sons to ARVN base camps precisely because the government had failed to provide adequately for its own troops and because the countryside, under Communist control, was no longer safe. "I remember going to a rally to support mothers who had sent two or more sons to the ARVN," remembered Duong Lan. "It was such a farce. First, our sons were drafted and had little choice. Second, the government politicians did little to support our sons once they were in the army. I needed to be near my son so that he had enough to eat."[43] Nguyen thi Linh wondered how her husband would have survived without her. "He had little to eat and his feet were constantly broken out in open sores. He had such terrible trouble with his feet before I got to the base."[44] Despite the government's effort, most ARVN families rejected the connection between women's work and patriotism. Instead they valued the close contact with each other and believed that they were "keepers of the flame of traditional Vietnam" even in the middle of "all this hell around us."[45]

Rejecting modern politics and patriotism for what they considered traditional family values, ARVN soldiers and their families tried to re-create their home lives in base camps. The goal was to take care of the individual soldiers but also to replicate village life "as closely as possible."[46] The ties to family and village are strong in Vietnam, yet one gets the sense that many ARVN families played to the stereotype. Much like Vietnam's neotraditionalists of the 1920s, these families may have created a whole host of traditions based on myth to preserve the family. In retrospect, many ARVN soldiers and their wives do suggest that they "acted" out village life at the army camps rather than duplicate the life they had known before the war and life in the army. One thoughtful former soldier, now a high school teacher in California, wondered if the focus on a romanticized domestic life was a key to his family's survival. "I think we pretended that our life had always been very traditional while I was in the army," explained Nguyen van Tien. "But we had seen ourselves as a very modern couple before I was drafted."[47] As Mayer suggested, this overly determined view of village life might have been a survival mechanism.

Still, it is undeniable that ARVN soldiers and their families took great comfort in being together. ARVN husbands and fathers joined their wives and children in thinking that the war was about "our little world."[48] If somehow the family could remain intact and survive the war, then the individual ARVN soldier could rescue victory from defeat. In scores of ARVN letters and diaries, we see references to the war in terms of domestic life. In one such letter, an ARVN soldier stationed in Long An province wrote, "For me dearest, the war is about you and our family. I know that the war will end one day, and then we can resume our normal lives. Yet, you have made my life in the army most normal by taking care of the children and me. This is the war's only blessing."[49]

Another soldier lamented sacrifices demanded by the war but was happy in the "thought that I will see you every day at camp. For us, that is the war."[50] Yet another suggested that the "war is about someone else's political concerns. For us, it has always been about my family and it always will be."[51] Regrettably, the Saigon government could never transfer this loyalty to family to the nation, perhaps its most serious shortcoming.

If ARVN soldiers took great solace in being with their families and viewed the war in terms of domestic tranquility, their wives, daughters, and mothers reinforced the idea that the war was about family survival. Nguyen thi Hanh suggested that her "highest calling" was service not to her country but rather to her husband. "My husband was trying to save our family by providing security and at least some food. We knew if we could somehow stay alive that our family would prosper in peace."[52]

This survival theme is repeated in numerous interviews with the wives, mothers, and daughters of ARVN soldiers, especially those who made their way to the United States after the war. "What mattered most to us was the survival of our family," recalled Mai Huong.[53] Another ARVN wife reported that her husband got up every day and "fought for our family. I remember telling my children that the war was about our survival. I mentioned nothing about the Republic or the politics of the war."[54] Perhaps most telling were the interviews with women who remembered camp life as constant preparations of food and gifts "to celebrate the anniversary deaths of our ancestors."[55] Phuong Thuy recalled the importance to her husband of "worshipping our ancestors." She concluded that it was her husband's tie to the past but also to his future. He understood that "the war was about keeping our family together no matter the military outcome."[56]

Some Americans criticized ARVN soldiers for bringing their families to camp. In most cases this was considered further evidence that the ARVN simply did not "have the fighting spirit" necessary to win the war.[57] For ARVN troops, however, the close proximity of family members was the only reason to carry on the fight. "The presence of our families was so important to us," reported Cao van Ngia. "We stayed energized for the war only by thinking that we were in the service of our families. I had refused to join my unit until I had permission to bring my family along. I know others felt the same way."[58] For many ARVN soldiers, domestic family life replaced the lost cause of national liberation during their time in the army.

READING THE WAR

This change did not come without some soul searching, nor was it ever discussed in official circles. Rather, we see individual ARVN soldiers struggling to find meaning in the war in their diaries, letters home, and memoirs. Another key source for understanding South Vietnamese sensibilities about the war and the nation is the voluminous collection of postwar fiction written by ARVN soldiers. All of these sources raise interesting questions about nationalism.

Historians have long been interested in what constitutes a nation. Benedict Anderson told us that nations are not natural but "imagined communities," requiring a great deal of blind faith. He believes that the creation of nations is often a purely cognitive undertaking. Common languages, customs, and history are often imagined or constructed by civilians to purposefully strengthen bonds for survival.[59] Eric Hobsbawm picked up on Anderson's theme, suggesting that most traditions that unite disparate people into a nation are invented.[60] Ernest Renan wrote that the nation is a "large-scale solidarity, constituted by the feeling of the sacrifices that one has made in the past and those that one is prepared to make in the future." He concluded, however, that the single variable that ties people to a nation is the "desire to continue a common life."[61]

Michael Howard took a different approach. For Howard, the principle of nationalism has always been "indissolubly linked, both in theory and practise, with the idea of war."[62] Barbara Ehrenreich agreed. In her book *Blood Rites: Origins and History of the Passions of War*, Ehrenreich argued that the nation is "our imagined link to the glorious deeds—or the terrible atrocities still awaiting revenge—that were performed by others long ago." She concluded by suggesting that the nation is "a warrior lineage in which everyone can now claim membership."[63]

If past sacrifice and a desire to share a common future are at the crux of nationhood, it is no wonder that the ARVN did not embrace national liberation as the war's ultimate meaning. Lacking history—real or invented—Saigon was simply no match for the Communists when it came to stirring up ancient passions or promoting what life would be like in postwar Vietnam. As one former ARVN enlisted man reported, "The very strength of South Vietnam as an idea was that it did not have ties to the traditions that had made Vietnam weak. We could reject the monarchy that had collaborated with the French. We could reject the corrupt temples that made us passive in the face of imperialism. We could reject the Confucian system that made us prisoners of the past. Yes, there was a way to sell the idea of a new, modern nation and our leaders failed to do this effectively."[64] Indeed, officials in Saigon seemed uninterested and even unwilling to promote this concept of nationalism, intent instead on the fringes of social scientific modernist theory. When the government did venture out to create a common history and common future for the people of South Vietnam, it did so on the Communist Party's terms, failing miserably against a powerful message from Hanoi.

The Communists had for decades promoted a brand of patriotism wrapped in nationalism that had broad appeal in Vietnam. Beginning in the 1920s, leaders of the Vietnamese revolution linked the modern struggle to past sacrifices against foreign invaders. The party skillfully created national heroes out of those who sacrificed for the revolution. Celebration of this sacrifice gave the party preponderant power to assemble a pantheon of champions with ties to Vietnam's glorious past. Throughout the war, party publications stressed revolutionary continuity and national sacrifice.[65] According to historian William Duiker, the party had used the personality of Ho Chi Minh to "cement the Party's reputation as the legitimate representative of Vietnamese national tradition as well as the leading force in the Vietnamese revolution."[66] One experienced reporter told Frances FitzGerald during the war that he finally realized the United States and its Saigon ally would never win "when I noticed the street signs in Saigon were named after Vietnamese heroes who fought against foreign invaders."[67]

It was virtually impossible for Saigon to lay claim to Vietnam's historic past, even though many southern families had contributed significantly to Vietnam's history. Many members of the Saigon government had ties to the French, and several ARVN generals, including some of Diem's closest advisers, had served with the Vietnamese National Army, created by France to defend the colony against Ho Chi Minh's Communists. Although President Diem was a staunch anticolonialist, his government was never able to shake the image that it had been created by the United States and that it had a colonial heritage. An unwillingness in Saigon to embrace any form of nationalism also made it impossible for South Vietnam to claim a share of Vietnam's past. Without these ties to the past, the Communists went unchallenged when they claimed to be the rightful heirs of the Trung sisters, Emperor Le Loi, and Nguyen Hue.

At times the Saigon government did try to show how its struggle was in line with Vietnamese traditions, but these efforts usually had unhappy results. In one such "celebration" an ARVN colonel spoke for three hours about "how the nation of South Vietnam was repelling an invasion just like the Trung sisters had against the Chinese in the first century." Many in attendance viewed the speech with "skepticism and boredom."[68] Many ARVN soldiers enlisted in the army because of their commitment to anticommunism and the rhetoric contained in these documents and speeches, but they soon discovered that the government could not deliver on the message.

Most ARVN soldiers would have preferred to live in a free and independent South Vietnam. Most would consider themselves patriots. However, ARVN records indicate that the ordinary infantry soldier lost confidence in his government and its officials early in the conflict and, therefore, believed that such a future for South Vietnam was doubtful. Once this doubt had crept in, there was little the government could do to keep ARVN troops committed to the nation-building experiment. Most troops rejected the sense of nationalism in favor of lives that gave precedence to individualism. Rather than willingly sacrifice themselves to the national cause, ARVN soldiers created a subnational culture that emphasized family survival and individual strength. The war against the Communists became a sideshow for many ARVN troops because they were all too aware of their government's own shortcomings. The troops fought to survive as members of extended families but not as members of a nation with rich memories of past sacrifices made together or a commitment to present-day common life.

That is not to say that ARVN soldiers were without a sense of nationhood or memories of Vietnam's past sacrifices. One important element in modern Vietnamese history often overlooked by Western historians of the war is that many ARVN troops felt the same sense of history as their adversaries in the PAVN and the PLAF. ARVN and Communist troops alike had a keen sense of the sacrifices made by Phan Boi Chau, Phan Chu Trinh, Nguyen An Ninh, and other anticolonial leaders in Vietnam's past. Even though the ARVN had been born out of the remnants of the Vietnamese National Army, which had collaborated with the French against the Communists, most individual ARVN soldiers interviewed for this book saw their own lives connected to the noncommunist, anticolonial activists of the early twentieth century. "We felt a strong connection to the work of Phan Chu Trinh," recalled Nguyen van Linh. "He was a patriot who wanted to free Vietnam from the yoke of colonialism and was one of us [southern]."[69] Indeed, Cochinchina (southern Vietnam) had been home to some of the more radical anticolonial activists of the early twentieth century. The first generation of Vietnamese literati who had rejected deterministic explanations for Vietnam's colonial status included many southerners, several of whom had strong connections to the families of the new republic.

These memories were not enough, however, to erase the fact that many of the ARVN's original officer corps had collaborated with the French and that many rural Vietnamese saw the ARVN as the *bo quan cong tac* (army of collaboration). The Communists were far more successful in convincing the citizens of Vietnam that they owned the nation's past sacrifices. The party was the self-proclaimed caretaker, therefore, of Vietnam's patriots, forcing the RVN government to create a nation from dust. The RVN's inability to use the past had a significant impact on its army's alienation and lack of ideological commitment to the national struggle. The lack of proper political conditioning meant that the idea of nationhood remained an abstract thought to most common soldiers. Few in the ARVN could articulate the "national essence"—a term used quite frequently in modern Vietnamese political discourses on nationhood—of South Vietnam.[70] Over time they would come to reject the concept of an independent South Vietnam altogether.

Essential for the survival of any nation is the commitment of its soldiers to a shared future. What separates modern nations from premodern communities is the abdication of the individual to the advantage of the community. National sacrifice has been the essence of modern armies, and it has been the key ingredient in turning subjects into citizens.

For the ARVN soldiers, the national question had already been settled, so the only remaining goal was to keep their families intact.

DEFEAT

Keeping loved ones safe and secure was not always easy to do. During the last months of the war, as PAVN forces marched south to victory, South Vietnam became a flood of refugees. Many families found themselves separated by the circumstances of the war, but it now seems clear that a majority of ARVN families were bound together even more tightly than before the Ho Chi Minh Campaign. "Despite the hell all around us," Nguyen van Linh recalled, "we did whatever was necessary to keep our family together."[71] Another former ARVN soldier said that "a surreal" quality filled the air in South Vietnam during those trying months. "It was the worst of times," remembered Nguyen van Chau, "but I knew at the time that my family was strong enough to take whatever that crazy war dished out."[72]

What the war dished out was one of the most bizarre and terrifying collapses of any government in modern history. Shortly after signing the Paris Peace Accord in 1973, RVN president Nguyen van Thieu declared that the "Third Indochina War" had begun, and he predicted a victory now that South Vietnamese forces were free to fight the war on their own terms without the constant meddling of American advisers. Thieu was not alone in this belief, and several South Vietnamese commanders urged the president to go on the offensive into North Vietnam. Given the realities of the war, Thieu's optimism, and that of many of his military commanders, amounted to little more than empty saber-rattling. Nothing government officials could say or do at this point was going to prevent a Communist victory.

In Hanoi the Military Commission of the Political Bureau announced its plan for a final offensive against the South. It had concluded that "with regard to both strategy and political-military forces, we have sufficient strength to overwhelm the enemy troops. The U.S. has proved to be completely impotent, and even if it increases its aid, it cannot save the puppets from collapse."[73] The decision was therefore made to grasp the strategic opportunity and end the war before the rains came and before Ho Chi Minh's birthday in mid-May. The Ho Chi Minh Campaign, as Hanoi called the final offensive, was months ahead of schedule, causing many ARVN troops increased fear for their future and their families.

The RVN government responded to Hanoi's military victories first with silence and then with a series of directives that made little sense to most ARVN troops. In early March 1975 Thieu ordered the ARVN to abandon key outposts in the Central Highlands and in some northern provinces in order to take up blocking positions along the eastern seaboard and near Saigon. The plan, Thieu told puzzled journalist Stanley Karnow, was to "lighten the top and keep the bottom."[74] Thieu believed such a strategic withdrawal would give the ARVN time to regroup in strong enclaves, buying time for an American return to Vietnam. Many among Saigon's urban upper class shared Thieu's deluded fantasy. According to Duong Van Mai Elliot, most of Saigon's elite believed, as late as January 1975, that the Americans and the Saigon government were planning a trap for the Communists. Indeed, the retreat was seen as a clever ploy to lure the PAVN deep into enemy territory just in time for the Americans to reenter the war and crush the Communists for good. One persistent rumor was that the huge U.S. air base at Da Nang was now full of American transport planes "disgorging brand new howitzers still glistening with lubricants, and powerful tanks."[75]

Despite these rumors and optimism in Saigon, Thieu's strategic withdrawal proved to be a fatal mistake. Once he had decided on the enclave strategy, Thieu ordered General Phan van Phu to retreat from Pleiku and Kontom in the Central Highlands. Phu left the area immediately by military transport, leaving nearly 200,000 troops and their families leaderless in the face of a massive Communist assault. The only hope for these ARVN families was a mass exodus to Da Nang, South Vietnam's second-largest city and home to an enormous seaport. ARVN troops led the way out of the highlands, across treacherous roads and dangerous jungles, toward Da Nang. On the way news of the fall of Hue reached them.

"After the fall of Hue," recalled Nguyen van Thien, "I knew that we were in for a horrific experience in Da Nang, but we had no place else to go. The Communists had cut off the routes south and west; our only hope was to get to the sea." Many ARVN families shared Thien's desperate vision. "There seemed little else to do but race to Da Nang and hope we beat the Communists."[76] All along the way, the ARVN troops provided for their families. "We marched as families; we ate as families," remembered Ngo van Trong.[77] Some families hurried home to sell their possessions, realizing that the war was lost and that they would have to buy their way to safety. Others stuck with the crowds heading east toward the coast, hoping for rescue at one seaside port or another. Through it all, though, the families remained together.

Nguyen van Ngo remembered that his wife wanted to return to their home in Pleiku before heading south. "She wanted to gather up our small supply of gold. We would need the gold to sell because by that time in the war, it was the only thing of value we had. Our money was no good, and there wasn't much of it. I made the decision that we would all go together. None of us would be separated during this ordeal."[78]

By late March 1975 the entire population of the Central Highlands, more than one million civilians, had joined the ARVN forces streaming toward Da Nang. In one of the most heart-wrenching chapters in the war, thousands of refugees poured into the city just ahead of the Communists. They waded into the sea to swim to safety. Many mothers carried their infants with them, only to have them drowned. Others were trampled to death as they struggled to get through Da Nang's busy streets and onto safe ships in the harbor. News photographs showed vastly overcrowded fishing boats dangerously close to capsizing because of the human cargo. The going rate for a berth on a protected boat was over $10,000VND. Private jumbo jets tried to take off from Da Nang's air base, many with refugees clinging to the stairways. One photographer captured this moment just before the hangers-on fell to their deaths. On Easter Sunday, March 30, 1975, Da Nang fell to the Communists, and the tide of refugees headed south to repeat this scene all along South Vietnam's eastern seaboard.

By mid-April the remaining ARVN forces had retreated to the strategic areas surrounding Saigon. There they engaged the PAVN in some of the war's most brutal fighting. At Xuan Loc, a small city located 37 miles (60 km) northeast of Saigon along National Highway 1, the ARVN's 18th Infantry Division stood and fought well for several days. For years U.S. advisers had claimed that the 18th Infantry Division, responsible for defense of the Xuan Loc region, was one of the worst units in South Vietnam's army.[79] At the war's end, however, the division had found new life. According to James Willbanks, Vietnam veteran and professor of combat studies at the U.S. Army's Command and General Staff College at Fort Leavenworth, the ARVN fought "valiantly" at Xuan Loc.[80] General Van Tien Dung, the PAVN officer in charge of the Ho Chi Minh Campaign, agreed. He was especially impressed by "the stubbornness of the enemy" and by the ARVN's "relentless pursuit" of PAVN soldiers.[81]

Following their defeat at Xuan Loc, many ARVN troops feared that there would be a bloodbath in Saigon and therefore did all they could to secure safe passage out of the country. The U.S. ambassador in Saigon, Graham Martin, was highly critical of the ARVN for these actions, claiming that the army was deserting the country in the hour of its greatest need. Martin was also in denial about the serious nature of the situation, refusing to make any plans for the safe evacuation of Saigon. According to Stanley Karnow, Martin was so deceived by his own optimism that he refused to allow for the evacuation of private citizens connected to IBM who generated the Saigon government payroll.[82] Even after President Gerald Ford declared in a speech at Tulane University on April 23, 1975, that the war was all but over, and the U.S. Congress refused to grant an emergency $700 million to save South Vietnam, Martin clung to his belief that the Saigon area could be defended and that the United States would eventually rejoin the fight.[83]

Martin's misreading of the situation cost the ARVN troops and their families dearly. Without formal plans for the safe evacuation of troops and South Vietnamese government officials, the city "resembled the third ring of hell."[84] With PAVN troops launching artillery attacks against Ton Son Nhut airport on the outskirts of Saigon, and the security ring around the capitol getting smaller each hour, Martin was finally pressed into action. He conceded on April 29, 1975, that Operation Frequent Wind—the air evacuation of Saigon—was the best hope for the most people. Martin himself refused to be airlifted before others, even though a severe fever threatened his physical abilities. Admiral Noel Gayler, the commander in chief of Pacific operations, was brought in to oversee the final evacuation. With PAVN troops controlling major vehicle escape routes, it was clear to Admiral Gayler that he needed to rely on Option IV of the withdrawal plan. That option called for helicopters to take Vietnamese refugees and Americans to ships offshore.

Over the course of the next twenty-four hours, thousands of ARVN officers, government officials, and their families were airlifted in CH-53s from the Ton Son Nhut airport compound to ships in the South China Sea. No plans had been made, however, to evacuate refugees who had made their way to the U.S. Embassy. Brigadier General Richard E. Carey ordered helicopters and marines to the embassy to oversee the hasty evacuation of some 1,200 Vietnamese and nearly 1,000 Americans. Thunderstorms and high winds made flying hazardous, and one marine had to illuminate the landing area inside the embassy compound with the light from a slide projector. When General Carey was finally forced to call off the rescue operation on

April 30, 1975, hundreds of thousands of ARVN troops and their families remained behind.[85]

For most Americans old enough to remember the fall of Saigon, the photographs and television coverage of the republic's last hours are indelibly etched in their minds. The most vivid images, no doubt, are of U.S. helicopters overloaded with ARVN troops and South Vietnamese citizens struggling to take off from the rooftops of buildings in the embassy compound (not the actual embassy building itself). What most viewers could not possibly understand, however, was that the evacuation of Saigon was the beginning of a process by which former ARVN soldiers tried to snatch a personal victory from national defeat by keeping their families intact.

DUNG CO LAM PHIEN

For many former ARVN troops, that process began with an uncertain future in reeducation camps as the reward for having belonged to what officials in Hanoi called "the rebel army." A perilous escape from Vietnam landed others in refugee camps throughout Southeast Asia and, if they were lucky, eventual resettlement with family members in a new country. Of course most former ARVN troops also suffered from the humiliation of defeat, negative racial stereotyping, and the cultural calling that led many Vietnamese to hide their troubles and sorrows in order not to burden others *(dung co lam phien)*. What kept them moving forward in their new homes was the clear understanding that they had survived with families intact.

Many ARVN veterans took solace in the fact that they had kept their families together despite enormous obstacles. "We survived the war, the Thu Duc reeducation camp, a refugee center in Hong Kong, and the American Orderly Departure Program [a U.S. government program to unite refugee families] to be together," remembered Nguyen van Hieu. "I held this day in my heart during the war, this day when all my family would live together in peace. It is what kept me going those many years."[86]

Indeed, ARVN soldiers were unique among refugee populations in that they did emigrate with their families. Most sociologists agree that the Vietnamese ability to leave with their families was atypical of flight patterns under hasty and traumatic circumstances such as the collapse of the RVN and the fall of Saigon.[87] As Tables 5.1 and 5.2 indicate, only 16,819 out of 124,493 Vietnamese refugees who came to the United States during the first year after the war came without families.

Table 5.1. Age and Sex of Vietnamese Immigrants (sample size 123,301; data correlated as of December 15, 1975)

Age	Male	Female	Total
0–5	10,572	9,817	20,389
6–11	9,704	8,611	18,315
12–17	9,519	8,296	17,815
18–24	13,591	9,105	22,696
25–34	12,063	8,821	20,884
35–44	6,364	5,068	11,432
45–62	4,706	4,569	2,495
Total	67,499	55,802	123,301

Source: Interagency Task Force for Indochina Refugees, "Report to the Congress," December 15, 1975, p. 11, as cited in Gail Paradise Kelly, *From Vietnam to America: A Chronicle of the Vietnamese Immigration to the United States* (Boulder, Colo.: Westview Press, 1977), p. 43.

Furthermore, according to official U.S. government statistics, Vietnamese households of over five persons accounted for roughly 62 percent of all immigrants.[88] These figures show that ARVN soldiers went to great lengths to get their families out of Vietnam. The large number of children and young people attests to the success of these efforts.

Many of the refugees ended up at Camp Pendleton in Orange County, California. Paul Graham, the commanding officer at Camp Pendleton, was in charge of constructing the makeshift "tent city" for nearly twenty thousand Vietnamese refugees. In a matter of days marines under Graham's command erected 140 Quonset huts and 1,040 squad-sized tents with plywood floors, put up 200 telephone poles, strung 20 miles (32 km) of power lines and 36 miles (58 km) of communication cable, installed 35,000 feet (10,700 meters) of water lines, and built 22 shower huts.[89] At Camp Pendleton, as was the case at other U.S. installations accepting Vietnamese refugees during that first year after the fall of Saigon, nearly 40 percent of the adult male population (over eighteen years of age) were veterans of the Republic of Vietnam armed forces.[90] Many of them were ARVN enlisted men who had brought their families.

Statistics from Camp Pendleton reveal that ARVN families were traditional, that is, the Vietnamese refugees had arrived "with a patriarchal, large-size household from five to twelve members, and including, besides the core family, the grandparents plus some siblings, their families, and even some in-laws."[91] Furthermore, 75 percent of heads of households were married, further evidence that ARVN soldiers had kept their families together.[92]

Table 5.2. Household Size of Vietnamese Refugees

Household Size	No. of Households	No. of People
1	16,819	16,819
2	4,524	9,048
3	3,166	9,498
4	2,952	11,808
5	2,537	12,685
6	2,185	13,110
7	1,663	11,641
8	1,357	10,856
9	960	8,640
10	620	6,200
10+	1,061	14,188

Source: Housing, Education, and Welfare Refugee Task Force, "Report to Congress," June 15, 1976, p. 27.

How the soldiers succeeded in keeping their families together while other refugee groups under similar conditions and circumstances failed remains a mystery. Some sociologists suggest that the Vietnamese refugee population had higher educational attainment levels than most refugee groups, and that this fact played a deciding role in the ability to escape with one's family.[93] This is certainly true of the ARVN. Even though the soldiers complained about educational opportunities inside the army, the educational system in Vietnam was superb up to the postsecondary level, meaning that many young men, even before they were drafted, had experienced some form of higher education. According to one survey, over 50 percent of the Vietnamese refugees had had some level of secondary education (ninth–twelfth grade), and nearly 20 percent had gone to a university.[94]

One explanation provided by some social scientists is that the Vietnamese were unlike many refugee populations. In most refugee groups, especially those that are the by-products of war, women and children dominate. The typical Vietnamese refugee in 1975, however, was an adult male who had served in the armed forces. According to most camp surveys, a substantial majority of the 1975 evacuees (about 55 percent) were male.[95] This number continued to climb over the next decade as former ARVN troops were released from reeducation camps and economic conditions in Vietnam worsened. For example, in 1982 nearly 60 percent of those Vietnamese arriving in the United States as political refugees were male.[96] Of this population, nearly 50 percent also claimed to have English-speaking ability, certainly a helpful tool in keeping families together as refugee workers reviewed cases in the camps.[97] ARVN enlisted men were twice as likely to have "good to adequate" English language skills as other men and three times as likely to be able to converse in English as were their female counterparts.[98]

Another possible reason for the ARVN soldiers' success in escaping was the fact that there were hundreds of Americans helping them. Even in the last chaotic days of Saigon the ARVN could draw upon the resources of its soon-to-be former ally. U.S. helicopters brought thousands of South Vietnamese to American ships offshore. Of the total Vietnamese refugee population living in the United States in 1975, over 90 percent had left within two weeks before April 30, 1975 (the fall of Saigon.)[99] In the 1980s the United States instituted what became known as the Orderly Departure Program (ODP), which reunited Vietnamese families. The ODP brought hundreds, if not thousands, of former ARVN soldiers to the United States.

Some former ARVN members have suggested that service in the army under extreme conditions prepared the enlisted men of South Vietnam for a refugee's life. "We knew what it would take to survive a life on the run," reported one former soldier. "I had learned how to become self-sufficient because the army had provided so little material comfort. In many ways, life in the refugee camps and then at Camp Pendleton resembled the life I had known in the army."[100] For Nguyen van Linh, the skills he learned in the army finally paid off "after the war was over."[101] "I was able to put the little training I had to use when we were in the refugee camp in Hong Kong. We were pretty much on our own, so my wife—who had been with me at the ARVN barracks for the last two years of the war—joined me in showing the rest of the family how to survive on very little and how to behave to survive in extreme conditions. I am sure that this is what kept us together."[102]

Still, the predominant view of ARVN enlisted men regarding their success in keeping their families together has been the creation of a subnational culture that gave the war its personalized meaning. As Cao van Ngia explained, "We had pressed on during the war—even under the most difficult circumstances— to save our families. We were not about to let that goal die just because the war ended so badly for South Vietnam."[103] Another ARVN veteran, Nguyen van Chau, concluded that this subnational culture was very familiar to most Vietnamese: "It was the way we lived our daily lives—protecting our families and caring for our elders; it really was not a stretch for us to keep this goal in the front of our minds through the war, our escape, and our journey to our new home in America. It was all very Vietnamese."[104]

Saving families did not come at the expense of saving the nation, however, as the government in Saigon was never a viable enterprise. Corruption, cronyism, incompetence, and a paralyzing fear of nationalism meant that the state never won the hearts and minds of those sworn to defend its interests. Most in the ARVN were committed anticommunists, but few found an outlet for their patriotism. For individual soldiers, this meant redefining the war's meaning. The focus on families in the absence of any meaningful national program based on the Vietnamese concept of *ai quoc* (patriotism) meant that ARVN soldiers reverted to the familiar: the comfortable, culture-bound dominance of family in their daily lives. Although the Communists had learned how to transfer this filial piety from the family to the village, then the state, the RVN never entertained such an idea. The blending of Marxism with nationalistic patriotism gave the Communists a decisive edge in the war.

For most ARVN soldiers, the focus on family gave them a way to make sense of the war and to continue to risk their lives for the republic. Keeping the family together required vigilance, patience, and sacrifice. At times the soldiers also had to alter their behavior from expected military norms to fight and live on their own terms, terms that made sense to them as individual members of extended families. Some government officials in Saigon saw the ARVN's actions as counterproductive, and their American allies often did not understand why the South Vietnamese soldiers behaved the way they did. Few armies have been as criticized by friend and foe alike, but former ARVN soldiers seem ready to accept this criticism as a small price to pay for keeping their families together against overwhelming odds, even when they knew in their hearts that the nation was lost.

Three decades after the fall of Saigon, Nguyen van Hieu returned to Vietnam for the first time since the war's end with his two daughters—both born in California. "We visited the graves of my mother, father, and grandparents," he offered. "It was a strange feeling—to be back in Vietnam—but something else also felt so comfortable, so familiar. I guess to be with one's family in Vietnam is as natural as breathing."[105] With that, he leaned back in his chair, smiled, and gazed at the ceiling, relieved that he could go home again.

NOTES

Preface

1. *Chong My, cuu nuoc thien anh hung ca vi dai* (National salvation against the U.S., a great and courageous chapter) (Hanoi: Nha xuat ban Quan Doi Nhan Dan, 1985), pp. 32, 38, 45, 89, and 91.

2. "Memorandum from Secretary of Defense McNamara to President Johnson, March 26, 1964," *Foreign Relations of the United States* (hereafter *FRUS*), *Vietnam, 1964–1968*, Vol. 4 (Washington, D.C.: Government Printing Office, 1994), p. 732.

3. "Letter from the Ambassador in Vietnam (Nolting) to the Deputy Assistant Secretary of State for Far Eastern Affairs (Cottrell), Oct. 15, 1962," *FRUS, Vietnam, 1961–1963*, Vol. 2 (Washington, D.C.: Government Printing Office, 1988), p. 648.

4. "Memorandum from George Carver of the Vietnamese Affairs Staff, Central Intelligence Agency, to Director of Central Intelligence Helms, July 7, 1966," *FRUS, Vietnam 1964–1968*, Vol. 4, p. 486.

5. "Letter from John Sylvester, Jr., Province Senior Advisor, Binh Long Province to Charles Whitehouse, Deputy for CORDS II FFV/III CTZ, September 19, 1969," The Francis N. Dawson, Papers, US Policy Towards Indochina 1940–53, Reports for Assist. Sec. State for Far Eastern Affairs, United States Military History Institute, Carlisle Barracks, Penn.

6. Ellen Frey-Wouters and Robert Laufer, *Legacy of a War: The American Soldier in Vietnam* (Armonk, N.Y.: M. E. Sharpe, 1986), p. 111.

7. Neil Sheehan, *A Bright Shining Lie: John Paul Vann and America in Vietnam* (New York: Random House, 1988), p. 90.

8. Frances FitzGerald, *Fire in the Lake: The Vietnamese and Americans in Vietnam* (New York: Vintage Books, 1972), pp. 263–266.

9. David Blight, *Race and Reunion: The Civil War in American Memory* (Cambridge, Mass.: Belknap Press of Harvard University Press, 2001), p. 191.

10. Roland Barthes, *Mythologies* (Paris: Editions du Seuil, 1957), p. 143.

Chapter One: Conscription

1. Lieutenant General Dong van Khuyen, *The RVNAF* (Washington, D.C.: U.S. Army Center of Military History, Indochina Monographs, 1984), pp. 34–50.

2. John Keegan, *A History of Warfare* (New York: Vintage Books, 1993), pp. 233–234.

3. *Quan Luc Vietnam Cong Hoa Trong Giai Doan Hinh Thanh, 1946–1955* (Republic of Vietnam Armed Forces during the formation period, 1946–1955) (Saigon: Co so dainam xuat ban, 1972), p. 441.

4. Interview with Hoang van Cao, Westminster, California, March 2002.

5. Phan Huy Le and Phan Dai Doan, *Khoi Nghia Lam Son va Phong Trao dau tranh giai phong dat nuoc vao dau the ky X!* (The Lam Son Revolution and liberation of the country in the eleventh century) (Hanoi: Nha xuat ban khao hoc xa hoi, 1969), pp. 22–38.

6. Buu Cam, *Quoc hieu nuoc ta tu An-Nam den Dai-Nam* (Our country's national symbolic history from An-Nam to Dai-Nam) (Saigon: Phu quoc vu khanh dac trac van hoa, 1969), pp. 1–7.

7. Nguyen van Xuan, "Lich su cuoc Nam Tien cua dan toc Viet Nam" (The history of the Vietnamese expansion to the south), *Su Dia* 19–20 (1970): 265–290.

8. Le Thanh Khoi, *Le Viet Nam histoire et civilisation* (Paris: Editions de Minuit, 1955), pp. 146–147.

9. Nguyen Khac Vien, "Confucianism and Marxism," in Nguyen Khac Vien, ed., *Tradition and Revolution in Vietnam* (Berkeley: Indochina Resource Center, 1974), p. 17.

10. Hoc Tu, *Nhung ngay dau cua mat tran Nam Bo* (First days on the South Vietnam battlefront) (Hanoi: Tran dau, 1945), p. 23.

11. This had been a major problem for the party since its birth. According to a 1932 newspaper article, the party focused its energies on getting rid of "intimate disassociations" that caused peasants to subordinate all questions to the family. Hai Au, "Vi sao nguoi minh thieu cai quan niem quoc gia?" (Why do our people lack the nation-state concept?), *Tieng dan* (Voice of the people), January 9, 1932, pp. 1–4. See also Alexander Woodside, *Community and Revolution in Modern Vietnam* (Boston: Houghton-Mifflin Company, 1976), pp. 28–29.

12. *Chong My, cuu nuoc thien anh hung ca vi dai* (National salvation against the U.S., a great and courageous chapter) (Hanoi: Nha xuat ban Quan Doi Nhan Dan, 1985), p. 113.

13. Hoang Minh Thao, "Quan diem chien tranh nhan dan cua Dang ta" (Our Party's viewpoint on people's war), *Hoc Tap* 12 (December 1966): 26–38.

14. See, for example, Bao Ninh, *Noi buon chien tranh* (The sorrow of war), English version by Frank Palmos based on the translation from Vietnamese by Vo Bang Thanh and Phan Thanh Hao, with Katherine Pierce (London: Secker and Warburg, 1991); Nguyen Huy Thiep, *Nhung ngon gio Hua Tat* (The winds of Hua Tat) and *The General Retires and Other Short Stories*, translated by Greg Lockhart (Singapore: Oxford University Press, 1992); and Duong Thu Huong, *Tieu thuyet vo de* (Novel without a name), translated by Phan Huy Duong and Nina McPherson (New York: William Morrow, 1995).

15. Duong Van Mai Elliot, *The Sacred Willow: Four Generations in the Life of a Vietnamese Family* (New York: Oxford University Press, 1999), p. 470.

16. Interview with General Dang Vu Hiep, Hanoi, Vietnam, June 1999.

17. The term "people's army" is a generic one, first used in Vietnam in 1945 during the French war. According to General Vo Nguyen Giap, the "Party advocated uniting all the elements that could be united, neutralizing all those that could be neutralized" to defeat the French in a people's war. General Vo Nguyen Giap, *People's War, People's Army* (Hanoi: Foreign Languages Publishing House, 1961), p. 16.

18. Ngo Dinh Diem, "Tu do va doc lap" (Freedom and independence), Trung Tam Luu Tru Quoc Gia–II (National Archives Center–II) Ho Chi Minh City, Vietnam (hereafter LTII).

19. Robert S. McNamara, James G. Blight, and Robert K. Brigham, *Argument without End: In Search of Answers to the Vietnam Tragedy* (New York: Public Affairs, 1999), p. 321.

20. Department of Defense, *U.S.-Vietnam Relations, 1945–1967*, Vol. 2, Section IV.A.5 (Washington, D.C.: House Committee on Armed Services, 1971), p. 2.

21. BDM Corporation, *A Study of Strategic Lessons Learned in Vietnam*, Vol. 5: *Planning the War* (McLean, Va.: BDM Corporation, 1980), 3.1–3.2.

22. General Tran van Don, *Our Endless War inside Vietnam* (San Rafael, Calif.: Presidio Press, 1978), pp. 148–149.

23. Bo Cong Dan Vu, *Tu ap chien luoc den ca tu ve* (From strategic hamlet to the self-defense village) (Saigon: Defense Ministry, 1962), pp. 23–24, LTII.

24. General Tran van Don, *Our Endless War,* p. 149.

25. "Msg, O'Daniel to CG, USARPAC, 10 August 1955," records of MAAG Indochina, U.S. Army Center of Military History, Washington, D.C. (hereafter CMH). See also Ronald Spector, *Advice and Support: The Early Years of the U.S. Army in Vietnam, 1941–1960* (New York: The Free Press, 1985), p. 263.

26. *Major Policy Speeches by President Ngo Dinh Diem*, 3rd ed. (Saigon: Presidential Office, 1957), pp. 34–35, 41, LTII.

27. *Interviews of Ngo Dinh Diem* (Saigon: Presidential Office, 1960), LTII.

28. Interview with former RVN official who requested anonymity, Los Angeles, California, March 2002.

29. Ibid.

30. As quoted in Philip Catton, *Diem's Final Failure: Prelude to America's War in Vietnam* (Lawrence: University Press of Kansas, 2002), p. 31. See also "Memorandum of a Conversation, May 10, 1957," *FRUS, Vietnam, 1955–1957*, Vol. 1 (Washington: Government Printing Office, 1985), pp. 814–815.

31. "Memorandum of a Conversation, April 4, 1957," *FRUS, Vietnam, 1955–1957,* Vol. 1, p. 770.

32. Interview with Nguyen Xuan Oanh, Ho Chi Minh City, Vietnam, July 1989.

33. Nguyen van Vy, personal letter, August 12, 1992.

34. Marguerite Higgins, *Our Vietnam Nightmare* (New York: Harper and Row, 1971), p. 168.

35. *Quan Doi Viet Nam Cong Hoa* (The Republic of Vietnam Armed Forces), p. 17, LTII.

36. Interview with former RVN official who requested anonymity, Los Angeles, California, March 2002.

37. Jeffrey Clarke, *Advice and Support: The Final Years, The U.S. Army in Vietnam* (Washington, D.C.: U.S. Army Center of Military History, 1988), p. 42.

38. Interview with Nguyen van Hieu, Westminster, California, March 2002.

39. For example, see Tran Ngoc Nhuan, *Doi Quan Ngu* (Life in the army) (Westminster, Calif.: Van Nghe, 1992).

40. "Command History, 1972–1973," Vol. 2, U.S. Military Assistance Command–Vietnam, prepared by the Military History Branch, Office of the Secretary, Joint Staff, Military Assistance Command–Vietnam, CMH; and "USMACV SEER Report, Part I, Combat Effectiveness of the Republic of Vietnam Armed Forces (RVNAF), March 30, 1970," CMH.

41. Dong van Khuyen, *The RVNAF*, p. 34.

42. Interview with Nguyen van Khai, Ho Chi Minh City, Vietnam, January 2003.

43. Interview with Huynh van Hung, Ho Chi Minh City, Vietnam, January 2004.

44. Ibid.

45. "Tinh hin va nhiem vu 59" (The situation and tasks for 1959), Communist Party document, ca. 1959, Trung Tam Luu Tru Quoc Gia I (National Archives Center I), Hanoi, Vietnam (hereafter LTI).

46. Le Duan, "Duong loi cach man mien Nam" (The revolutionary path in the South), ca. 1956, LTI.

47. *Cuoc khang chien chong My, cuu nuoc, 1954–1975: Nhung su kien quan su* (The anti-U.S. resistance war for national salvation of the fatherland, 1954–1975: military events) (Hanoi: Nha xuat ban quan doi nhan dan, 1988), p. 20.

48. Interview with Nguyen van Vinh, Ho Chi Minh City, Vietnam, March 1996.

49. *Cuoc khang chien chong My*, p. 30.

50. Ta Xuan Linh, "Armed Uprisings," *Vietnam Courier* (October 1974): 20.

51. George C. Herring, *America's Longest War: The United States and Vietnam, 1950–1975*, 4th ed. (New York: McGraw Hill, 2002), p. 100.

52. Clarke, *Advice and Support*, p. 12

53. *Mot so van kien cua Dang ve chong My*, Vol. 1: 154–210, LTI; Le Duan, *Some Questions Concerning the International Tasks of Our Party: Speech at the Ninth Party Plenum of the Third Central Committee of the Vietnam Workers' Party, December 1963* (Peking: Foreign Languages Press, 1964); and "The Viet-Nam Workers' Party's 1963 Decision to Escalate the War in the South," *Vietnam Documents and Research Notes*, document no. 96, July 1971.

54. Le Duan, *Thu vao Nam* (Letters to the South) (Hanoi: Nha xuat ban su that, 1986), p. 74.

55. "Working Paper on the North Vietnamese Role in South Viet Nam: Captured Documents and Interrogation Reports," Department of State, May 1968. See also William S. Turley, *The Second Indochina War* (New York: Mentor, 1986), p. 44.

56. Dong van Khuyen, *The RVNAF*, p. 36.

57. "Comparison of Ground Forces, October 1966," RVNAF Assessments Folder, CMH.

58. Michael Beschloss, ed., *Taking Charge: The Johnson White House Tapes, 1963–1964* (New York: Simon and Schuster, 1997), p. 264.

59. Herring, *America's Longest War*, p. 178.

60. "Command History, 1968," Vol. 1, United States Military Assistance Command–Vietnam, prepared by the Military History Branch, Office of the Secretary, Joint Staff, Military Assistance Command–Vietnam, CMH.

61. "Msg, COMUSMACV MAC 06882 to CINPCPAC, 091250 March 1968," Southeast Asia Branch, CMH.

62. Clarke, *Advice and Support*, p. 293.

63. Cao Xuan Huy, *Thang Ba Gay Sung* (The march of the broken rifles) (Westminster, Calif.: Van Khoa, 1986), p. 34; and "Command History, 1968," Vol. 1, CMH.

64. Dong van Khuyen, *The RVNAF*, p. 37.

65. *State Department Briefing Book on Vietnam*, Section 2 (February 1968), pp. 4–9.

66. "Army Organization, ARVN, Army HQ, Concurrently JGS," RVNAF Assessments Folder, CMH.

67. Dong van Khuyen, *The RVNAF*, pp. 37–40. See also Nguyen Vu, *12 Nam Linh* (Twelve years of being a soldier) (Westminster, Calif.: Van Hoa, 1990).

68. Interview with Ngo van Linh, Westminster, California, March 2002.

69. Roger Morris, *An Uncertain Greatness: Henry Kissinger and American Foreign Policy* (New York: Harper and Row, 1977), p. 4.

70. Jeffrey Kimball, *Nixon's Vietnam War* (Lawrence: University Press of Kansas, 1998), pp. 130–131.

71. *New York Times*, May 9, 1969.

72. Dong van Khuyen, *The RVNAF*, p. 38.

73. Ibid.

74. Interview with Nguyen van Hieu, Westminster, California, March 2002.

75. Herring, *America's Longest War*, p. 285.

76. "Assessment of ARVN/VNMC Organizations, February 10, 1970," Fact Sheet File, CMH.

77. Interview with Nghiem Khoa, Ho Chi Minh City, Vietnam, January 2004.

78. Interview with Huynh Thuy, Da Lat, Vietnam, March 1996.

79. Interview with Ngo Chao Minh, Ho Chi Minh City, Vietnam, January 2003.

80. Interview with Ngo Chao Minh, Ho Chi Minh City, Vietnam, January 1999.

81. Interview with Nguyen Xuan Oanh, Ho Chi Minh City, Vietnam, July 1989.

82. Ibid.

83. Gabriel Kolko, *Anatomy of a War: Vietnam, the United States, and the Modern Historical Experience* (New York: Pantheon, 1985), p. 261.

84. Interview with Nguyen van Luong, Westminster, California, March 2002.

85. Interview with former RVN official who requested anonymity, Westminster, California, March 2002.

86. Gerald Hickey, *Village in Vietnam* (New Haven, Conn.: Yale University Press, 1964), p. 138.

87. Interview with Huynh van Cam, New York, New York, March 2002.

88. Republic of Vietnam, Ministry of Agriculture, Agriculture and Statistics Service, "Census of Agriculture, 1960–1961" (Saigon: Ministry of Agriculture, 1964), p. 80, LTII.

89. Interview with Cao van Thu, San Francisco, California, June 1999.

90. Interview with Hoang van Cao, Westminster, California, March 2002. See also Jeffrey Race, *War Comes to Long An: Revolutionary Conflict in a Province* (Berkeley: University of California Press, 1972), pp. 218, 252.

91. Interview with Nguyen Truc, New York, New York, March 2002.

92. "Economic and Social Assistance to the Republic of Vietnam," (Saigon: Government of the Republic of Vietnam, 1973), p. 3, CMH.

93. Interview with Nguyen Thao, Ho Chi Minh City, Vietnam, January 2003.

94. Robert Sansom, *The Economics of Insurgency in the Mekong Delta of Vietnam* (Cambridge, Mass.: Massachusetts Institute of Technology Press, 1970), p. 8.

95. Ibid., p. 125.

96. Ibid., p. 124.

97. Ibid., p. 136.

98. Xu Uy Nam Bo (Southern Regional Command), "Chanh sach dien da" (Policy on land), ca. 1962, LTI.

99. James W. Trullinger, *Village at War: An Account of Conflict in Vietnam* (Stanford, Calif.: Stanford University Press, 1994), pp. 91–92, 104, 176, 188, 192; and Frances FitzGerald, *Fire in the Lake: The Vietnamese and Americans in Vietnam* (New York: Vintage Books, 1972), p. 153.

100. *Luat Su Nguyen Huu Tho* (Lawyer Nguyen Huu Tho) (Ho Chi Minh City: Nha xuat ban van hoc, 1995), pp. 23–28; and Hoang van Thai, "Tu tuong chien luoc chien thuat cua chien tranh nhan dan—duong loi xay dung luc luong vu trang nhan dan" (Thoughts on tactics and strategy of people's war—the direction to build the armed forces), *Hoc Tap* 11 (July 1965): 44–51.

101. Interview with Nguyen van Hieu, Westminster, California, March 2002.

102. Interview with Nguyen van Nhon, Ho Chi Minh City, Vietnam, January 2003.

103. Kolko, *Anatomy of a War*, p. 261.

104. Interview with Nguyen van Hieu, Westminster, California, March 2002.

105. Duong Van Mai Elliot, *The Sacred Willow*, p. 314.

106. Dong van Khuyen, *The RVNAF*, p. 76.

107. Clarke, *Advice and Support*, pp. 41–42.

108. Interview with Hoang Thuy, Westminster, California, March 2002.

109. "Effectiveness of ARVN, RF and PF, June 1967," RVNAF Assessments Folder, CMH.

110. Robert White, "Anthropometric Survey of the Armed Forces of the Republic of Vietnam," U.S. Army Natick Laboratories, Advanced Research Projects Agency, Natick, Massachusetts, October 1964.

111. Kolko, *Anatomy of a War*, p. 255.

112. General Arthur S. Collins, Jr., "Writings, Published and Unpublished, 1945–1983," The Arthur S. Collins, Jr., Papers, U.S. Army Military History Institute, Carlisle, Pennsylvania.

113. General Nguyen Duy Trinh and General Tran Dinh Tho, *The South Vietnamese Society*, reprinted as part of the Indochina Monographs Series (Washington, D.C.: U.S. Army Center of Military History, 1984).

114. Interview with Tran van Chat, Ho Chi Minh City, Vietnam, July 1989.

115. Interview with Nguyen Thanh, Washington, D.C., March 2002.

116. James Scott, *The Moral Economy of the Peasant* (New Haven, Conn.: Yale University Press, 1976).

117. Samuel L. Popkin, *The Rational Peasant: The Political Economy of Rural Society in Vietnam* (Berkeley: University of California Press, 1979), p. ix.

118. Interview with former village elder who requested anonymity, My Tho, Vietnam, July 1989.

119. Dong van Khuyen, *The RVNAF*, p. 35.

120. "Effectiveness of ARVN, RF and PF, June 1967."

121. Interview with citizens of Republic of Vietnam who requested anonymity, Ho Chi Minh City, Vietnam, January 2003.

122. Ibid.

123. Interview with Nguyen Thanh, Washington, D.C., March 2002.

124. Interview with Ngo van Linh, Westminster, California, March 2002.

125. Interview with Ngo van Chuong, Westminster, California, March 2002.

126. Dong van Khuyen, *The RVNAF,* pp. 41–42.

127. Interview with Nguyen van Hieu, Westminster, California, March 2002.

128. Dong van Khuyen, *The RVNAF,* pp. 42–43.

129. "MACV Study on RVNAF Morale, July 10, 1970," Folder 102424, National Archives, Suitland, Maryland. This document was declassified for this study.

130. Interview with former student from Saigon who requested anonymity, London, England, November 2003.

131. "Actions in Support of RVNAF, Westmoreland Study, 1965–1967," CMH.

132. Ibid.

133. Interview with Nguyen Truc, New York, New York, March 2002.

134. "Analysis of RVNAF, CY 1966," RVNAF Assessments Folder, CMH.

135. Interview with Ngoc Cao Huynh, Westminster, California, March 2002.

136. Bui Diem, *In the Jaws of History* (Bloomington: Indiana University Press, 1999), p. 166.

137. Ibid., p. 99.

138. Interview with Ngoc Cao Huynh, Westminster, California, March 2002.

139. Interview with former Buddhist monk who requested anonymity, Ho Chi Minh City, Vietnam, January 2003.

140. Dong van Khuyen, *The RVNAF,* p. 302.

141. Interview with Huong Cong Thanh, Westminster, California, March 2002.

142. Interview with Nguyen van Hieu, Westminster, California, March 2002.

143. Interview with Ngo van Linh, Westminster, California, March 2002.

144. Interview with Nguyen van Hieu, Westminster, California, March 2002.

145. Interview with Nguyen van Luong, Westminster, California, March 2002.

146. Dong van Khuyen, *The RVNAF,* p. 41.

147. Ibid., p. 42.

148. Chu Bang Linh, *Dang Can Lao* (The Can Lao Party) (San Diego: Me Viet Nam, 1993), p. 3.

149. Interview with Roger Spence, former MACV official, Washington, D.C., June 2003.

150. As reported in the *Saigon Post,* April 18, 1975.

151. "Chieu long, Can Lao Nhan Vi Cach Mang" (Complaint, The Revolutionary Personalist Worker's Party), LTII.

152. Interview with Nguyen van Hieu, Westminster, California, March 2002.

153. Interview with former Can Lao official who requested anonymity, Washington, D.C., June 2003.

154. Dong van Khuyen, *The RVNAF,* p. 70.

155. Interview with Nguyen van Phuoc, New York, New York, March 2003.

156. Interview with Dang van Thuy, New York, New York, February 2005.

157. Keegan, *A History of Warfare,* p. 233.

158. Interview with Nguyen Thao, Ho Chi Minh City, Vietnam, January 2003.

159. Interview with Nguyen van Hieu, Westminster, California, March 2002.

Chapter Two: Training

1. Interview with Nguyen van Hieu, Westminster, California, March 2002.

2. See for example, Tran Ngoc Nhuan, *Doi Quan Ngu* (Life in the army) (Westminster, Calif.: Van Nghe, 1992).

3. Interview with Huynh van Hung, Ho Chi Minh City, Vietnam, January 2004.

4. "Support of RVNAF, 1965–1967," Westmoreland Study, U.S. Army Center of Military History, Washington, D.C. (hereafter CMH).

5. Interview with Hoang van Cao, Westminster, California, March 2002.

6. For example, see Tran Ngoc Nhuan, *Doi Quan Ngu*.

7. Interview with Nguyen van Linh, Westminster, California, March 2002.

8. Interview with Nguyen van Luong, Westminster, California, March 2002.

9. Neil Jamieson, *Understanding Vietnam* (Berkeley: University of California Press, 1993), p. 31.

10. Interview with Nguyen Thanh, New York, New York, March 2002.

11. Philip Katcher, *Armies of the Vietnam War* (London: Osprey, 1996), p. 26.

12. Interview with Nguyen van Khoi, San Francisco, California, May 1999.

13. Ibid.

14. Interview with Roger Banning, Washington, D.C., June 1999.

15. Interview with Nguyen van Hieu, Westminster, California, March 2002.

16. Interview with Timothy Brandon, New York, New York, January 2004.

17. Interview with Nguyen van Hiep, New York, New York, November 1999.

18. Lieutenant General Dong van Khuyen, *The RVNAF* (Washington, D.C.: U.S. Army Center of Military History, Indochina Monographs, 1984), p. 48.

19. Interview with former Saigon official who requested anonymity, Denver, Colorado, February 2001.

20. Dong van Khuyen, *The RVNAF*, p. 48.

21. "Quang Trung," Trung Tam Luu Tru Quoc Gia–II (National Archives Center–II) Ho Chi Minh City, Vietnam (hereafter LTII).

22. Interview with former Saigon official who requested anonymity, Denver, Colorado, February 2001.

23. "Increasing the Effectiveness of RVNAF, 22 April 1967," Section 3, p. B-11, RVNAF Assessments Folder, CMH.

24. Unpublished memoir of Nguyen Dinh, Westminster, California.

25. Interview with Nguyen van Long, Boston, Massachusetts, June 1999.

26. Interview with Nguyen van Hieu, Westminster, California, March 2002.

27. Form QD-1 5A was used for enlisted men.

28. Dong van Khuyen, *The RVNAF*, p. 46.

29. *Saigon Post*, October 27, 1966.

30. "Assessment of ARVN, February 2, 1968," Fact Sheet File, CMH.

31. *Quan Luc Vietnam Cong Hoa Trong Giai Doan Hinh Thanh, 1946–1955* (Republic of Vietnam Armed Forces during the formation period, 1946–1955) (Saigon: Co so dainam xuat ban, 1972), p. 444.

32. Dong van Khuyen, *The RVNAF*, p. 46.

33. Ibid.

34. Interview with Hoang van Cao, Westminster, California, March 2002.

35. Interview with Nguyen van Hieu, Westminster, California, March 2002.

36. Dong van Khuyen, *The RVNAF*, p. 48.

37. Interview with Pham van Cao, Los Angeles, California, June 1999.

38. *Saigon Post*, July 18, 1968.

39. Interview with former Saigon resident who requested anonymity, March 1996.

40. Interview with Pham van Thuy, San Jose, California, June 1999.

41. Interview with Thomas White, Washington, D.C., June 2003.

42. Interview with Nguyen van Dinh, Ho Chi Minh City, Vietnam, January 2004.

43. Nguyen Vu, *12 Nam Linh* (Twelve years of being a soldier) (Westminster, Calif.: Van Hoa, 1990).

44. Van Thanh Hao, *Mau va Nuoc Mat* (Blood and tears) (Westminster, Calif.: Van Nghe Press, 1999), p. 34.

45. Ibid., pp. 61–66.

46. Cao Xuan Huy, *Thang Ba Gay Sung* (The march of the broken rifles) (Westminster, Calif.: Van Khoa, 1986), p. 31.

47. General James Lawton Collins, Jr., *The Development and Training of the South Vietnamese Army, 1950–1972* (Washington, D.C.: Department of the Army, 1975), p. 123.

48. Interview with former ARVN officer who requested anonymity, New York, New York, November 1999.

49. Dong van Khuyen, *The RVNAF*, p. 212.

50. Interview with former ARVN officer who requested anonymity, San Francisco, California, June 1999.

51. Collins, *Development and Training of the South Vietnamese Army*, pp. 33, 103.

52. Interview with former ARVN officer who requested anonymity, New York, New York, February 2003.

53. "Improvement of the RVNAF, January 11, 1968," RVNAF Assessments Folder, CMH.

54. Interview with Huynh van Cuong, San Jose, California, June 1999.

55. Dong van Khuyen, *The RVNAF*, p. 211.

56. Ibid., pp. 209–210.

57. Interview with Nguyen van Nhon, Ho Chi Minh City, Vietnam, March 1996.

58. Interview with Nguyen van Hieu, Westminster, California, March 2002.

59. Interview with Ngo Ca Cong, New York, New York, November 2002.

60. Interview with Hoang van Cao, Westminster, California, March 2002.

61. Jamieson, *Understanding Vietnam*, p. 310.

62. Hoang van Minh, personal letter, April 1966.

63. Nguyen van Huynh, personal letter, August 1967.

64. Nguyen van Son, personal letter, March 1968.

65. Interview with Nguyen van Son's surviving relatives, Ho Chi Minh City, Vietnam, January 2004.

66. Ibid.

67. Interview with Nguyen van Hieu, Westminster, California, March 2002. See also Collins, *Development and Training of the South Vietnamese Army*, p. 135.

68. Collins, *Development and Training of the South Vietnamese Army,* p. 33.

69. Interview with Colonel Herbert Schandler (U.S. Army, retired), Bellagio, Italy, July 1998.

70. Interview with William Jackson, Boston, Massachusetts, June 1999.

71. "Command History, 1968," Vol. 1, CMH.

72. Lieutenant General Ngo Quang Truong, *RVNAF and U.S. Operational Cooperation and Coordination* (Washington, D.C.: U.S. Army Center of Military History, 1980), pp. 115–116.

73. Interview with Roger Timmelson, Cleveland, Ohio, February 2000.

74. Interview with Nguyen Hung, Washington, D.C., March 2002.

75. Dong van Khuyen, *The RVNAF,* pp. 211–214.

76. Collins, *Development and Training of the South Vietnamese Army,* pp. 103–105, 109–110, 117–119, and 126–127. See also Ngo Quang Truong, *RVNAF and U.S. Operational Cooperation and Coordination,* pp. 119–127 and 135–140; and Dong van Khuyen, *The RVNAF,* pp. 199–200.

77. Interview with Nghiem Tam Ngoc, New York, New York, June 2002.

78. "Command History, 1968," Vol. 1, CMH.

79. Philip Catton, *Diem's Final Failure: Prelude to America's War in Vietnam* (Lawrence: University Press of Kansas, 2002), p. 39.

80. Wesley Fishel, *Problems of Freedom: South Vietnam since Independence* (East Lansing, Mich.: Bureau of Social and Political Research, 1961), pp. 29–68.

81. *Saigon Post,* May 12, 1964.

82. Emmanuel Mounier, *Personalism* (South Bend, Ind.: University of Notre Dame Press, 1952), pp. 97–124.

83. *Interviews of Ngo Dinh Diem* (Saigon: Presidential Office, 1960), LTII.

84. Catton, *Diem's Final Failure,* p. 43.

85. "Sac Lenh" (Decree), LTII.

86. "Cu xu tot" (Behave well), LTII.

87. Mark P. Bradley, *Imagining Vietnam and America: The Making of Postcolonial Vietnam* (Chapel Hill: University of North Carolina Press, 2000), pp. 68–71.

88. *Interviews of Ngo Dinh Diem.*

89. Interview with Nguyen van Hieu, Westminster, California, March 2002.

90. Nguyen Trang, unpublished essay.

91. Interview with Ngo Quynh, London, England, November 2003.

92. Dong van Khuyen, *The RVNAF,* p. 312.

93. See, for example, *Quan Doi Viet Nam Cong Hoa,* LTII.

94. Interview with Nguyen van Chau, New York, New York, June 1999.

95. Paul Mus, "Foreword," in Gerald Hickey, *Village in Vietnam* (New Haven, Conn.: Yale University Press, 1964), p. xxi.

96. Interview with Nguyen van Ngo, London, England, November 2003.

97. Interview with Nguyen van Chau, New York, New York, June 1999.

98. Gregory Lockhart, *Nation in Arms: The Origins of the People's Army of Vietnam* (Sydney, Australia: Allen and Unwin, 1989), p. 44.

99. Dong van Khuyen, *The RVNAF,* pp. 323–324.

100. Ibid.

101. Interview with former Saigon official who requested anonymity, London, England, November 2003.

102. Interviews with former ARVN enlisted men, Westminster, California, March 2002.

103. Dong van Khuyen, *The RVNAF,* p. 325.

104. Interview with Huynh van Cuong, San Jose, California, June 1999.

105. Interview with Pham van Thuy, San Jose, California, June 1999.

106. Interview with Nguyen van Hieu, Westminster, California, March 2002.

107. Interview with Nguyen van Thanh, Los Angeles, California, June 1999.

108. Interview with Nguyen van Dinh, Ho Chi Minh City, Vietnam, January 2004.

109. Interview with Nguyen van Thanh, Los Angeles, California, June 1999.

110. National Archives, RG 472, Records of U.S. Forces in Southeast Asia, HQ-MACV, Army Advisory Group, Training Directorate, Service Scholars Division, "Vietnamese National Military Academy, Advisor," Box 3, Folder: Senior Advisor.

111. See, for example, "Si quan chi huy va bo doi," LTII.

112. Dong van Khuyen, *The RVNAF,* p. 322.

113. Victor Davis Hanson, *The Western Way of War* (New York: Alfred A. Knopf, 1989), p. 118.

114. Ibid.

115. David McCullough, *1776* (New York: Simon and Schuster, 2005).

116. William Manchester, *Goodbye Darkness: A Memoir of the Pacific War* (New York: Random House, 1979), p. 391.

117. Samuel Andrew Stouffer, C. I. Hovland, A. A. Lumsdaine, and F. D. Sheffield, *The American Soldier: Combat and Its Aftermath,* Vol. 2 (Princeton: Princeton University Press, 1949), p. 112.

118. John Keegan, *The Face of Battle: A Study of Agincourt, Waterloo, and the Somme* (New York: Penguin, 1976), pp. 173–174.

119. Interview with Nguyen van Thanh, Los Angeles, California, June 1999.

120. Ibid.

121. Interview with Ngo van Son, Minneapolis, Minnesota, February 2001.

122. "Assessment of ARVN/VNMC Organizations, February 10, 1970," Fact Sheet File, CMH.

123. "Analysis of RVNAF, CY 1970," RVNAF Assessments Folder, CMH.

124. "Increasing the Effectiveness of RVNAF, April 1967," Section 3, p. B-13. CMH.

125. Ibid., Section 3, p. B-10.

126. Interview with former Saigon official who requested anonymity, London, England, November 2003.

127. Interview with former ARVN officer who requested anonymity, Los Angeles, California, June 1999.

128. Interview with Huynh van Cuong, San Jose, California, June 1999.

129. Interview with Nguyen van Hieu, Westminster, California, March 2002.

Chapter Three: Morale

1. General Hamilton Howze, "Vietnam: An Epilogue," *Association of the United States Army* 25 (July 1975): 1–2.

2. Jeffrey Race, *War Comes to Long An: Revolutionary Conflict in a Province* (Berkeley: University of California Press, 1972), p. 141.

3. Ibid., p. 165.

4. Howze, "Vietnam: An Epilogue," p. 2.

5. Frances FitzGerald, *Fire in the Lake: The Vietnamese and Americans in Vietnam* (New York: Vintage Books, 1972), p. 264.

6. "RVNAF Assessments, 1970, Assessment of ARVN/VNMC Operations, February 1970," p. 4, U.S. Army Center of Military History, Washington, D.C. (hereafter CMH).

7. U.S. Army Service Forces, Office of the Provost Marshall, General, "World War II: A Brief History," Mimeo, Washington, D.C., 1946, pp. 363–372, CMH.

8. Neil Sheehan, *A Bright Shining Lie: John Paul Vann and America in Vietnam* (New York: Random House, 1988), p. 90.

9. Lieutenant General Dong van Khuyen, *The RVNAF* (Washington, D.C.: U.S. Army Center of Military History, Indochina Monographs, 1984), p. 138. Before 1964 a soldier was listed as absent without leave when he did not report for morning muster. He was given a six-day grace period if he was a new recruit with less than ninety days in service and fifteen days if he had already served over ninety days. In 1965 the ARVN command raised the grace period to thirty days. However, in 1966 Law 15/66 reduced the grace period to fifteen days for all servicemen.

10. "Desertions Not Defections from ARVN, July 1967," Office of Media Services, Bureau of Public Affairs, Department of State Publication No. 260, East Asian Pacific Series 163, U.S. Government Printing Office, 1967, CMH.

11. Ibid.

12. Ibid.

13. "1966 Evaluation of RVNAF: The Desertion Problem," pp. 103–105, CMH.

14. "RVNAF Assessment 1970, Assessment of ARVN/VNMC Operations, February 1970," p. 4, CMH.

15. "RVNAF Assessment 1967, Desertion Control Report, Republic of Vietnam Armed Forces," CMH.

16. "RVNAF Assessment 1967, Quality Improvement of RVNAF, January 9, 1968," pp. 2–4, CMH.

17. Interview with Nguyen van Hieu, Los Angeles, California, June 1999. See also Cao Xuan Huy, *Thang Ba Gay Sung* (The march of the broken rifles) (Westminster, Calif.: Van Khoa, 1986); and Nguyen Vu, *12 Nam Linh* (Twelve years of being a soldier) (Westminster, California: Van Hoa, 1990).

18. Official sources suggest that nearly 250,000 ARVN soldiers died in combat and that another 499,067 were wounded. Charles Hirschman, Samuel Preston, and Vu Manh Loi, "Vietnamese Casualties during the American War: A New Estimate," *Population and Development Review* 21 (December 1995): 783–812; and David A. Savitz, Nguyen Minh Thang, Ingrid E. Swenson, and Erika Stone, "Vietnamese Infant and Child Mortality in Relation to the Vietnam War," *American Journal of Public Health* 83 (1993): 1134–1138. Most American scholars accept these numbers. For example, see Ronald Spector, *After Tet: The Bloodiest Year in Vietnam* (New York: The Free Press, 1993); Thomas C. Thayer, *War without Fronts: The American Experience in Vietnam* (Boulder, Colo.: Westview Press, 1985); Guenter

Lewy, *America in Vietnam* (New York: Oxford University Press, 1978); and William S. Turley, *The Second Indochina War* (Boulder, Colo.: Westview Press, 1986).

19. Interview with Nguyen van Hieu, Los Angeles, California, June 1999.

20. Interview with Nguyen Hue, Ho Chi Minh City, Vietnam, January 2004.

21. "Memorandum to C. E. Mehlert from Lacy Wright, April 24, 1970, Conversation with Captain Tram Buu, Interpreter for Generals Nguyen Viet Thanh and Nguyen Huu Hanh, April 23, 1973, Can Tho, Vietnam," Francis N. Dawson Papers, U.S. Army Military History Institute, Carlisle Barricks, Carlisle, Pennsylvania.

22. "Command History, 1969," Vol. 2, U.S. Military Assistance Command, Vietnam, prepared by the Military History Branch, Office of the Secretary, Joint Staff, Military Assistance Command, Vietnam, p. 76, CMH.

23. "Draft Report—Deputy Senior Advisor, II Corps Tactical Zone," U.S. Army Advisory Group, John W. Barnes, Brigadier General, USA Commanding, CMH.

24. Gerald Hickey, *Village in Vietnam* (New Haven, Conn.: Yale University Press, 1964), p. 277.

25. Interview with Le van Duong, Ho Chi Minh City, Vietnam, March 1996.

26. Interview with Nguyen Tang, Gia Dinh, Vietnam, January 1999.

27. Brian M. Jenkins, "A People's Army for South Vietnam: A Vietnamese Solution," R-897-ARPA, November 1971 (Santa Monica: Rand Corporation, 1971), pp. 5–9.

28. "Abrams MAC 9093 to Major Subordinate Commands, 150305, July 1969," Abrams Papers, Historical Records Branch, CMH.

29. General Vo Nguyen Giap was fond of saying that there were few morale problems in the PAVN. Still, he urged his officers to care for the men because morale is the "soul of the army." Quoted in Phillip B. Davidson, *Vietnam at War: The History, 1946–1975* (Oxford: Oxford University Press, 1991), p. 60.

30. Philip Catton, *Diem's Final Failure: Prelude to America's War in Vietnam* (Lawrence: University Press of Kansas, 2002), pp. 25–31.

31. Interview with Nguyen Co Thach, former foreign minister of the Socialist Republic of Vietnam, Hanoi, Vietnam, June 1997.

32. *Cuoc khang chien chong My, cuu nuoc, 1954–1975: Nhung su kien quan su* (The anti-U.S. resistance war for national salvation of the fatherland, 1954–1975: military events) (Hanoi: Nha xuat ban quan doi nhan dan, 1988).

33. Greg Lockhart, *Nation in Arms: The Origins of the People's Army of Vietnam* (Sydney, Australia: Allen and Unwin, 1989), pp. 41–51. See also Hue-Tam Ho Tai, *Radicalism and the Origins of the Vietnamese Revolution* (Cambridge, Mass.: Harvard University Press, 1992), p. 86.

34. Vietnam Dan Chu Cong Hao, *Van quoc ngu* (Learning the national language) (Hanoi: Bo Quoc Gia Giao Giup, 1945), pp. 23–24.

35. Lockhart, *Nation in Arms*, p. 45.

36. Bui Diem, *In the Jaws of History* (Bloomington: Indiana University Press, 1999), p. 125.

37. FitzGerald, *Fire in the Lake*, pp. 263–266.

38. John Keegan, *A History of Warfare* (New York: Vintage Books, 1993), pp. 301, 305–306.

39. See Race, *War Comes to Long An.*

40. Interview with Vu Huy Phuc, Hanoi, Vietnam, June 1992.

41. Truong Nhu Tang, *A Viet Cong Memoir: An Inside Account of the Vietnam War and Its Aftermath* (New York: Vintage Books, 1985), p. 158.

42. Bui Tin, *From Cadre to Exile: The Memoirs of a North Vietnamese Journalist* (Chiang Mai, Thailand: Silkworm Books, 1995), p. 51.

43. Interview with General Nguyen Dinh Uoc, Hanoi, Vietnam, June 1997.

44. Interview with Dr. Hoang Quang Ho, Hanoi, Vietnam, June 1992.

45. "Combat After Action Report, September 12, 1968," Records of the U.S. Forces in Southeast Asia, MACV, Assistant Chief of Staff of Operations (J3), Evaluation and Analysis Division (MAC J3-05), Report No. 981–1022, Box 28, Folder MACV J3 No. 1002–1008, National Archives, Suitland, Maryland.

46. Interview with Nguyen van Hieu, Los Angeles, California, June 1999.

47. "Combat After Action Report, December 1, 1967," Records of the U.S. Forces in Southeast Asia, MACV, Assistant Chief of Staff of Operations (J3), Evaluation and Analysis Division (MAC J3-05), Report No. 531–560, Box 9, Folder MACV J3 No. 544, National Archives, Suitland, Maryland.

48. Interview with Nguyen van Hieu, Los Angeles, California, June 1999.

49. "Combat After Action Report, June 24, 1969," Records of the U.S. Forces in Southeast Asia, MACV, Assistant Chief of Staff of Operations (J3), Evaluation and Analysis Division (MAC J3-05), Report No. 155–169, Box 41, Folder MACV J3 No. 168–169, National Archives, Suitland, Maryland.

50. Interview with Nguyen Manh, Ho Chi Minh City, Vietnam, March 1996.

51. Tran Ngoc Nhuan, *Doi Quan Ngu* (Life in the army) (Westminster, Calif.: Van Nghe, 1992), pp. 114–115.

52. Interview with Phan Thuy, San Francisco, California, June 1999.

53. "Combat After Action Report, May 11, 1970," Records of the U.S. Forces in Southeast Asia, MACV, Assistant Chief of Staff of Operations (J3), Evaluation and Analysis Division (MAC J3-05), Report No. 26–70, Box 43, Folder MACV J3 No. 40–70, National Archives, Suitland, Maryland.

54. Interview with Nguyen Hue, Ho Chi Minh City, Vietnam, March 1996.

55. Interview with Nguyen Co Huong, San Francisco, California, June 1999.

56. "RVNAF Assessment 1967, Quality Improvement of RVNAF, January 9, 1968," pp. 2–4, CMH.

57. Interview with Nguyen van Hieu, Los Angeles, California, June 1999.

58. Dong van Khuyen, *The RVNAF*, p. 225.

59. Jeffrey Clarke, *Advice and Support: The Final Years, The U.S. Army in Vietnam* (Washington, D.C.: U.S. Army Center of Military History, 1988), p. 45.

60. Tran Ngoc Nhuan, *Doi Quan Ngu*, p. 151.

61. Interview with Thinh Pham, Ho Chi Minh City, Vietnam, March 2003.

62. Interview with George C. Davis, Washington, D.C., July 1999.

63. "Support of RVNAF, 1965–1967," Westmoreland Study, CMH.

64. FitzGerald, *Fire in the Lake*, p. 466.

65. Interview with Pham van Khai, prime minister of the Socialist Republic of Vietnam, Hanoi, Vietnam, June 1997.

66. Interview with Nguyen van Pham, Los Angeles, California, June 1999.

67. Interview with Nguyen Hue, Ho Chi Minh City, Vietnam, March 2003.

68. Interview with Nguyen van Hieu, Los Angeles, California, June 1999; and interview with Nguyen Pham and Hoang van Thuy, Westminster, California, March 2002.

69. Kil Yi, "The U.S.-Korean Alliance in the Vietnam War," in Lloyd Gardner and Ted Gittinger, eds., *International Perspectives on Vietnam* (College Station, Tex: Texas A&M University Press, 2000), p. 154. See also Charles K. Armstrong, "America's Korea, Korea's Vietnam," *Critical Asian Studies* 33 (2001): 527–539.

70. Interview with Cao van Ngia, Los Angeles, California, June 1999.

71. Interview with Nguyen Khang, New York, New York, March 2002.

72. Interview with Ngo Hien Quoc, Westminster, California, March 2002.

73. Interview with Nguyen van Thien, My Tho, Vietnam, July 1989.

74. Interview with Nguyen Binh, Ho Chi Minh City, Vietnam, January 2004.

75. "Memo for the Secretary of Defense, JCS, Briefing for Secretary of Defense, August 7, 1968," CMH.

76. Dong van Khuyen, *The RVNAF,* p. 252.

77. Interview with Nguyen thi Thuy, Los Angeles, California, June 1999.

78. "Support of RVNAF, 1965–1967," Westmoreland Study, CMH.

79. Interview with former Saigon official who requested anonymity, Washington, D.C., June 1996.

80. Clarke, *Advice and Support,* p. 503.

81. Ibid.

82. Dong van Khuyen, *The RVNAF,* pp. 252–253.

83. Interview with Nguyen Tin Thanh, Los Angeles, California, June 1999.

84. Interview with Cao van Thu, San Jose, California, June 1999.

85. Interview with Nguyen van Hieu, Los Angeles, California, June 1999.

86. Allan Goodman, *An Institutional Profile of the South Vietnamese Officer Corps* (Santa Monica, Calif.: Rand Corporation, 1970).

87. Interview with Nguyen van Hieu, Los Angeles, California, June 1999.

88. B1 was the diploma given at the end of eleventh grade, B2 given at the end of twelfth grade. CC1 or CC2 were ARVN technical courses.

89. Interview with Huynh van Hung, Ho Chi Minh City, Vietnam, January 2004.

90. Interview with Colonel Herbert Schandler (U.S. Army, retired), Washington, D.C., June 1999.

91. Lieutenant General Ngo Quang Truong, *RVNAF and U.S. Operational Cooperation and Coordination* (Washington, D.C.: U.S. Army Center of Military History, 1980), p. 7. See also Nguyen Cao Ky, *Twenty Years and Twenty Days* (New York: Stein and Day, 1976), p. 132.

92. Clarke, *Advice and Support,* p. 101.

93. Dong van Khuyen, *The RVNAF,* p. 254.

94. Interview with Colonel Herbert Schandler (U.S. Army, retired), Washington, D.C., June 1999.

95. Interview with Ngo Ca Cong, Los Angeles, California, June 1999.

96. Interview with Huynh van Man, Ho Chi Minh City, Vietnam, March 1996.

97. Interview with Robert S. McNamara, Washington, D.C., June 1999.

98. "Support of RVNAF, 1965–1967," Westmoreland Study, CMH.

99. Interview with Nguyen van Hieu, Los Angeles, California, June 1999.

100. Dong van Khuyen, *The RVNAF,* p. 238.

101. Social Welfare Directorate of Vietnam (SWD), "Housing Concerns," Trung

Tam Luu Tru Quoc Gia–II (National Archives Center–II) Ho Chi Minh City, Vietnam (hereafter LTII).

102. Dong van Khuyen, *The RVNAF*, p. 242.

103. Social Welfare Directorate of South Vietnam (SWD), "Housing Concerns," LTII.

104. *Saigon Post*, October 14, 1962.

105. SWD, "New RVNAF Housing Guidelines," LTII.

106. Ibid.

107. "Command History, 1970," Vol. 2, U.S. Military Assistance Command, Vietnam, prepared by the Military History Branch, Office of the Secretary, Joint Staff, Military Assistance Command, Vietnam, p. 55, CMH.

108. Interview with Ngo van Chuong, Ho Chi Minh City, Vietnam, January 2003.

109. Interview with Nguyen van Mui, Ho Chi Minh City, Vietnam, January 2004.

110. "Inspector General History, 1964–1972," MACV 1 G Files, Box 1, Number 77/0074, RG 334, pp. 11–12, National Archives, Suitland, Maryland. See also Clarke, *Advice and Support*, p. 44.

111. Dong van Khuyen, *The RVNAF*, p. 239.

112. Interview with Roger LaFelice, Los Angeles, California, June 1999.

113. "Westmoreland MAC 6191 to Wheeler 280530, November 1964—Assessment of the Military Situation," COMUSMACV Message File, Westmoreland Papers, CMH.

114. Clarke, *Advice and Support*, p. 156.

115. "Support of RVNAF, 1965–1967," Westmoreland Study, CMH.

116. Ibid.

117. Clarke, *Advice and Support*, p. 320.

118. "Support of RVNAF, 1965–1967," Westmoreland Study, CMH.

119. "Command History, 1969," Vol. 2, p. 64, CMH.

120. *New York Times*, November 22, 1972.

121. Interview with Nguyen van Dinh, Ho Chi Minh City, Vietnam, January 2004.

122. Interview with Nguyen van Hieu, Los Angeles, California, June 1999.

123. Interview with Dr. Hoang van Cong, Ho Chi Minh City, Vietnam, March 1996.

124. Interview with Colonel Huynh van Cuong, San Jose, California, June 1999.

125. Interview with Ho van Dien, Ho Chi Minh City, Vietnam, January 2004.

126. Interview with Nguyen van Hieu, Los Angeles, California, June 1999.

127. Interview with Nguyen van Thanh, Los Angeles, California, June 1999.

128. Interview with Ho van Dien, Ho Chi Minh City, Vietnam, January 2004.

129. Interview with former Saigon official who requested anonymity, Washington, D.C., June 1996.

130. Dong van Khuyen, *The RVNAF*, p. 269.

131. Ibid., p. 275.

132. *Saigon Post*, December 13, 1973.

133. *Saigon Post*, June 12, 1970.

134. "Quang Doi Viet Nam Cong Hoa-nu y ta" (Republic of Vietnam Armed Forces—nurses), LTII.

135. John Prados, *The Hidden History of the Vietnam War* (Chicago: Ivan R. Dee, 1995), p. 105.

136. Interview with Thinh Pham, Los Angeles, California, June 1999.

137. Dong van Khuyen, *The RVNAF*, pp. 268–269.

138. Interviews conducted with former ARVN enlisted men from June 1992 through January 2004.

139. Nguyen Phuc Tran, *Dai nguc* (Hell) (San Jose, Calif.: Truth Press, 1985), p. 31.

140. "After Action Report, June 24, 1965," RG 472, Records of the U.S. Forces in Southeast Asia–MACV, Assistant Chief of Staff for Operations (J3), Evaluation and Analysis Division (MACJ3-05), Report No. 9-130, Box No. 1, HM 1988, Folder MACV J3 AAR 28, National Archives, Suitland, Maryland.

141. "After Action Reports, January–August 1968," RG 472, Records of the U.S. Forces in Southeast Asia–MACV, Assistant Chief of Staff for Operations (J3), Evaluation and Analysis Division (MACJ3-05), Report No. 1031–1038, Box No. 30, Folder MACV J3, No. 1035, Folder II, National Archives, Suitland, Maryland.

142. "After Action Report, Interview with Staff Sergeant Robert S. Douty," RG 338, Records of the U.S. Army Command, 1942– , Records of Headquarters, U.S. Army, Pacific Military Historian's Office Command Reporting Files, 1963–1972, Box No. 206, Folder "Mobile Advisory Team, the 1968 ARVN unit," National Archives, Suitland, Maryland.

143. Dong van Khuyen, *The RVNAF,* p. 264.

144. Interview with Phan van Thuy, San Jose, California, June 1999.

145. Interview with Pham van Cao, Los Angeles, California, June 1999.

146. Interview with Nguyen van Ngo, Ho Chi Minh City, Vietnam, January 2004.

147. *Saigon Post,* October 15, 1972.

148. A phrase used by a village elder in a small hamlet outside My Tho, Vietnam, January 2004.

Chapter Four: Battles

1. John Keegan, *The Face of Battle: A Study of Agincourt, Waterloo, and the Somme* (New York: Penguin, 1976), p. 28.

2. Gabriel Kolko, *Anatomy of a War: Vietnam, the United States, and the Modern Historical Experience* (New York: Pantheon, 1985); Jeffrey Race, *War Comes to Long An: Revolutionary Conflict in a Province* (Berkeley: University of California Press, 1972); Guenter Lewy, *America in Vietnam* (New York: Oxford University Press, 1978); and Phillip B. Davidson, *Vietnam at War: The History, 1946–1975* (Oxford: Oxford University Press, 1991), to name but a few.

3. Interview with George White, Boston, Massachusetts, June 1999.

4. For good descriptions of the Battle of Ap Bac, see Charles Neu, *America's Lost War, Vietnam: 1945–1975* (Wheeling, Ill.: Harlan Davidson, 2005), pp. 58–62; George C. Herring, *America's Longest War: The United States and Vietnam, 1950–1975,* 4th ed. (New York: McGraw Hill, 2002), p. 106; Stanley Karnow, *Vietnam: A History* (New York: Penguin Books, 1983), pp. 259–262; Kolko, *Anatomy of a War,* pp. 146–147; Andrew Krepinevich, *The Army and Vietnam* (Baltimore, Md.: Johns Hopkins University Press, 1986), pp. 78–81; and Marilyn Young, *The Vietnam Wars* (New York: HarperCollins, 1991), pp. 89–90.

5. Neil Sheehan, *A Bright Shining Lie: John Paul Vann and America in Vietnam* (New York: Random House, 1988), pp. 198–199.

6. Interview with Nguyen van Hinh, Ho Chi Minh City, Vietnam, January 2004.

7. *Mot so van kien cua Dang ve chong My, cuu nuoc* (Selected party documents related to the anti-U.S. resistance war for national salvation of the fatherland), Vol. 2 (Hanoi: Nha xuat ban su that, 1985), pp. 49–50.

8. Sheehan, *A Bright Shining Lie,* p. 206.

9. *Mot so van kien cua Dang ve chong My, cuu nuoc,* Vol. 2, pp. 38–44.

10. "After Action Report by the Senior Advisor, 7th Infantry Division, January 9, 1963," JCS Files, U.S. Army Center of Military History, Washington, D.C. (hereafter CMH).

11. Ibid.

12. Interview with Nguyen Thiep, Ho Chi Minh City, Vietnam, March 1996.

13. Ironically, Diem was eventually assassinated in the back of an M-113.

14. *Foreign Relations of the United States* [hereafter *FRUS*], *Vietnam, 1961–1963: January–August 1963,* Vol. 3 (Washington: Government Printing Office, 1991), pp. 1–3, 98.

15. "After Action Report by the Senior Advisor, 7th Infantry Division, January 9, 1963," JCS Files, CMH.

16. Interview with Huynh van Cuong, San Jose, California, June 1999.

17. "After Action Report by the Senior Advisor, 7th Infantry Division, January 9, 1963," JCS Files, CMH.

18. Ibid.

19. Interview with General Vo Nguyen Giap, Hanoi, Vietnam, June 1997.

20. Merle Pribbenow, *Victory in Vietnam,* translation of the Military History Institute of Vietnam official history of the People's Army of Vietnam (Lawrence: University Press of Kansas, 2002), pp. 119–120.

21. *Cuoc khang chien chong My, cuu nuoc, 1954–1975: Nhung su kien quan su* (The anti-U.S. resistance war for national salvation of the fatherland, 1954–1975: military events) (Hanoi: Nha xuat ban quan doi nhan dan, 1988), p. 53.

22. Ibid., p. 54.

23. Le Duan, *Thu vao Nam* (Letters to the South) (Hanoi: Nha xuat ban su that, 1986), p. 71.

24. William Prochnau, *Once upon a Distant War* (New York: Times Books, 1995), p. 235.

25. *Washington Post,* January 3, 1963.

26. *Washington Post,* January 7, 1963. For a reprint of the article, see *Reporting Vietnam: American Journalism, 1959–1969,* Part 1 (New York: The Library of America, 1998), pp. 68–70.

27. *New York Times,* January 3, 1963.

28. *New York Times,* January 4, 1963.

29. *New York Times,* January 6, 1963.

30. *FRUS, Vietnam, 1961–1963: January–August 1963,* Vol. III, p. 2.

31. Prochnau, *Once upon a Distant War,* p. 239.

32. Ibid., p. 240.

33. David Halberstam, *The Making of a Quagmire* (New York: Random House, 1964), p. 158.

34. *FRUS, Vietnam, 1961–1963: January–August 1963,* Vol. 3, p. 3.

35. Halberstam, *The Making of a Quagmire,* p. 158.

36. Interestingly, many authors suggest that Felt's comments were directed at others, not Malcome Browne. Stanley Karnow suggested the remark was meant for Peter Arnett of the Associated Press (Karnow, *Vietnam,* p. 262); John Clarke Pratt argued that Felt directed his response at Neil Sheehan of the United Press International (John Clarke Pratt, *Vietnam Voices* [New York: Penguin, 1984], pp. 126–127); and William Prochnau claimed that Browne was indeed the intended recipient of Felt's anger (Prochnau, *Once upon a Distant War,* p. 244).

37. *FRUS, Vietnam, 1961–1963: January–August, 1963,* Vol. 3, p. 2.

38. Ibid., p. 3.

39. Ibid.

40. National Defense University, Taylor Papers, T-182-67, McClean, Virginia. See also "Report by an Investigative Team Headed by the Chief of Staff, United States Army (Wheeler), to the Joint Chiefs of Staff, Washington, January 1963," National Defense University, Taylor Papers, T-181-69, McClean, Virginia. Reprinted in *FRUS, Vietnam, 1961–1963: January–August 1963,* Vol. 3, pp. 73–94.

41. Krepinevich, *The Army and Vietnam,* p. 79.

42. *New York Times,* January 11, 1963.

43. Halberstam, *The Making of a Quagmire,* p. 159.

44. Ibid.

45. Ibid., p. 167.

46. *FRUS, Vietnam, 1961–1963: January–August 1963,* Vol. 3, p. 1.

47. For example, Hoang van Coa, unpublished memoir titled "My Years in the Army."

48. Nguyen van Thanh, personal letters, May 1965.

49. Bui Diem, *In the Jaws of History* (Bloomington: Indiana University Press, 1999), p. 91.

50. Interview with Nguyen Co Huong, San Francisco, California, June 1999.

51. Interview with Cao van Ngia, Los Angeles, California, June 1999.

52. Interview with Pham Huong, New York, New York, May 2002.

53. Interview with former ARVN officer who requested anonymity, London, England, November 2003.

54. Nguyen van Huong, *Problems of War: A Memoir of the War for the Independence of South Vietnam* (San Jose, Calif.: Right Way Press, 1990), pp. 32–33.

55. Interview with "Jim" Nguyen, Westminster, California, March 1999.

56. Robert S. McNamara, James G. Blight, and Robert K. Brigham, *Argument without End: In Search of Answers to the Vietnam Tragedy* (New York: Public Affairs, 1999), p. 322.

57. Ibid.

58. Prochnau, *Once upon a Distant War,* p. 90.

59. *Reporting Vietnam,* Part 1, p. 112.

60. Krepinevich, *The Army and Vietnam,* pp. 166–167; General Bruce Palmer, *The 25-Year War: America's Military Role in Vietnam* (Lexington: University of Kentucky Press, 1984), pp. 178–179; and Herbert Schandler, *Lyndon Johnson and Vietnam: The Unmaking of a President* (Princeton, N.J.: Princeton University Press, 1977), pp. 294–295.

61. Interview with Hoang van Cao, Westminster, California, June 1999.

62. Interview with Huynh van Hung, Ho Chi Minh City, Vietnam, January 2004.

63. Sheehan, *A Bright Shining Lie*, p. 65.

64. Ibid., p. 66.

65. General William Westmoreland, *A Soldier Reports* (Garden City, N.Y.: Doubleday, 1976), p. 126.

66. Neu, *America's Lost War*, pp. 102–105.

67. Interview with Nguyen van Thanh, Los Angeles, California, June 1999.

68. Interview with Nguyen van Hieu, Los Angeles, California, June 1999.

69. Interview with Nguyen van Vinh, Ho Chi Minh City, Vietnam, March 1996.

70. Interview with former ARVN enlisted man who requested anonymity, New York, New York, September 2004.

71. Interview with Dinh Phuong, Westminster, California, March 2002.

72. Pribbenow, *Victory in Vietnam*, pp. 155–156.

73. *Cuoc khang chien chong My, cuu nuoc*, p. 75.

74. Le Duan, *Thu vao Nam*, p. 129.

75. Ibid.

76. Neil Sheehan, Fox Butterfield, Hedrick Smith, and E. W. Kenworthy, *The Pentagon Papers as Published by the New York Times: The Secret History of the Vietnam War* (New York: Quadrangle Books, 1971), p. 419.

77. Karnow, *Vietnam*, p. 423.

78. *Communist Strategy as Reflected in Lao Dong Party and COSVN Resolutions* (Saigon: U.S. Military Assistance Command, 1964); and "The Viet-Nam Workers' Party's 1963 Decision to Escalate the War in the South," in Robert Lester, ed., *Viet-Nam Documents and Research Notes*, Document Number 96, July 1971 (Bethesda, Md.: University Publications of America, 1991).

79. Le Duan, *Some Questions Concerning the International Tasks of Our Party: Speech at the Ninth Party Plenum of the Third Central Committee of the Vietnam Workers' Party, December 1963* (Peking: Foreign Language Press, 1964).

80. Le Duan, *Thu Vao Nam*, p. 117.

81. As reported in Shelby Stanton, *The Rise and Fall of an American Army* (Novato, Calif.: Presidio Press, 1985), p. 6.

82. Interview with Huynh van Cuong, San Jose, California, June 1999.

83. Stanton, *The Rise and Fall of an American Army*, p. 6.

84. Sheehan et al., *The Pentagon Papers*, p. 419.

85. Ibid., p. 420.

86. As quoted in William Gibbons, *The U.S. Government and the Vietnam War*, Part 3 (Princeton, N.J.: Princeton University Press, 1989), p. 275.

87. Sheehan et al., *The Pentagon Papers*, pp. 419–420.

88. General William Westmoreland, *Report on Operations in South Vietnam, January 1964–June 1968* (Washington: Government Printing Office, 1969), p. 109, CMH.

89. Westmoreland, *A Soldier Reports*, p. 181.

90. Robert Shaplen, *The Lost Revolution: The U.S. in Vietnam, 1946–1966* (New York: Harper and Row, 1966), p. 347.

91. Ibid., p. 347. There is a great deal of controversy surrounding the 173rd Airborne's role in rescuing the ARVN at Dong Xoai. *The Pentagon Papers* suggested that the battalion was not involved in the rescue operation at Dong Xoai (Sheehan et al., *The Pentagon Papers*, p. 421).

92. Sheehan et al., *The Pentagon Papers,* p. 412.

93. Schandler, *Lyndon Johnson and Vietnam,* p. 27.

94. Sheehan et al., *The Pentagon Papers,* p. 422.

95. Michael Beschloss, ed., *Taking Charge: The Johnson White House Tapes, 1963–1964* (New York: Simon and Schuster, 1997), pp. 123, 293.

96. Herring, *America's Longest War,* p. 167.

97. Westmoreland, *A Soldier Reports,* pp. 144, 146.

98. Lyndon Johnson, *The Vantage Point: Perspectives of the Presidency, 1963–1969* (New York: Holt, Rinehart, and Winston, 1971), p. 153.

99. Jeffrey Clarke, *Advice and Support: The Final Years, The U.S. Army in Vietnam* (Washington, D.C.: U.S. Army Center of Military History, 1988), p. 99.

100. Department of Defense, *U.S.-Vietnam Relations, 1945–1967,* Vol. 5, Sec. IV.C.6 (Washington, D.C.: House Committee on Armed Services, 1971), p. 5.

101. Ibid.

102. Clarke, *Advice and Support,* p. 101.

103. Interview with Pham van Cao, Los Angeles, California, June 1999.

104. Interview with Nguyen van Cam, Westminster, California, March 2002.

105. Interview with Pham van Thuy, San Jose, California, June 1999.

106. Interview with Nguyen Phuong, London, England, November 2003.

107. Interview with Huynh van Cuong, San Jose, California, June 1999.

108. Interview with Nguyen Dinh, New York, New York, June 1999.

109. *U.S.-Vietnam Relations,* Vol. 5, Sec. IV.C.6., p. 17.

110. Ibid.

111. As quoted in Clarke, *Advice and Support,* pp. 121–122.

112. Interview with former PAVN officer who requested anonymity, Hanoi, Vietnam, June 1997.

113. Many southern military leaders, especially COSVN director Nguyen Chi Thanh, had long advocated an all-out offensive against the Saigon army and its American allies. They saw the compromise at the party plenum as a halfway measure that only prolonged the war in the South. Instead, they argued that leaders in Hanoi should commit all of the party's resources to offensive military action in South Vietnam. See Robert Brigham, "Why the South Won the Vietnam War," in Marc Gilbert, ed., *Why the North Won the Vietnam War* (New York: Palgrave, 2002), pp. 108–110.

114. McNamara et al., *Argument without End,* pp. 151–217.

115. Interview with Pham van Thuy, San Jose, California, June 1999.

116. Interview with Nguyen van Vinh, San Francisco, California, May 1999.

117. "Politics and Decisions Relative to the Current RVNAF Posture, 1965–1967," Westmoreland Study, Part 5, RVNAF, 1965–1967, CMH.

118. "Bunker's Weekly Report to the President, November 1967–April 1968, Wednesday, December 13, 1967," CMH.

119. "RVNAF, 1965–1967," Westmoreland Study, Part 5, Tab A and Tab B, CMH.

120. "Bunker's Weekly Report to the President, June–November 1967, June 7, 1967," CMH.

121. Ibid.

122. "Bunker's Weekly Report to the President, June–November 1967, August 9, 1967," CMH.

123. Interview with former U.S. Information Service officer who requested ano-nymity, Washington, D.C., June 2003.

124. "Actions in Support of RVNAF, 1965–1967," Westmoreland Study, CMH.

125. "After Action Report, Operation Hancock I," RG 472, Records of U.S. Forces in Southeast Asia, MACV, J3, MACJ 3-05, Report No. 671–705, Box 14, Folder MACV J3; "Combat After Action Report, February 9, 1967," RG 472, Records of U.S. Forces in Southeast Asia, MACV, J3, MACJ 3-05, Report No. 531–560, Box 9, Folder MACV J3; "After Action Report on the Defense of Phuoc Qua," RG 472, Records of U.S. Forces in Southeast Asia, MACV, J3, MACJ 3-05, Report No. 722–750, Box 16, Folder MACV J3; and "After Action Report, Opera-tion Xuy Dung," RG 472, Records of U.S. Forces in Southeast Asia, MACV, J3, MACJ 3-05, Report No. 671–705, Box 14, Folder MACV J3, National Archives, Suitland, Maryland.

126. Stanton, *The Rise and Fall of an American Army*, p. 83.

127. "Secret Operation: Fairfax/Rang Dong Staff Study, December 1, 1967," National Archives, Suitland, Maryland. This document was declassified for this study, July 17, 1997.

128. "Bunker's Weekly Report to the President, June–November 1967, July 19, 1967," CMH.

129. Ibid.

130. "Actions in Support of RVNAF, 1965–1967," Westmoreland Study, CMH.

131. "Effectiveness of ARVN, RF and PF, June 1967," RVNAF Assessments Folder, CMH.

132. "Quan Doi Viet Nam Cong Hoa, Tet Mau than" (The Republic of Vietnam Armed Forces, Tet Offensive), Trung Tam Luu Tru Quoc Gia–II (National Archives Center–II) Ho Chi Minh City, Vietnam.

133. "Command History, 1967," U.S. Military Assistance Command–Vietnam, prepared by the Military History Branch, Office of the Secretary, Joint Staff, Military Assistance Command–Vietnam, CMH.

134. Robert S. McNamara, *In Retrospect: The Tragedy and Lessons of Vietnam* (New York: Times Books, 1995), pp. 284–290.

135. Ibid., p. 286.

136. "Memorandum for the President, Subject: A Fifteen Month Program for Military Operations in Southeast Asia," November 1, 1967, Robert S. McNamara Papers, Lyndon Baines Johnson Presidential Library, Austin, Texas.

137. Lawrence Korb, *The Joint Chiefs of Staff: The First Twenty-Five Years* (Bloomington: Indiana University Press, 1976), p. 166.

138. George C. Herring, *LBJ and Vietnam: A Different Kind of War* (Austin: University of Texas Press, 1994), p. 60.

139. Sheehan et al., *The Pentagon Papers,* pp. 560–565.

140. *Saigon Post,* November 12, 1967.

141. *Saigon Post,* October 23, 1967.

142. *Mau than Saigon* (The Tet Offensive in Saigon) (Ho Chi Minh City: Nha xuat ban van nghe, 1988), p. 34.

143. *Tap chi lich su quan su: So dac biet 20 nam Tet mau than* (Journal of mili-tary history: Special twentieth anniversary issue on the Tet Offensive) (February 1968): 2–3.

144. Bui Tin, *From Cadre to Exile: The Memoirs of a North Vietnamese Journalist* (Chiang Mai, Thailand: Silkworm Books, 1995), pp. 61–62.

145. General Tran van Tra, *A History of the Bulwark B-2 Theater,* Vol. 5, *Concluding the Thirty Years War*, in *Southeast Asia Report*, no. 1247, JPRS 82783, February 2, 1983, Foreign Broadcast Information Service.

146. I am indebted to historian Ngo Vinh Long for lengthy conversations on this topic and for a copy of his paper "The Tet Offensive and Its Aftermath," delivered at the conference Remembering Tet 1968: An Interdisciplinary Conference on the Vietnam War, Salisbury State University, Salisbury, Maryland, November 18–21, 1992.

147. As quoted in Don Oberdorfer, *Tet!* (Garden City: Doubleday, 1971), p. 158.

148. Westmoreland, *Report on Operations in South Vietnam*, Section 2, p. 159, CMH.

149. Ronald Spector, *After Tet: The Bloodiest Year in Vietnam* (New York: The Free Press, 1993), p. 24.

150. Herring, *America's Longest War,* p. 217.

151. *New York Times*, July 17, 1968.

152. Herring, *America's Longest War,* p. 281.

153. *New York Times*, February 2, 1969.

154. A. J. Langguth, "General Abrams Listens to a Different Drummer," *New York Times Magazine,* May 5, 1968, p. 28.

155. Interview with Huong Cong Thanh, New York, New York, March 2002.

156. Interview with Ngoc Cao Huynh, New York, New York, March 2002.

157. Interview with Nguyen van Phuoc, New York, New York, March 2003.

158. Interview with Ngo Quynh, San Francisco, California, June 1999.

159. Interview with Nguyen van Hieu, Los Angeles, California, June 1999.

160. Interview with Nguyen van Linh, New York, New York, March 2002.

161. Interview with former ARVN officer who requested anonymity, New York, New York, September 2002.

162. Interview with Nguyen van Hieu, Westminster, California, March 2002.

163. "Command History, 1969," Vol. 2, Military History Branch, Headquarters, U.S. Military Assistance Command, Vietnam, CMH.

164. Interview with Hoang van Cao, Boston, Massachusetts, March 2002.

165. George C. Herring, "'Peoples Quite Apart': Americans, South Vietnamese, and the War in Vietnam," *Diplomatic History* 14 (Winter 1990): 17–18.

166. Herring, *America's Longest War,* p. 284.

167. Interview with Nguyen van Hieu, Westminster, California, March 2002.

168. Interview with Nguyen van Ngo, London, England, November 2003; and interview with Nguyen van Tien, New York, New York, March 2002.

169. Interview with Nguyen van Chau, New York, New York, June 1999.

170. Interview with Nguyen van Vinh, San Francisco, California, May 1999.

171. Jeffrey Kimball, *Nixon's Vietnam War* (Lawrence: University Press of Kansas, 1998), pp. 258–263.

172. "Collins Memorandum, April 25, 1970," General Arthur S. Collins Papers, U.S. Army Military History Institute, Carlisle Barracks, Pennsylvania.

173. Interview with Nguyen van Hieu, Westminster, California, March 2003.

174. *Congressional Record,* 93rd Congress, 2nd Session (Washington, D.C.: Government Printing Office, 1974), pp. 29176–29180.

175. Interview with Nguyen van Phuoc, New York, New York, March 2003.

176. Interview with Dan van Thuy, New York, New York, February 2005.

177. Interview with Nguyen van Thien, My Tho, Vietnam, July 1989.

178. Interview with Nguyen van Hao, Ho Chi Minh City, Vietnam, July 1989.

179. Interview with Nguyen van Luong, New York, New York, March 2002.

Chapter Five: Families

1. Interview with Nguyen van Son, Ho Chi Minh City, Vietnam, January 2004.

2. Interview with Nguyen van Hieu, Westminster, California, March 2002.

3. Interview with Nguyen van Ninh, San Francisco, California, May 1999.

4. Barton C. Hacker, "Women and Military Institutions in Early Modern Europe: A Reconnaissance," *Signs: Journal of Women in Culture and Society* 6 (Summer 1981): 644.

5. Ibid., p. 653.

6. Geoffrey Parker and Angela Parker, *European Soldiers, 1550–1650* (Cambridge: Cambridge University Press, 1977), p. 34.

7. Geoffrey Parker, *The Army of Flanders and the Spanish Road, 1567–1659: The Logistics of Spanish Victory and Defeat in the Low Countries' Wars* (Cambridge: Cambridge University Press, 1972), p. 86.

8. Holly A. Mayer, *Belonging to the Army: Camp Followers and Community During the American Revolution* (Columbia: University of South Carolina Press, 1996), p. 2.

9. Nguyen Khac Vien, *Vietnam: A Long History* (Hanoi: The Gioi Publishers, 1999), p. 16.

10. Keith Taylor, *The Birth of Vietnam* (Berkeley: University of California Press, 1983), pp. 334–336.

11. Interview with Nguyen van Son, Ho Chi Minh City, Vietnam, January 2004.

12. Exhibit text, National Women's Museum, Hanoi, Vietnam.

13. Interview with Vu Huy Phuoc, Tran Huu Dinh, and Tran Quynh Cu, History Institute, Social Sciences Committee, Hanoi, Vietnam, June 1992.

14. Taylor, *The Birth of Vietnam,* 339.

15. *Lich Su Viet Nam* (The history of Vietnam) (Hanoi: Khoa hoc xa hoi, 1971), pp. 46–47.

16. As cited in Le thi Nham Tuyet, *Phu nu Viet Nam qua ca Thoi Dai* (Vietnamese women across the ages) (Hanoi: Khoa hoc xa hoi, 1973), p. 17.

17. Interview with Vu Huy Phuoc, History Institute, Hanoi, Vietnam, June 1992.

18. Bui Tin, *From Cadre to Exile: The Memoirs of a North Vietnamese Journalist* (Chiang Mai, Thailand: Silkworm Books, 1995), p. 49.

19. *30 nam Duong Ho Chi Minh, 19-5-1959–19-5-1989* (Thirty years on the Ho Chi Minh Trail, May 19, 1959–May 19, 1989) (Hanoi: Binh doan truong son xuat ban, 1989), p. 23.

20. Robert K. Brigham, *Guerrilla Diplomacy: The NLF's Foreign Relations and the Vietnam War* (Ithaca, N.Y.: Cornell University Press, 1998), pp. 90–101. See also Karen Turner, *Even the Women Must Fight: Memories of War from North Vietnam* (New York: John Wiley and Sons, 1998), pp. 35–37, 126, 130; Sandra Taylor, *Vietnamese Women at War: Fighting for Ho Chi Minh and the Revolution* (Lawrence: University Press of Kansas, 1999), pp. 36, 38, 43–47, 68–70, 75–78; and Nguyen thi Dinh, *Khong con duong nao khac* (No other road to take) (Hanoi: Nha xuat ban phu nu, 1968).

21. Truong Nhu Tang, *A Viet Cong Memoir: An Inside Account of the Vietnam War and Its Aftermath* (New York: Vintage Books, 1985), p. 167.

22. Jeffrey Clarke, *Advice and Support: The Final Years, The U.S. Army in Vietnam* (Washington, D.C.: U.S. Army Center of Military History, 1988), p. 44.

23. Interview with Nguyen van Hieu, Westminster, California, March 2002.

24. Interview with Nguyen thi Mai, Westminster, California, March 2002.

25. Interview with Truong Thu, New York, New York, July 1999.

26. Nguyen thi An, diary entry, August 12, 1971, Ho Chi Minh City, Vietnam.

27. Hoang Que, diary entry, March 1972, Ho Chi Minh City, Vietnam.

28. Interview with Ton Nu Mai, Westminster, California, March 2002

29. Interview with Nguyen thi Mai, Westminster, California, March 2002.

30. "Quan niem doc tai va Quan niem dan chu," *Thoi Luan*, August 20, 1955.

31. Phan Boi Chau, *Tuong Trung nu vuong, truyen Pham Hong Thai* (The play of the Trung queens, the story of Pham Hong Thai) (Hanoi: nha xuat ban Van Hoc, 1967); Nguyet Tu, *Chi Minh Khai* (Sister Minh Khai) (Hanoi: Nha xuat ban Phu Nu, 1980), pp. 83–85; and David G. Marr, *Vietnamese Anticolonialism* (Berkeley: University of California Press, 1971), pp. 153–154.

32. Mayer, *Belonging to the Army*, p. 124.

33. "Quan Doi Viet Nam Cong Hoa, Chuong Trinh, Tang 9 Nam 1960" (The Republic of Vietnam Armed Forces, program, September 1960), Trung Tam Luu Tru Quoc Gia–II (National Archives Center–II) Ho Chi Minh City, Vietnam.

34. As quoted in ibid., pp. 38–39, 89.

35. Interview with Nguyen van Chau, New York, New York, June 1999.

36. Hoang Ngoc Thanh and Thanh thi Nhan Duc, *Ngay Cuoi Cung cua Tong Thong Ngo Dinh Diem* (Days of President Ngo Dinh Diem) (San Jose, Calif.: Xuat Ban lan thu tu, 2001), p. 200.

37. Interview with Duong Lan, Ho Chi Minh City, Vietnam, January 2004.

38. *New York Times*, June 12, 1962.

39. *Saigon Post*, August 12, 1962.

40. Interview with Nguyen thi Thu, Ho Chi Minh City, Vietnam, January 2004.

41. Interview with Duong Lan, Ho Chi Minh City, Vietnam, January 2004.

42. *Saigon Post*, November 15, 1967.

43. Interview with Duong Lan, Ho Chi Minh City, Vietnam, January 2004.

44. Interview with Nguyen thi Linh, Westminster, California, March 2002.

45. Interview with Nguyen thi Mai, Westminster, California, March 2002.

46. Interview with Duong Lan, Ho Chi Minh City, January 2004.

47. Interview with Nguyen van Tien, Westminster, California, March 2002.

48. Interview with Nguyen van Vinh, San Francisco, California, May 1999.

49. Nguyen van Hieu, personal letter, March 1970.

50. Hoang van Cao, personal letter, July 1972.

51. Tran van Kim, personal letter, June 1972.

52. Interview with Nguyen thi Hanh, Minneapolis, Minnesota, February 2001.

53. Interview with Mai Huong, Westminster, California, March 2002.

54. Interview with Duong Lan, Ho Chi Minh City, Vietnam, January 2004.

55. Interviews with Nguyen thi Mai, Nguyen thi Linh, and Mai Huong, Westminster, California, March 2002.

56. Interview with Phuong Thuy, Ho Chi Minh City, Vietnam, March 1996.

57. Charles Levy, "The ARVN as Faggots: Inverted Warfare in Vietnam," *transaction* 8 (1971): 22.

58. Interview with Cao van Ngia, New York, New York, November 2004.

59. Benedict Anderson, *Imagined Communities: Reflections on the Origin and Spread of Nationalism* (London: Verso, 1991).

60. Eric Hobsbawm, *Nations and Nationalism Since 1780: Programme, Myth, and Reality* (Cambridge: Cambridge University Press, 1990); and Eric Hobsbawm and Terence Ranger, *The Invention of Tradition* (Cambridge: Cambridge University Press, 1983).

61. Ernest Renan, "What Is a Nation?" translated and annotated by Martin Thom, in Geoff Eley and Renald Grigor Suny, eds., *Becoming National: A Reader* (New York: Oxford University Press, 1996), p. 52.

62. Michael Howard, *The Lessons of History* (New Haven, Conn.: Yale University Press, 1991), p. 2.

63. Barbara Ehrenreich, *Blood Rites: Origins and History of the Passions of War* (New York: Henry Holt and Company, 1997), p. 200.

64. Interview with Nguyen van Chau, New York, New York, June 1999.

65. *May van de tong ket chien tranh va viet lich su quan su* (Selected issues related to the conclusions and the writing of the military history of the war) (Hanoi: Nha xuat ban su that, 1987); Pham van Dong, "Phat huy chu nghia anh hung cach mang, day manh su nghiep chong My, cuu nuoc den thang loi hoan toan" (Promote revolutionary heroism, strengthen the anti-U.S. resistance war for national salvation of the fatherland to lead to complete victory), *Hoc Tap* 13 (January 1967): 17–20; and Robert K. Brigham, "Revolutionary Heroism and Politics in Postwar Vietnam," in Charles Neu, ed., *After Vietnam: Legacies of a Lost War* (Baltimore, Md.: Johns Hopkins University Press, 2000), pp. 85–104.

66. William Duiker, *Vietnam: Revolution in Transition,* 2nd ed. (Boulder, Colo.: Westview Press, 1995), p. 123.

67. Frances FitzGerald, *Fire in the Lake: The Vietnamese and Americans in Vietnam* (New York: Vintage Books, 1972), p. 512.

68. Interview with Nguyen van Chau, New York, New York, June 1999.

69. Interview with Nguyen van Linh, Westminster, California, March 2002.

70. Hue-Tam Ho Tai, *Radicalism and the Origins of the Vietnamese Revolution* (Cambridge, Mass.: Harvard University Press, 1992), pp. 48–50.

71. Interview with Nguyen van Linh, Westminster, California, March 2003.

72. Interview with Nguyen van Chau, New York, New York, June 1999.

73. *Cuoc khang chien chong My, cuu nuoc, 1954–1975: Nhung su kien quan su* (The anti-U.S. resistance war for national salvation of the fatherland, 1954–1975: military events) (Hanoi: Nha xuat ban quan doi nhan dan, 1988), p. 179.

74. Stanley Karnow, *Vietnam: A History* (New York: Penguin Books, 1983), p. 665.

75. Duong Van Mai Elliot, *The Sacred Willow: Four Generations in the Life of a Vietnamese Family* (New York: Oxford University Press, 1999), p. 385. See also Minh Duc Haoi Trinh, *This Side . . . the Other Side* (Washington, D.C.: Occidental Press, 1980); and Duong Nghiem Mau, "The Day the Milk-Breast Tree Was Cut Down," translation by Vo Dinh Mai, in Nguyen Ngoc Bich, ed., *War and Exile: A Vietnamese Anthology* (San Francisco: Vietnamese PEN Abroad, 1989).

76. Interview with Nguyen van Thien, Westminster, California, March 2002.

77. Interview with Ngo van Trong, Westminster, California, March 2002.

78. Interview with Nguyen van Ngo, London, England, November 2003.

79. Shelby Stanton, *The Rise and Fall of an American Army* (Novato, Calif.: Presidio Press, 1985), p. 217.

80. James H. Willbanks, *Abandoning Vietnam: How America Left and South Vietnam Lost Its War* (Lawrence: University Press of Kansas, 2004), p. 267.

81. General Van Tien Dung, *Dai thang mua xuan* (Our great spring victory) (Hanoi: Nha xuat ban Quan Doi Nhan Dan, 1977), p. 167.

82. Karnow, *Vietnam*, 667.

83. David Butler, *The Fall of Saigon: Scenes from the Sudden End of a Long War* (New York: Dell, 1985), p. 333 and "Graham Martin to Henry Kissinger, April 18, 1975," Kissinger/Scowcroft File, Box A1, Gerald Ford Presidential Library, Grand Rapids, Michigan.

84. Interview with Nguyen Xuan Oanh, former RVN financial minister, Ho Chi Minh City, Vietnam, July 1989.

85. Butler, *The Fall of Saigon*, pp. 446–463.

86. Interview with Nguyen van Hieu, Westminster, California, March 2002.

87. David Haines, Dorothy Rutherford, and Patrick Thomas, "Family and Community among Vietnamese Refugees," *International Migration Review* 15 (Summer 1981): 310.

88. "Refugee Statistical Data," Fort Indian Town Gap, Pennsylvania, October 1975 as cited in Gail Paradise Kelly, *From Vietnam to America: A Chronicle of the Vietnamese Immigration to the United States* (Boulder, Colo.: Westview Press, 1977), p. 45.

89. *Los Angeles Times*, May 5, 1985.

90. "Evacuee/INS Longitudinal File," Immigration and Naturalization Services, as cited in Reginald Baker and David North, *The 1975 Refugees: Their First Five Years in America* (Washington, D.C.: New TransCentury Foundation, 1984) p. 36.

91. As quoted in William T. Liu, Maryanne Lamanna, and Alice Murata, *Transition to Nowhere: Vietnamese Refugees in America* (Nashville, Tenn.: Charter House Publishers, 1979), p. 44.

92. Ibid, p. 47.

93. Baker and North, *The 1975 Refugees*, p. 30.

94. "Survey of the Social, Psychological, and Economic Adaptation of Vietnamese Refugees in the U.S., 1975–1979" (Washington, D.C.: Bureau of Social Science Research, 1982), p. 69.

95. Thanh van Tran, "Ethnic Community Supports and Psychological Well-Being of Vietnamese Refugees," *International Migration Review* 21 (Autumn 1987): 833–844.

96. Baker and North, *The 1975 Refugees,* p. 27.

97. Thanh van Tran, "Sponsorship and Employment Status among Indochinese Refugees in the United States," *International Migration Review* 25 (Autumn 1991): 536–550.

98. Ibid.

99. Le thi Que, A. Terry Rambo, and Gary Martin, "Why They Fled: Refugee Movement during the Spring 1975 Communist Offensive in South Vietnam," *Asian Survey* 16 (September 1976): 860–863.

100. Interview with Nguyen van Hieu, Westminster, California, March 2002.

101. Interview with Nguyen van Linh, Westminster, California, March 2002.

102. Ibid.

103. Interview with Cao van Ngia, New York, New York, January 2004.

104. Interview with Nguyen van Chau, New York, New York, June 1999.

105. Interview with Nguyen van Hieu, Westminster, California, March 2002.

SELECTED BIBLIOGRAPHY

Archival Collections

Center for Military History, U.S. Army, Washington, D.C.
John F. Kennedy Presidential Library, Dorchester, Massachusetts
Lyndon Baines Johnson Presidential Library, Austin, Texas
National Archives, College Park, Maryland
Trung Tam Luu Tru Quoc Gia–II (National Archives Center–II), Ho Chi Minh City,
    Vietnam
U.S. Army Military History Institute, Carlisle Barracks, Pennsylvania
Vietnam Archive, Lubbock, Texas

Interviews

Roger Banning, Washington, D.C., June 1999
Timothy Brandon, New York, New York, January 2004
Can van Thu, San Francisco, California, June 1999
Cao van Ngia, Los Angeles, California, June 1999
Cao van Thu, San Jose, California, June 1999
Dang van Thuy, New York, New York, February 2005
Dang Vu Hiep, Hanoi, Vietnam, June 1999
George C. Davis, Washington, D.C., July 1999
Dinh Phuong, Westminster, California, March 2002
Duong Lan, Ho Chi Minh City, Vietnam, January 2004
Ho van Dien, Ho Chi Minh City, Vietnam, January 2004
Hoang Quang Ho, Hanoi, Vietnam, June 1997
Hoang Thuy, Westminster, California, March 2002
Hoang van Cao, Westminster, California, March 2002
Huynh Thuy, Da Lat, Vietnam, March 1996
Huynh van Cuong, San Jose, California, June 1999
Huynh van Hung, Ho Chi Minh City, Vietnam, January 2004
Huynh van Man, Ho Chi Minh City, Vietnam, March 1999
William Jackson, Boston, Massachusetts, June 1999
Roger LaFalice, New York, New York, July 2002
Le van Duong, Ho Chi Minh City, Vietnam, March 1996
Robert S. McNamara, Washington, D.C., April 1997, June 1999
Nghiem Tam Ngoc, New York, New York, June 2002
Ngo Ca Cong, Los Angeles, California, June 1999
Ngo Chao Minh, Ho Chi Minh City, Vietnam, January 2003

Ngo Hien Quoc, Westminster, California, March 2002
Ngo Quynh, London, England, November 2003
Ngo Quynh, San Francisco, California, June 1999
Ngo van Chuong, Westminster, California, March 2002
Ngo van Chuong, Ho Chi Minh City, Vietnam, January 2004
Ngo van Linh, Westminster, California, March 2002
Ngo van Trong, New York, New York, March 2002
Ngoc Cao Huynh, Westminster, California, March 2002
Nguyen Co Huong, San Francisco, California, June 1999
Nguyen Co Thach, Hanoi, Vietnam, June 1997
Nguyen Cong Thanh, Westminster, California, March 2002
Nguyen Dinh Uoc, Hanoi, Vietnam, June 1997
Nguyen Hue, Ho Chi Minh City, Vietnam, March 1996
Jim Nguyen, Westminster, California, March 1999
Nguyen Pham, Westminster, California, March 2002
Nguyen Phuong, London, England, November 2003
Nguyen Tang, Gia Dinh, Vietnam, January 1999
Nguyen Thao, Ho Chi Minh City, Vietnam, January 2003
Nguyen thi Hanh, Minneapolis, Minnesota, February 2001
Nguyen thi Linh, Westminster, California, March 2002
Nguyen thi Mai, Westminster, California, March 2002
Nguyen thi Thuy, Los Angeles, California, June 1999
Nguyen Thiep, Ho Chi Minh City, Vietnam, March 1996
Nguyen Tin Thanh, Los Angeles, California, June 1999
Nguyen van Cam, Westminster, California, March 2002
Nguyen van Chau, New York, New York, June 1999
Nguyen van Dinh, Ho Chi Minh City, Vietnam, January 2004
Nguyen van Hiep, New York, New York, November 1999
Nguyen van Hieu, Westminster, California, March 2002
Nguyen van Hinh, Ho Chi Minh City, Vietnam, January 2004
Nguyen van Khai, Ho Chi Minh City, Vietnam, January 2003
Nguyen van Long, Boston, Massachusetts, June 1999
Nguyen van Luong, Westminster, California, March 2002
Nguyen van Mui, Ho Chi Minh City, Vietnam, January 2004
Nguyen van Ngo, Ho Chi Minh City, Vietnam, January 2004
Nguyen van Ngo, London, England, November 2003
Nguyen van Nhon, Ho Chi Minh City, Vietnam, January 2003
Nguyen van Pham, Los Angeles, California, June 1999
Nguyen van Phuoc, New York, New York, March 2003
Nguyen van Son, Minneapolis, Minnesota, February 2001
Nguyen van Son, Ho Chi Minh City, Vietnam, January 2004
Nguyen van Thanh, Los Angeles, California, June 1999
Nguyen van Thien, My Tho, Vietnam, July 1989
Nguyen van Vinh, Ho Chi Minh City, Vietnam, March 1996
Nguyen van Vinh, San Francisco, California, May 1999
Nguyen Vinh, Ho Chi Minh City, Vietnam, January 2004
Nguyen Xuan Oanh, Ho Chi Minh City, Vietnam, July 1989

Pham Huong, New York, New York, May 2002
Pham van Cao, Los Angeles, California, June 1999
Pham van Thuy, San Jose, California, June 1999
Phan van Cao, Los Angeles, California, June 1999
Phuong Thuy, Ho Chi Minh City, Vietnam, March 1996
Herbert Schandler, Bellagio, Italy, July 1998
Roger T. Spence, Washington, D.C., June 2003
Thinh Pham, Ho Chi Minh City, Vietnam, March 2003
Thinh Pham, Los Angeles, California, June 1999
Roger Timmelson, Cleveland, Ohio, February 2000
Ton Nu Mai, Westminster, California, March 2002
Tran Huu Dinh, Hanoi, Vietnam, June 1992
Tran Quynh Cu, Hanoi, Vietnam, June 1992
Tran van Chat, Ho Chi Minh City, Vietnam, July 1989
Vo Nguyen Giap, Hanoi, Vietnam, June 1997
Vu Huy Phuoc, Hanoi, Vietnam, June 1992
Thomas Waite, Washington, D.C., June 2003
George White, Boston, Massachusetts, June 1999

Published Collections

Department of Defense, *U.S.–Vietnam Relations, 1945–1967*, Vols. 1–12. Washington, D.C.: Government Printing Office, 1971.
Foreign Relations of the United States, Vietnam, 1955–1957. Vol. 1. Washington, D.C.: Government Printing Office, 1985.
Foreign Relations of the United States, Vietnam, 1958–1960. Vol. 1. Washington, D.C.: Government Printing Office, 1986.
Foreign Relations of the United States, Vietnam, 1961–1963. Vols. 1–4. Washington, D.C.: Government Printing Office, 1988–1991.
Interviews of Ngo Dinh Diem. Saigon: Presidential Office, 1960.
Major Policy Speeches by President Ngo Dinh Diem, 3rd ed. Saigon: Presidential Office, 1957.
Sheehan, Neil, Fox Butterfield, Hedrick Smith, and E. W. Kenworthy. *The Pentagon Papers as Published by the New York Times: The Secret History of the Vietnam War*. New York: Quadrangle, 1972.

Government Publications

Bo Cong Dan Vu. *Tu ap chien luoc den ca tu ve* (From strategic hamlet to self-defense village). Saigon: Defense Ministry, 1962.
Collins, James Lawton, Jr. *The Development and Training of the South Vietnamese Army, 1950–1972*. Washington, D.C.: Department of the Army, 1975.
Dong van Khuyen. *The RVNAF*. Washington: U.S. Army Center of Military History, Indochina Monographs, 1984.
Hickey, Gerald. *The American Military Advisor and His Foreign Counterpart: The Case of Vietnam*. Santa Monica, Calif.: Rand, 1965.

Jenkins, Brian. *A People's Army for South Vietnam: A Vietnamese Solution*. Santa Monica, Calif.: Rand, 1971.

Ngo Quang Truong. *RVNAF and U.S. Operational Cooperation and Coordination*. Washington, D.C.: U.S. Army Center of Military History, Indochina Monographs, 1980.

Nguyen Duy Trinh and Tran Dinh Tho. *The South Vietnamese Society*. Washington, D.C.: U.S. Army Center of Military History, Indochina Monographs, 1984.

Quan Doi Viet Nam Cong Hoa (The Republic of Vietnam Armed Forces). Saigon: Presidential Office, 1963.

Quan Luc Vietnam Cong Hoa Trong Giai Doan Hinh Thanh, 1946–1955 (Republic of Vietnam Armed Forces during the formation period, 1946–1955). Saigon: Co so dainam xuat ban, 1972.

Survey of the Social, Psychological, and Economic Adaptation of Vietnamese Refugees in the U.S., 1975–1979. Washington, D.C.: Bureau of Social Science Research, 1982.

White, Robert. *Anthropometric Survey of the Armed Forces of the Republic of Vietnam*. Natick, Mass.: U.S. Army Advanced Research Projects Agency, 1964.

Memoirs

Bui Diem. *In the Jaws of History*. Bloomington: Indiana University Press, 1999.

Elliot, Duong Van Mai. *The Sacred Willow: Four Generations in the Life of a Vietnamese Family*. New York: Oxford University Press, 1999.

Hoang Khoi Phong. *Ngay + . . . : Hoi ky* (Day N+ . . . : memoirs). Westminster, Calif.: Van Nghe, 1988.

Huy Xuan Cao. *Thang ba gay sung* (The march of the broken rifles). Westminster, Calif.: Van Khoa, 1986.

Johnson, Lyndon. *The Vantage Point: Perspectives of the Presidency, 1963–1969*. New York: Holt, Rhinehart, and Winston, 1971.

Lu van Thanh. *The Inviting Call of the Wandering Souls: A Memoir of an ARVN Liaison Officer to United States Forces in Vietnam*. Jefferson, N.C.: McFarland, 1997.

Nguyen Cao Ky. *Twenty Years and Twenty Days*. New York: Stein and Day, 1976.

Nguyen Tan Hung. *Mot doi de hoc* (A life to learn). Toronto: Lang Van, 1988.

Nguyen Vu. *12 Nam Linh* (Twelve years of being a soldier). Westminster, Calif.: Van Hoa, 1990.

Pham Kim Tuan. *The ARVN: A Stoic Army*. Washington, D.C.: U.S. Army Center for Military History, 1983.

Tran Ngoc Nhuan. *Doi Quan Ngu* (Life in the army). Westminster, Calif.: Van Nghe, 1992.

Tran van Don. *Our Endless War inside Vietnam*. San Rafael, Calif.: Presidio Press, 1978.

Truong Duy Hy. *Toi tham chien tu thu can cu hoa luc 30 tai ha Lao* (I fought at base 30 in lower Laos). Westminster, Calif.: Van Nghe, 1999.

Van Thanh Hao. *Mau va nuoc mat* (Blood and tears). Westminster, Calif.: Van Thanh Hoa, 1991.

Westmoreland, William. *A Soldier Reports*. Garden City, N.Y.: Doubleday, 1976.

Books and Articles

Anderson, David. *Trapped by Success: The Eisenhower Administration and Vietnam, 1953–1961.* New York: Columbia University Press, 1991.

Appy, Christian. *Patriots: The Vietnam War Remembered from all Sides.* New York: Penguin, 2003.

Bergerud, Eric. *The Dynamics of Defeat: The Vietnam War in Hau Nghia Province.* Boulder, Colo.: Westview Press, 1991.

Berman, Larry. *No Peace, No Honor: Nixon, Kissinger, and Betrayal in Vietnam.* New York: Free Press, 2000.

Beschloss, Michael. *Taking Charge: The Johnson White House Tapes, 1963–1964.* New York: Simon and Schuster, 1997.

Bradley, Mark. *Imagining Vietnam and America: The Making of Postcolonial Vietnam.* Chapel Hill: University of North Carolina Press, 2000.

Butler, David. *The Fall of Saigon: Scenes from the Sudden End of a Long War.* New York: Dell, 1985.

Buzzanco, Robert. *Masters of War: Military Dissent and Politics in the Vietnam Era.* Cambridge: Cambridge University Press, 1996.

Cao van Vien. "The Strategy of Isolation." *Military Review* 52 (April 1972): 22–30.

Catton, Philip. *Diem's Final Failure: Prelude to America's War in Vietnam.* Lawrence: University Press of Kansas, 2002.

Clarke, Jeffrey. *Advice and Support: The Final Years, The U.S. Army in Vietnam.* Washington: U.S. Army Center of Military History, 1988.

Duiker, William. *Sacred War: Nationalism and Revolution in a Divided Vietnam.* Boston: McGraw Hill, 1995.

Elliot, David. *The Vietnamese War: Revolution and Social Change in the Mekong Delta, 1930–1975.* Two volumes. Armonk, N.Y.: M. E. Sharpe, 2003.

FitzGerald, Frances. *Fire in the Lake: The Vietnamese and Americans in Vietnam.* New York: Vintage Books, 1972.

Gardner, Lloyd. *Approaching Vietnam: From World War II through Dien Bien Phu.* New York: W. W. Norton, 1988.

Halberstam, David. *The Making of a Quagmire.* New York: Random House, 1964.

Herring, George C. *America's Longest War: The United States and Vietnam, 1950–1975,* 4th ed. New York: McGraw Hill, 2002.

———. "'Peoples Quite Apart': Americans, South Vietnamese, and the War in Vietnam." *Diplomatic History* (Winter 1990): 1–23.

Hickey, Gerald. *Village in Vietnam.* New Haven, Conn.: Yale University Press, 1964.

Hue-Tam Ho Tai. *Radicalism and the Origins of the Vietnamese Revolution.* Cambridge, Mass.: Harvard University Press, 1992.

Hy van Luong. *Revolution in the Village: Tradition and Transformation in North Vietnam, 1925–1988.* Honolulu: University of Hawaii Press, 1992.

Jamieson, Neil. *Understanding Vietnam.* Berkeley: University of California Press, 1993.

Keegan, John. *A History of Warfare*. New York: Vintage Books, 1993.

Kimball, Jeffrey. *Nixon's Vietnam War*. Lawrence: University Press of Kansas, 1998.

Kolko, Gabriel. *Anatomy of a War: The United States and the Modern Historical Experience*. New York: Pantheon, 1985.

Krepinevich, Andrew. *The Army and Vietnam*. Baltimore, Md.: Johns Hopkins University Press, 1986.

Langguth, A. J. *Our Vietnam: The War, 1954–1975*. New York: Simon and Schuster, 2000.

Latham, Michael. *Modernization as Ideology: American Social Science and Nation Building in the Kennedy Era*. Chapel Hill: University of North Carolina Press, 2000.

Lockhart, Gregory. *Nation in Arms: The Origins of the People's Army of Vietnam*. Sydney, Australia: Allen and Unwin, 1989.

Logevall, Fredrik. *Choosing War: The Lost Chance for Peace and the Escalation of War in Vietnam*. Berkeley: University of California Press, 1999.

McHale, Shawn. *Print and Power: Confucianism, Communism, and Buddhism in the Making of Modern Vietnam*. Honolulu: University of Hawai'i Press, 2004.

McMahon, Robert. *The Limits of Empire: The United States in Southeast Asia since World War II*. New York: Columbia University Press, 1999.

Marr, David. *Vietnamese Anticolonialism, 1885–1925*. Berkeley: University of California Press, 1971.

———. *Vietnamese Tradition on Trial, 1920–1945*. Berkeley: University of California Press, 1984.

Moise, Edwin. *Land Reform in China and North Vietnam: Consolidating the Revolution at the Village Level*. Chapel Hill: University of North Carolina Press, 1983.

Neu, Charles. *America's Lost War: Vietnam, 1945–1975*. Wheeling, Ill.: Harlan Davidson, 2005.

Palmer, Bruce. *The 25-Year War: America's Military Role in Vietnam*. Lexington: University of Kentucky Press, 1984.

Popkin, Samuel. *The Rational Peasant: The Political Economy of Rural Society in Vietnam*. Berkeley: University of California Press, 1979.

Prados, John. *The Hidden History of the Vietnam War*. Chicago: Ivan Dee, 1995.

Pratt, John Clarke. *Vietnam Voices*. New York: Penguin, 1984.

Pribbenow, Merle. *Victory in Vietnam*. Lawrence: University Press of Kansas, 2002.

Prochnau, William. *Once upon a Distant War*. New York: Times Books, 1995.

Race, Jeffrey. *War Comes to Long An: Revolutionary Conflict in a Province*. Berkeley: University of California Press, 1972.

Rotter, Andrew. *The Path to Vietnam: Origins of the American Commitment to Southeast Asia*. Ithaca, N.Y.: Cornell University Press, 1987.

Sansom, Robert. *The Economics of Insurgency in the Mekong Delta of Vietnam*. Cambridge: Massachusetts Institute of Technology Press, 1970.

Schandler, Herbert. *Lyndon Johnson and the Vietnam War: The Unmaking of a President*. Princeton, N.J.: Princeton University Press, 1977.

Schulzinger, Robert. *A Time for War: The United States and Vietnam, 1941–1975*. New York: Oxford University Press, 1997.

Scott, James. *The Moral Economy of the Peasant*. New Haven, Conn.: Yale University Press, 1976.

Shaplen, Robert. *The Lost Revolution*. New York: Harper and Row, 1966.

Sheehan, Neil. *A Bright Shining Lie: John Paul Vann and America in Vietnam*. New York: Random House, 1988.

Spector, Ronald. *Advice and Support: The Early Years of the U.S. Army in Vietnam*. New York: The Free Press, 1985.

Stanton, Shelby. *The Rise and Fall of an American Army*. Novato, Calif.: Presidio Press, 1985.

Taylor, Keith. *The Birth of Vietnam*. Berkeley: University of California Press, 1983.

Thanh van Tran. "Ethnic Community Supports and Psychological Well-Being of Vietnamese Refugees." *International Migration Review* 21 (Autumn 1987): 833–844.

Trullinger, James. *Village at War: An Account of Conflict in Vietnam*. Stanford, Calif.: Stanford University Press, 1994.

Willbanks, James. *Abandoning Vietnam: How America Left and South Vietnam Lost Its War*. Lawrence: University Press of Kansas, 2004.

Woodside, Alexander. *Community and Revolution in Modern Vietnam*. Boston: Houghton Mifflin, 1976.

Young, Marilyn. *The Vietnam Wars*. New York: Harper Collins, 1991.

Unpublished Works

Chapman, Jessica. "Debating the Will of Heaven: South Vietnamese Politics and Nationalism in International Perspective, 1954–1956." Ph.D. dissertation, University of California, Santa Barbara, 2006.

INDEX